Edmonton

Vancouver

Friday
Harbor

San Juan Islands

Seattle

Anacortes

Depot
Bay

Newport

Albany

C A N A D A

U N I T E D   S T A T E S

Monterey

Los
Angeles

*Palos Verdes
Peninsula*

San Diego

M E X I C O

B A J A   C A L I F O R N I A

Sea of Cortez

Guerrero
Negro

Ojo de Liebre

N
E
S
W

Praise for *Soundings*

"This book is a gorgeous journey. Cunningham guides us elegantly from Mexico to Alaska, riding along with wild gray whales. And she excels as well at bringing the reader along on her personal journey of motherhood, struggle, and epiphany. You will be glad you've joined her."

—Susan Orlean, author of *On Animals* and *The Library Book*

"A raw and rapturous work of nature writing. Or is it memoir? Adventure journalism? Pop science? Climate cri de coeur? This foulmouthed, gimlet-eyed, big-hearted chimera of a book is all of those—and more."

—Robert Moor, bestselling author of *On Trails: An Exploration*

"In this fascinating book, Doreen Cunningham takes us on an intimate journey through a world already altered by climate change. As her own travel companions become ours—the indigenous people of Utqiaġvik, the whales of the Pacific, the world's scientists, and her little son Max—we learn that it is only by coming together as people and species that we will be able to navigate our way ahead in the vast troubled waters of our shared future."

—Sjón, author of *The Whispering Muse*

"Through her journey from Mexico to Alaska, Doreen Cunningham develops what can only be described as a spiritual relationship with the gray whales. Readers will be further enriched by her ability to seamlessly integrate traditional Indigenous knowledge and science of the sea, ice, and world of the Iñupiat who hunt the mammoth baleen whales."

—Rosita Ḵaaháni Worl, PhD, president of the
Sealaska Heritage Institute

"*Soundings* is a story of whales and people, of kinship and questing, and, perhaps most of all, of the connections among our human selves and across species. With a lyrical voice and tremendous emotional honesty, Doreen Cunningham defies genre and skips easy romance to bring us a cetacean journey—and a journey into the tough, transformative stuff of making community in this beautiful, harsh, and changeable world."

—Bathsheba Demuth, PhD, author of *Floating Coast:
An Environmental History of the Bering Strait*

"Defiant, despairing, hopeful, restless, and compelled—Doreen Cunningham grabs our hands and takes us with her on a wild journey through danger, motherhood, upheaval, and love. *Soundings* is resonant with the voices of endangered whales and the essential truth that our failures and imperfections are tangled with our unique strengths and beauty. This is a book that grips and doesn't let go."
    —Rebecca Schiller, author of *A Thousand Ways to Pay Attention*

"Beautiful and brave, and startling in its raw emotional honesty."
    —Neil Ansell, author of *Deep Country* and *The Circling Sky*

"An intimate and fascinating story of one woman's journey with our most charismatic species."
    —Mark Boyle, author of *The Way Home*

"Soulful, honest, insightful, humane, and best of all, propulsive . . . I was deeply moved and fell in love with Doreen's story."
    —Jini Reddy, author of *Wanderland*

"Beautifully written, insightful, and gripping."
    —Daniel Lavelle, author of *Down and Out*

SOUNDINGS

Journeys in the Company of Whales

— A Memoir —

DOREEN
CUNNINGHAM

SCRIBNER

New York   London   Toronto   Sydney   New Delhi

Scribner
An Imprint of Simon & Schuster, Inc.
1230 Avenue of the Americas
New York, NY 10020

First Scribner hardcover edition July 2022

SCRIBNER and design are registered trademarks of The Gale Group, Inc., used
under license by Simon & Schuster, Inc., the publisher of this work.

For information about special discounts for bulk purchases, please contact Simon &
Schuster Special Sales at 1-866-506-1949 or business@simonandschuster.com.

The Simon & Schuster Speakers Bureau can bring authors to your live event. For more
information or to book an event, contact the Simon & Schuster Speakers Bureau at
1-866-248-3049 or visit our website at www.simonspeakers.com.

Interior design by Wendy Blum

Manufactured in the United States of America

1   3   5   7   9   10   8   6   4   2

Library of Congress Cataloging-in-Publication Data

Names: Cunningham, Doreen, author.
Title: Soundings : journeys in the company of whales / Doreen Cunningham.
Description: First Scribner hardcover edition. | New York, NY : Scribner, 2022. |
Includes bibliographical references.
Identifiers: LCCN 2021055684 (print) | LCCN 2021055685 (ebook) |
ISBN 9781982171797 (hardcover) | ISBN 9781982171803 (paperback) |
ISBN 9781982171810 (ebook)
Subjects: LCSH: Cunningham, Doreen. | Cunningham, Doreen—Travel. | Women
journalists—Great Britain—Biography. | Single mothers—Great Britain—Biography. |
Whales—Behavior. | Inupiat—Hunting. | Nature—Effect of human beings on.
Classification: LCC CT788.C8763 A3 2022 (print) | LCC CT788.C8763
(ebook) | DDC 941.092 [B]—dc23/eng/20220303
LC record available at https://lccn.loc.gov/2021055684
LC ebook record available at https://lccn.loc.gov/2021055685

ISBN 978-1-9821-7179-7
ISBN 978-1-9821-7181-0 (ebook)

To my children, all children,
human and nonhuman.

CONTENTS

SOUNDINGS

PROLOGUE

Wind spits spray in my face. Water slops against the sides of our small fishing boat as it shudders out of the harbor, into a dawn that billows fire above and below the horizon. Max, my two-year-old, is up front "helping" drive the boat. I met the skipper, Chris, just twelve hours ago. We are borrowing a dad, one who has lived at sea and might be able to open a door into this secretive ocean. Today there is one last chance for things to go right. There is nothing to do except trust in this generous stranger, give myself over to the wind and the water, keep my eyes fixed on the waves, examining every curve, every roll, every swirl, every ripple.

"Look that old rust bucket," shouts Max from inside the cabin, pointing. We are cruising slowly past the rust-streaked blue-and-white hulk of a commercial fishing boat. He's channeling Grandpa Pig arguing with Granddad Dog from the *Peppa Pig* cartoon. The boat's name, *Faith*, is written in strident white capital letters on the bow. I have to look away. I have lost faith in my idea of following the gray whale migration, in the whales themselves, and most of all in myself. I wanted to show Max how the mothers and calves travel thousands of miles from the lagoons of Baja California in Mexico to the Arctic Ocean, to prove to him that it is possible to do anything, to overcome anything, with just the two of us. It was me who needed convincing, though, and things haven't gone to plan.

Kodiak Island, our final stop, is a major milestone on the gray whale highway and is our last chance to see them before we have to leave. On the map, the island looks as though it's been carelessly thrown from the Alaskan mainland, as carelessly as I've thrown away ten thousand pounds of bank loan to finance this trip. Our visas are spent too. The journey was supposed to help me start anew. It distracted me for a while, but now that it's ending I'm confronted by all I ran from, a list of my failings. I failed to set up a life for us that I could tolerate, failed to earn enough money to support us, failed to just get on with it like everyone else. I've repeatedly and spectacularly failed at love and of course failed to see what a stupid idea this journey was in the first place. I'm reeling with so much failure that my legs are unsteady and I grip the side of the boat, press my hands onto the wood. My fingers leave no impression. We slide past *Arctic Hunter*, *Resolution*, *Provider*, and *Lady Kodiak* on the final row of moorings. The boat throttles up. The water gets agitated. We creep out from behind a hook of land. The sea, which is now a jagged industrial gray, withholds judgment, unlike me. It could drown me without it being anything personal. Its indifference is comforting. The freezing rip of air anesthetizes the sorrow in my chest. The moving mass of water that backs with a noise like thunder against the far-off cliffs drowns out my head wreck.

Max is sitting on Chris's knee, a small pair of hands and a large pair of hands in company on the wheel, guiding our course. Max is enjoying himself so much he hasn't called for me once. I see the corner of a wide smile, round cheek framed by blond tangles and the ruff of his hood. He turns and fixes his eyes on me. Large, slightly elongated, and usually blue, they are softened to gray by the light from the clouds.

The island shuttles off through the ocean behind us. This is the

Gulf of Alaska, where the Bering Sea breaks its back on the Aleutian Islands, which stretch westward toward Russia. The Unangan or Aleut people call one of these islands the Birthplace of the Winds. Chris, who used to be a fisherman and is now a landlocked electrician, is treating himself to a fishing trip for Father's Day. His wife and their two young daughters bump happily on the benches in the cabin as we skitter across the swells. Max and I are tagging along because Chris says he knows where the gray whales feed.

As well as being home to the ominous specter that is the Kodiak bear and this miraculously kind family, the island is special for its benthic mud. So far, the place has been shrouded in too much fog to spot any sea life, and in my dispirited mood the cold sludge at the bottom of the sea invites me. I hold on to the gunwale and close my eyes, sink down through layers of water in my mind.

I am the whale diving. The light shrinks to a shining hole above. My blood pump slows, lungs close, body shuts down. Color slips away. I'm lost in a deep mist. I hear the ocean floor, twisting, flowing. Water sizzles, hums with life, shrimp snap. I probe the dark for voices, call out, try to summon the grays.

Scientist now, I examine the muck, a teeming city of multitudes. Clams surf the currents or dig in with their feet, ribbon worms writhe and slip. A fork-tailed comma shrimp, Diastylidae, a cumacean, swarms and spawns. These tiny shrimp are the prize the whales have traveled so far to gorge on. It's hard to believe such giants are sustained by prey only millimeters long. Mud plumes spew like lava flows as they suck up the sea floor and extrude silt through a curtain of baleen plates. With shifts in the ocean due to climate change, gray whales can't be fussy about their diet. The cumaceans they feed on here are a less calorific and crustier shrimp than the one the whales prefer.[1] Luckily they're basically vacuum cleaners.

I've learned a lot about grays on this journey. I've read whenever Max has slept.

You are unique and spectacular beings, sentinels of the sea, eco-system engineers, harbingers of the climate change that will affect us all. But where the fuck are you? How could you let me down?

Before my son was born, I had a home in London, a busy social life, and a successful career as a journalist. When I became a mother, things began to twist and snap. When Max was one, in 2012, I found myself living in a hostel, a shared house for single mothers, in Jersey, the island off the coast of northern France, where I grew up. I'd spent my savings on lawyers' fees, fighting my ex, Pavel, in court, arguing that Max should live with me.

In the hostel, I kept a low profile, wore my body like armor, tried not to attract attention from anyone or anything. So much had slipped away so quickly. Regular paid work, sleep, friends whom I no longer had the money to call, my own home. I owned a flat in east London but could neither sell it, because it was in negative equity, nor afford to pay the mortgage and live in it. And there were other reasons not to live in London.

It felt as if I were learning to walk and talk all over again. The world did not seem to recognize me, so I focused on taking care of what was now at the center of it, my one-year-old son.

One winter's day I'd walked down a side street, away from the main shopping precinct in St Helier, Jersey's capital, to the food bank housed above the Salvation Army charity shop. A smiling man had led us past the clothes rails and up the stairs to a series of walk-in cupboards on the first floor.

"Take whatever you need," he'd said, "as much as you can carry." I'd taken more than I could carry. One bag was already splitting. The doorbell of the shop jangled as I stepped out onto the pavement, three bags of tins in one hand and Max's small palm in the other.

A familiar voice: "Doreen!" An old school friend stood on the street with an easy smile I remembered from two decades ago. As teenagers we'd been close. "You're back."

"Hey! Yes, I am." I put my bags down.

"I didn't know you had a little one. Hello, handsome." She nodded at Max and looked back at me. "Your husband, he's from England?" Max jumped up and down, pulling at my hand.

"No husband, it's just Max and me. How are you? It's been ages."

Her next question was airborne already: "Are you back home with your parents then?"

My jaw tensed. "No, my mum's too ill." I lifted the bags off the pavement.

"Where are you staying then?" She frowned. "How are you managing? Is someone helping you?"

My head began to hurt. The plastic bags cut into my hand. I let Max tug me backward away down the street. "We're fine. Lovely to see you. Sorry, I have to go, we're late."

On the way back to the hostel we passed a bakery with trays of soft rolls in the window. A bag lady was in the glass, wearing my clothes, clutching the hand of a lovely child.

A few weeks later, an encounter set me on a different path. There were perks for the likes of me, mothers who'd recently stayed at or who were currently living in the women's refuge. A church group was putting on a pamper day especially for us. I'd arrived a few minutes early and pushed the heavy wooden doors open, admiring the size of the light-filled hall inside.

"Dear Lord, help these poor women . . . the right path . . . away from Satan . . ." The huddle of women hadn't noticed me come in. I considered going straight back out again but the group had broken up and were already greeting me with smiles. I scowled back. Needed saving, did I? One woman homed in on Max and led us to the crèche, staffed by professional childcare volunteers, she assured me. He took her hand and tottered over to explore the toys. Another woman in a navy-striped sailor top and deck shoes tried to shepherd me toward an array of massages, manicures, and footbaths. I would not be their charity case. I had to get Max out. I peered around her and saw my son sitting on a woman's knee, unwrapping a present, a toy cement mixer complete with driver and rotating drum. Delight shone out of him. I looked around the room again. Other families were starting to arrive. If I was stuck being Satan's woman for the afternoon, I might as well make the most of it.

"I'd love a head massage, thank you," I said to the nautical woman, then sat down and closed my eyes. Her fingers stroking down my scalp felt like water. At first I pretended I was in a spa. But the spa transmogrified into the sea. I wasn't in the church hall anymore. I was a child again, running wild on beaches in Jersey and Ireland. Then a different coast appeared in my mind, an Arctic coast, and I was looking across a vast expanse of sea ice, stretching up toward the north pole. I was back in Alaska, where I'd traveled seven years earlier, back in the city of Utqiaġvik, then known as Barrow, living with an Iñupiaq family. The city teeters on the edge of the Arctic Ocean at the northernmost point of the United States. The Iñupiat have thrived there, in a place periodically engulfed in ice and darkness, for thousands of years, bound closely together by their ancient culture and their relationships with the animals they hunt, most notably the magnificent and mysterious bowhead whale. I hadn't just seen whales there, I'd joined a family hunting crew, traveling with them in a landscape of astonishing beauty and danger. I'd felt so alive then, so connected to other people and to the natural world. If only I could feel that way again and give that feeling to Max.

"Mummy."

I came back from the Arctic and opened my eyes to find him standing in front of me. The woman lifted her hands from my scalp. My head felt lighter.

"Out." Max pointed in the direction of the door. I thanked my masseur, took his hand, and left.

That night, while Max slept, I ignored my freelance research work and read online about bowhead whales. Moving on to blue whales, I watched my favorite David Attenborough clip, where the giant creature surfaces next to his tiny boat. I strayed onto an article about gray whales, a species I knew nothing about. There were two populations, I learned, in the western and eastern Pacific. It was then I discovered how, every year, the eastern population traveled from the Arctic to the Mexican birthing lagoons, before migrating north again with their calves. It was more than ten thousand miles round trip, like swimming around the moon twice. The whales usually traveled close to shore in shallow kelp beds, and people watched them all the way up the west coast of North America. The mothers fought off predators, parented, and breastfed, while swimming halfway across the planet. They were endurance incarnate.

As I read about them, I felt new strength. Mothers and newborns, the article said, could be seen in Baja California from December to April. Perhaps I could take Max to see them. I laughed out loud at the idea, but my mind kept working. I could imprint them on his subconscious, teach him what freedom felt like, erase any claustrophobia or despair he might have picked up on in the hostel. I could share the inspiration I found in the wonders of undersea life. It would be like the Attenborough documentaries I'd grown up on but even better because it would be real. It was January. The mothers and babies must already be there, in Baja.

Hunched over my computer on the edge of the mattress next to Max, I heard a voice, Billy's voice, deep and close, as though he were sitting right next to me, on the sea ice in Alaska seven years before, watching for whales.

"Sometimes," he said slowly, "we see a gray." It was as if Billy were speaking to me across the miles that separated us.

From there, everything happened quickly. A string was pulling me out the window, into the sky, across the sea. The next day I left the hostel and moved into a friend's attic room. I got a loan, organized visas. We would follow the mothers and babies from Mexico to the top of the world, I told Max. They would swim and we would take the bus, the train, and the boat alongside them.

"Train?" Max wasn't so fussed about whales, but he certainly loved all forms of transport. "Me take Flash, Mummy." He picked up his fluffy toy dog and stood by the door, ready to go.

I told myself I would relearn from the whales how to mother, how to endure, how to live.

Beneath the surface, secretly, I longed to get back to northernmost Alaska, to the community who'd kept me safe in the harsh beauty of the Arctic, and to Billy, the whale hunter who'd loved me.

LOS ANGELES

Latitude: 33° 59' 40" N
Longitude: 118° 28' 57" W

The immigration man in Los Angeles glares at me, then looks down at Max and gives a beautiful smile. Toddling along like a penguin, carrying his mini-rucksack, shouting his name when asked, he's like a magic spell that lights people up. I clutch my paperwork but the official doesn't look at it, just waves us straight through.

My friend Marie is waiting for us in the arrivals hall and stretches her arms wide when she sees us. She has a six-month-old asleep in a buggy. The air outside is warm and dry, making Max and me wriggle out of our coats while Marie drives us across LA. Spindly palm trees look down from above, their fronds tousled by the wind. It's late when we arrive at her apartment in Venice Beach. She has a little boy, Max's age, as well as the baby. The toddlers scribble chalk on a blackboard together while Marie and I have tea and talk about the trip I've booked. We're meeting a tour group in San Diego and will drive to Baja for two weeks of whale watching.

"Then to the Arctic?" she says. "That's far." Marie knows the north. I first met her on the plane to Utqiaġvik. Squashed into adjacent seats, we'd admired each other's ski jackets as the aircraft landed. The view was white in whichever direction you looked, and the bottle of water I was carrying had begun to form ice crystals before we'd walked ten yards off the plane. By the end of my stay the cold had transformed me too. Some places are just like that. You come back different or perhaps you don't come back at all. Marie's having been to Utqiaġvik helps me. I guess astronauts must like to see each other sometimes too, after coming back from the moon.

"We're splitting the journey," I tell her. Max and I can't travel for more than a month without first jumping through legal hoops. "Two one-month trips. Mexico first, then home, and then we'll come back to follow the whales north."

"I'll get to see you twice!"

Marie asks how I can afford it all, so I tell her about the phone call to the bank. We were on the beach, Max racing barefoot on the sand, squealing as he watched his footprints trailing off behind him. I was on the phone, cupping my hand against the wind.

"Are you still working, still staff?" the man in the call center asked. I was inquiring, ever so casually, about the possibility of a loan.

"Yes." I held my breath. He had my account in front of him. It must have been clear that I absolutely was not staff anymore, was barely working. There was a pause. If I could hold my breath until he spoke, it would be a yes, I told myself.

"Okay, that's all done for you. Ten thousand pounds should be in your account within five days."

Marie tells me I'm brave. "You boys have drawn a storm," she says, admiring their chaotic chalk artwork. Max and I curl together on her sofa bed in the living room for the night, savoring the pleasure of being in a family home.

The hostel was almost full when we moved in. Our room was on the second floor, four fire doors and eight stair gates from the outside world, sealed off from it. Ashley, in the room beside ours, was a legal secretary, originally from South Africa. She had a boy of five. Magda, next one along, was Polish with three children. Angelina, down one floor, was from Madeira. There was a yard with trikes and a plastic slide where the children played. We swapped court experiences while we cooked in the shared kitchen. When we talked about the events that had brought us here, we could have been reading from the same script. Angelina and I didn't receive benefits, she because of her immigration status, I because I owned a flat. But I had a laptop and freelance work that was reasonably paid, while Angelina's only option was to work long shifts in a CD warehouse, for minimum wage. I was privileged. On the days Angelina's ex let her down with childcare, the rest of us babysat her daughter so she could still work. On the days I was tired from working at night, I was careful not to complain.

Gradually, my new friends moved into local authority flats or rooms in shared houses. Over Christmas the hostel was empty, apart from Max and me.

Then it started to fill up again, and Nicola moved in.

"Your hair is lovely," I said, while sitting on Nicola's bed one evening. She and her four-year-old, Will, were the only other family on my floor. The doors to our rooms were open so I'd hear from down the corridor if Max, now eighteen months old, woke.

"You should try using mousse, it would give your hair some body," Nicola said, picking up a canister from her dressing table. Hair wasn't my thing, but Nicola used to be a hairdresser and I was trying to be friendly, to give us something to talk about. Her hair moved in a shimmering chestnut curtain, drawing the light, as she walked the corridors of the hostel. She reminded me of the ringleader girls at school, the ones I avoided in the playground, who laughed and sang "ugly" as I passed. She examined her perfectly polished red nails as she talked.

"I need to go soon," I said. "I've got a deadline." I yawned, exhausted just thinking about it.

Nicola lifted her chin and looked at me sideways, down her nose. "I'm not interested in working." She'd returned to Jersey from Manchester when she and her boyfriend split, she said, and hoped to be allocated a flat by the States of Jersey soon. "You don't get anywhere in life by being nice, you know. I read this book, *Gusty Girls Have Better Lives*. When I read it, I thought, 'That's me, I'm gusty.'"

"*Gusty?* Do you mean *g*—"

The windows rattled and we both looked up. It was a windy night. An image of Nicola being blown around came to mind, hair streaming out behind her like a superhero's cape as she gusted through the room.

"*Gusty Girls Get Ahead, Good Girls Don't.* That was the title." She paused. "You should read it."

I nodded. "Got to do some work. Thanks for the mousse."

Max lay spread-eagled on the mattress in his striped sleep suit. I went downstairs to get a glass of water before starting.

Kayleigh was in the kitchen. Of all the new residents, I liked her best. She was foulmouthed like me, streetwise as I would never be. She'd told me about the fights with her boyfriend and family. "I just want all the control freaks out of my life," she'd said. I could relate. I'd given her a pair of silk-lined black leather gloves, a present from Pavel that I couldn't quite bring myself to donate to a charity shop. She'd tried them on, danced her fingers through the air, and pushed back her white-blond hair. "I look like Marilyn Monroe!"

Kayleigh was unlocking her food cupboard. She took out a bag of penne and moved across the kitchen with balletic grace, despite her growing pregnant belly. A group was smoking and chatting in the concrete yard outside the kitchen, Nicola among them. They looked up and I waved through the open door. Nicola turned away. She said something and the group laughed. I busied myself with nothing in the sink.

"Don't worry about it," Kayleigh said quietly, tilting her head toward the door. "They can't stand to see anyone doing something with their life, who's on their way out of here."

I wasn't sure what she meant. I smiled and said good night, nothing more. Going up the stairs, I felt heavy. A woman in the room underneath me started shouting down the phone, waking Max. I fed him until his body relaxed against mine. The shouting from the floor below started again. I couldn't understand what was being said, but she was getting really angry. Max sat up and started to cry. I banged on the floor. It went quiet. I fed him back to sleep and worked until 3:00 a.m.

The next day I had a Skype meeting with a client in Geneva. The hostel had no Wi-Fi and my mobile connection was unreliable, so I took Max to a nearby café. I chose a table with a backdrop of blank wall and angled Max opposite me in his buggy. He had his face in a croissant. I put on my headset and waited for the call.

"Yes. We need to talk about periods," I said loudly as the meeting got going. We were discussing girls in low-income countries missing school when menstruating. A room of customers in suits turned to look. I'd made a big effort that morning, actually brushed my hair, but was scruffy from the shoulders down. I narrowed my focus to the screen to block out the staring. Amrita, the sanitation expert, felt frustrated at how little attention the issues were getting and used the word *shit* liberally, for shock value. I had to say *shit* a lot too, to show commitment.

"Do you have the figures for the rural shit?" I asked. "If people shit in the fields and it goes into the water, then . . . Yes, I'll make sure that point is strong."

A customer loudly ordered a latte as I finished speaking.

"Are you in a café?" asked Amrita.

"It's a communal work space." I wasn't sure my café setup was professional enough for this team. Max finished his croissant and squawked. I clamped my hand over the mic.

"Is there something wrong with the line?" said Amrita.

"Yes, there seems to be a bit of interference."

By the end of the call I could smell my sweat. How did other broke single parents of small children survive? How long could I keep this up?

Half a year passed by. The hostel got smaller, the corridors narrower, the staircases steeper. Nicola mostly ignored me, but whenever we met, Will would joyfully charge into Max. At half Will's age and size, Max always came off worse. I walked in on Nicola's birthday party one lunchtime. A group were sitting around the kitchen table. The chocolates I'd given her were placed on the side.

"Party, Mummy!" said Max. Nicola looked up. I smiled. She resumed her conversation. I didn't know where to look. We ate in our room.

Whenever I had time for a break, I met Angelina and Ashley in parks. Pushing the children on the swings, watching them on the slide, looking out beyond the fence of the playground, I felt as if I were in a cage for mothers. Sometimes at night, when Max was asleep, I'd carefully unpack and put on the fur cap Billy had given me when I was in Utqiaġvik.

"Beaver fur," he'd said. "The warmest." I'd remember his voice as I pulled the earflaps down to muffle the world and think about being out on the sea ice, watching the dark ocean rise and fall against the white edge.

One morning in January, after another late night in front of the laptop, I wandered groggily with Max into the hostel kitchen. A few families were making breakfast, Nicola too. Will ran across the room into Max, knocking him over. His head bounced off the floor. Not again. Every time we were in the same room as Will, Max got hurt.

That morning I was too sleepy to control my reaction. "Oh, for God's sake, Will." I picked up Max and held him until he stopped crying, then climbed over the baby gate to get to my food cupboard.

"I think it's up to me to tell off my child," said Nicola.

The air around me went cold. Taking a stand was not my usual style, but I was somehow unable to bring myself to apologize.

"Are you talking to me?" I tried to sound blasé. Although practiced at challenging people from behind microphones, in real life my usual strategy was to go quiet or run away.

"Yeah."

"If Will hurts Max, I will tell him not to." I was short of breath, had to push out each word.

"You have to let them sort it out themselves or they will get bullied."

My stomach jolted. Was it fight or flight? "Oh, piss off," said a voice. My voice. "He's only two years old." It was fight. I was surging anger and blood. I was going to war. The last time I'd felt like that I'd been eleven. I'd hit Lisa Clark on the netball court because she wouldn't stop calling me names. "Fuck off," I added loudly, knowing then that I would have to leave the hostel. Nicola disappeared. The kitchen emptied around me. I was no longer pretending any of this was okay. Fuck this. Fuck Nicola. Fuck everyone. Fuck the whole fucking world. Fuck off.

When I wake up on the sofa bed, it takes me a few seconds to realize Max and I are in Marie's house, to remember how far we've traveled. There's an orange and a lemon tree bathing in Californian spring sunshine outside the window. We eat breakfast with the family, and when her husband goes to work, Max and I join Marie at mommy-and-baby yoga. We're surrounded by moms in LA Fitness uniforms.

"Stand like a froggy, Mummy," Max shouts, climbing all over me when we are doing downward dog. The others shush him. I want to get out. We are asked to share what gives us fire and passion. I try to talk about loving my son but speak so quietly no one can hear and I can't make it louder. Walking back, Marie wonders aloud what it's like for Max, me being a single mother. Her son is always asking for Daddy, she says. I want to get out again, but I'm out already.

Marie is having lunch with her work colleagues so I walk with Max to Venice Beach. It's huge and open. Lots of little shells. I take long, deep breaths and start to feel lighter. I always feel at home when I'm by the sea, watching the waves. Even more at home when I'm in them. This ocean is vast and wild, though, not suitable for Max and me to swim in. I sketch a map of the migration route on the sand. The thin Baja Peninsula, a wiggling line up the North American west coast, a dramatic swerve out into the Gulf of Alaska past the Aleutian Islands chain, and a jagged hump over the top of the continent. I take a little boxwood sperm whale out of my pocket for Max to play with. The whale travels everywhere with me. It's intricately carved, with a gentle curve to the mouth, a hint of a smile. Max scoots it across the sand.

When I was four, my mother gave me a children's Bible, large and beautifully illustrated. On the first page was a yellow map of the kingdoms of Judah and Israel, and right in the middle, in the Mediterranean Sea, was a sperm whale, mouth slightly agape. It was the only real character on the map, with the train of camels and men in the boat too small to hold any expression. The whale was a clue, like seeing a letter before you have learned the alphabet but already know it's a symbol, with secrets to impart. It was more spellbinding than any unicorn. In my Bible, Jonah and the Whale was the final story of the Old Testament section. A picture showed Jonah kneeling, bowed, praying, in the swirling gray vortex of the whale's insides. In the story, after three days and three nights, the whale, a benevolent force, had delivered Jonah to safety.

When I was six, we moved from Wales to Jersey, into a former stables in a ramshackle granite farm complex. As an island child, I knew the sea was all around. At any given time I'd know if the tide was high or low, and I tested my strength in the currents. On Friday evenings Dad took me, my sister, and my brother to swimming lessons, but I dreaded them. I'd thought I was drowning once, when the instructor had shouted at us to let go of the side. One Friday I hid, on the top shelf of the airing cupboard.

"Doreen?" Dad called, sounding cross. I heard his footsteps coming up the stairs, held my breath in my cave behind the towels and sheets. He went down again and called for me outside. Then I heard the car leave. I stayed curled up, safe and happy in invisibility. After this success I hid on Sunday morning too, to avoid going to mass with my mother. She, though, was a more determined sleuth and routed me out. Once Dad realized I didn't like swimming lessons, he didn't make me go. Instead he would book a Ping-Pong table and we'd play while the others swam. I was awful at Ping-Pong but I loved the time alone with him. And instead of in the chlorinated pool, I mostly learned to swim, by trial and error, in the sea.

Dad was a quiet man, often lost to the world in his hobbies. A biologist, he had a way with animals that I copied studiously. On workdays, he regularly came in without saying hello and didn't speak until asked a direct question or unless he had something functional to express. He would usually eat breakfast in silence, only speaking to say goodbye to my mom when he kissed her.

"I wonder if there is a word for the silent way he is?" she said once, as the door clicked shut behind him. My parents often argued. My father would be quiet, my mother shouting. I did not want to be like her, I decided, with her yelling and blaming. I wanted to be like him.

There was a time when Dad took us swimming nearly every day. This was a period when my mother had very bad depression. Cold, wavy days were the best, when the sea played rough, uninhibited and violently free. It was so exciting being tossed up on top of the breakers. All the colors muted, nothing fancy. Deep greens, muddy brown, and the smashed-up gray of the tumbling clouds. I liked being in the same body of water as my dad. On the calmer days, when you could see where you were going, I would follow his long white shape as he frog-stroked. We were sea mammals then, with the cold current on our skin. Fingers welded together like fins. My brother, sister, and I would swim between each other's legs underwater or terrify each other by pretending to have seen a shark approaching. The whole family, Mom included, took night swims in the phosphorescence, an experience so astonishing that when I hauled myself out in the moonlight, I wasn't sure I had fully retrieved me, that part of me wasn't left there among the sparks in the water.

On the highest tide of the century, we drove to Archirondel, a shingle beach on the east coast. Men in waders were fishing from the parking lot. The water had risen to shining puddles on the tarmac. The change was too much to take in. I felt terror as slick as the night-bright water and added sea-level rise to the list of silent bidding prayers, inspired by school and the news, that I would reel off at mass. On Sundays I'd kneel, like Jonah in the picture, in the pew. *Dear God, please don't let there be a nuclear bomb, or another ice age, please stop anything else going extinct like the dodo, please stop the acid rain, please stop people killing the whales and dolphins and seals.* If I forgot an item on the list, I'd feel uneasy all week.

By the time I was seven, Save the Whales was in full swing, Greenpeace having selected whales as their first ecological campaign in the year I was born. Whales were either blue-tinged angels gliding peacefully below the waves, leaping into the air with wings outstretched, or huge, collapsed, bloody carcasses being dragged onto factory ships. Sometimes they were on TV, as the people in Zodiac inflatables, which flashed orange against the dark water, tried to get in the way of the harpooners' sights. The *Rainbow Warrior*, Greenpeace's flamboyant three-masted campaign ship, once docked in St. Helier harbor to refuel, following an escape from a naval base in northern Spain, where it had been held after harassing the Spanish whaling fleet. The public were allowed onboard. I spoke to a bearded sailor, told him I loved whales, and asked to join the crew. He laughed, showed me around, and gave me a handful of stickers and badges to add to my collection. I've still got one of my Greenpeace badges. Most showed rorquals, the largest group of baleen whales, which include humpbacks, minkes, and blues. I didn't recognize one of the whales, so I put that badge away in a box and it survived. It shows a mother and a baby, swimming together. They do not have a dorsal fin, just knobbles on their backs, and they are gray.

Another ship, which would not make the news until decades later, was also at sea during this period of my childhood. The *Esso Atlantic* was a supertanker, the fourth-largest ship in the world and flagship of the Exxon International fleet. As it cruised the Atlantic, crossing paths with humpbacks and southern right whales, sophisticated sampling equipment in the belly of the ship took measurements from surface waters and the air to investigate the carbon cycle and the role of the ocean in storing CO_2 emissions.[1] It was unprecedented research, led by world-class scientists.

This project came after a warning the company, then Esso, had received in 1978 from one of its own employees, James Black.[2] He explained to executives that burning fossil fuels was increasing CO_2 levels, which would accumulate in the upper atmosphere and warm the planet. "Some countries would benefit but others would have their agricultural output reduced or destroyed," Black wrote in his presentation notes. There was a "five- to ten-year time window to establish what must be done."

The researchers working on the supertanker project made projections about CO_2 levels and global temperatures that would prove startlingly accurate today. The research was published and formed the basis of a 1982 technical briefing[3] prepared by Exxon's environmental affairs office and marked "not to be distributed externally." The document stated that some uncertainties needed further research, but it pointed clearly to "potentially catastrophic events that must be considered." These included the melting of the Antarctic ice sheet and agricultural disruption. Page five held an ominous warning: "There is concern among some scientific groups that once the effects are measurable, they might not be reversible."

By the time I was in my midteens, things had moved on for the energy companies. Exxon had ended the supertanker CO_2 research project. Inside the company, a communications strategy was taking shape. On an internal draft memo in 1988,[4] a public affairs manager wrote that what was then called the greenhouse effect "may be one of the most significant environmental issues for the 1990s." The spokesperson laid out "the Exxon position," which included to "emphasize the uncertainty" in any science on predicted climate effects. Exxon began to buy space in leading papers, such as the *New York Times*, for regular pieces that mimicked the look of a *Times* op-ed. These advertorials, as they became known, reached a readership of millions.[5] "Unsettled Science," read the title of one in 2000.[6] It wasn't only Exxon. A 1998 American Petroleum Institute memo,[7] developed by a group including Exxon, Chevron, and Southern Company, had laid out a draft Global Climate Science Communications Plan. The document described an effort to start a national media relations program "to inform the media about uncertainties in climate science." It said "victory would be achieved" when uncertainties became "conventional wisdom," and when those promoting the Kyoto treaty on the basis of existing science appeared to be "out of touch with reality." The journalists at *Inside Climate News* who worked on the Exxon story two decades later were nominated for a Pulitzer Prize. The oil giant said it was part of an orchestrated campaign to stigmatize and misrepresent the company on climate.[8]

"I cannot see into Exxon management's heart," said physicist Martin Hoffert, who had worked on climate models for Exxon. He was testifying to a US congressional committee in 2019, during a hearing examining oil industry efforts to suppress the truth on climate.[9] "Exxon was publicly promoting views that its own scientists knew were wrong. What they did was immoral."

In Jersey, I grew and swam. After dog paddle, I learned breaststroke, and to count myself down to a leap off the cobbled slipways. Held safe by the sea, I dreamed of whales.

Marie pulls her car up outside Union Station. "I feel nervous for you, doing this all by yourself."

Max and I are leaving LA, catching a train to San Diego. I look at him sleeping in his car seat. "Do you think I shouldn't be going?"

A pause, a clearing of the throat. "I think you've got to get it out of your system."

"But do you think it's okay to take him?"

"Well, you've spent so much money."

"But do you think it's too risky?"

A longer pause. "No."

Having squeezed out the response I need to hear, fairly or not, I hug her goodbye.

"Dis is train at Wenyee Park," says Max as he wakes to a departures announcement. "Bee-bee-beep."

I'm struggling with the buggy, car seat, rucksacks, bags.

The train attendant glares. "That buggy needs to be folded up, upstairs." She turns away before I can ask for help.

The train ride is a beauty. We shoot out of the station in our capsule, in glorious limbo, past the Wun Fun meat company buildings and a viaduct.

"Will be full of gin in twenty-five minutes," I mishear over the PA. My ears are clearly taking awhile to adjust to the American accent. Max and I stare out the window, transfixed. Muddy-brown snake of river and yellow conveyor-belt-plant flash past. Glittering heaps and in the distance mountains. I can feel the landscape filling my head. Toilet brush trees. Pale yellow earth. Pennzoil tank. Land site for sale. I count forty-two truck containers. Power lines crisscross the sky. This is how my heart is furnished, like the view from a train. I like to be totally occupied in the immediate. And am always, always, longing for something in the distance.

Max is sitting quietly next to me and then he is not. He is retching. I launch myself toward him just in time to catch a stream of brown vomit on my front. Chocolate milk shake while we waited for the train had seemed a great idea at the time. Passengers nearby look around, then quickly turn away. A towel, some tissues, I have nothing. I can't open my bag because my hands are covered in brown. When the retching stops, I shuffle backward into the aisle, carrying Max and cradling the brown lake between us on my T-shirt. I walk down the train toward the toilets. The carriage is full.

"Sorry, sorry," I say to each person as we pass.

A tall woman in a white blouse leaps up, her eyes wide. "Oh my."

I apologize frantically.

"What can I do?" she asks. She's joined by another woman offering help. They excavate items from my rucksack and pass them to me in the lavatory. Baby wipes, shampoo, diaper, clean clothes. Finally, they magic up a plastic bag to stuff the dirty clothes in, although our T-shirts aren't worth saving and go in the bin. I want to hug them but worry I might still smell of vomit, so I thank them instead.

"Been there," says the tall woman knowingly. The other smiles and wishes me luck.

"Nee-nee, Mummy," Max interrupts. It's our code word for "boobs." He breastfeeds sporadically for the remaining journey. I keep a towel and baby wipes close to hand.

It's getting dark when we arrive in San Diego.

"I need to go on a tram," Max shouts as the trams stream around us.

"Maxim," I say firmly, "we're getting a bus."

"Not a bus, I need to go on a *tram*," he screams. A man gives him a quarter and tells him I will buy him something later, but Max shrieks, at earsplitting volume, all the way through the bus journey and into check-in at the hotel. That night he sleeps peacefully but I can't. I take his temperature and check for rashes every few hours. What am I doing? Was it really that bad in the hostel? At least it was safe there.

I carefully remind myself that I tried hard to carve out a space for us in Jersey. I looked for jobs and even got an interview at the Environment Department, dredging up parts of my science CV for the application form. After university I'd worked on storm prediction, building a statistical model that predicted rainfall intensity, and for a year I'd assisted with an experiment about elevated levels of CO_2 and plant growth. For the job interview I crammed on insect-population sampling methods and was asked to prepare a talk on the Jersey grasshopper, *Euchorthippus pulvinatus elegantulus*. It looks like a pointy-headed mint humbug and is a species found nowhere else on earth. When Jersey was cut off from Europe, when sea levels rose and the land bridge was submerged about eight thousand years ago, this little creature was cut adrift from other grasshopper populations. It defined itself with unique evolutionary steps and likes resting vertically on grass stalks, in the sand dunes that huddle and sprawl opposite the bay that sweeps up the entire west coast of the island. As a child I'd liked throwing myself down the dunes and lying, sheltered from the wind, watching the insects crawl. I was sure I'd met the grasshopper before. It was an iconic animal, I told the interview panel, Jersey's equivalent of charismatic megafauna. It showcased the unique biodiversity of the island, and its quirky story of survival and adaptation could help people engage with environmental protection. I didn't get the job. It went to someone who'd discovered his own species of louse, a sympathetic insider told me later. As I watched Max sleep, I thought of the grasshopper, navigating its own path, with no other grasshopper relatives around to make it feel different, or to complain that it was doing something wrong.

At half past four in the morning I wheel Max out in the buggy, dropping things everywhere. He's still out for the count. A warm wind blows around a group of mainly elderly people standing by a minibus. I thought there would be other kids, other ages, families. Everyone's quiet, shocked to be up so early.

"I'm Ralph," a man who looks like a handsome Droopy the Dog introduces himself. He's tying things onto the roof and grumbles when he sees all my stuff. I fit the car seat into an empty row in the bus. Max wakes as I lift him in and stares sleepily out the window. No one speaks. We've got hours of driving ahead.

At the Mexican border the officials peer in and wave us on. The checkpoint guards are attractive, two women and one man, with tight trousers and guns. I fancy all of them. It feels so good to be out in the world again, brings back memories of traveling for work. I'm reminded that I once had a paid job, was self-supporting, judged useful by society. It's hot and dawn hasn't yet broken. We pass through Tijuana, where colorful roadside businesses are just starting to wake up.

"We're getting closer to the whales," I tell Max.

"Look, Flash, whales." He holds his toy dog up to the window.

"Not yet, we'll be there soon."

He gives me a dubious look and goes back to sleep.

We'll join the whales where the ocean is geographically blessed by the tropical and subtropical desert climate. The lagoons are their safe place, their birthing grounds. I've read that whale-watching pangas are not allowed to get close, but occasionally whales approach the boats and might even allow themselves to be touched.

I imagine a gray whale mother giving birth, raising her tail vertically from the water and lowering it again, repeating the movement while a comparatively tiny head emerges close to her flukes, from a beautiful long slit. Surrounded by seawater and amniotic fluid, the unborn calf will have been hearing everything, will know his mother's voice. He appears, inch by inch, then it's all in a rush, all five meters of newborn in the water, fins unfurling. The umbilical cord breaks and then they are two, the baby still depending on the mother for her milk, to regulate his heart rate and blood pressure, to provide immunity and safety, to teach him how to live. She supports him with her body; he scatters the surface, breaks the light with his first breath.

I remember breathing and blowing, calling out into the water as my body produced my son. Whales and humans are both mammals. I wonder if we experience birth similarly. Our babies both seek out the nipple, make sounds that communicate that they are upset or scared. We share the same survival instinct, feelings that tell us to go toward things or get away. I haven't managed to provide much in the way of close family for Max, but I want to show him his place in this more-than-human family. I want to tell the whales thank you, just for being here.

The windows start showing us desert and scrub. I love scrub. It looks angry. As if it's just got up. *Fuck you,* it says, *you try surviving here. See how you'll look.* Yeah, I think. We drive through more checkpoints. Ralph says we'll be searched and it might take some time. He says something about *ballenas* to the guards. They look at Max and me, at the buggy on top of the van, and wave us straight through. I gloat inwardly that we and our troublesome luggage have made things easier for the group. On the narrow mountain roads, trucks come by fast and close. Cacti give us the finger as we pass. We arrive in Guerrero Negro as the clouds curdle with orange.

I carry Max to our room, his face and arms licked amber by the sunset. I know whales see in monochrome. But do they play in the changing light as night falls? They wrap their lives around their young in these lagoons, and by seeking them out I'm finding the space to do that too. The rest of the world can wait awhile. I wonder if the baby whales are sleeping. Are the mothers watching the sky? Do they feel the wonder too?

UTQIAĠVIK: AĠVIQ

Latitude: 71° 17' 26" N
Longitude: 156° 47' 19" W

In the dark of winter, under the sea ice of the northern Bering Sea, there are voices. *Aġviġit*,[1] bowhead whales, *Balaena mysticetus*, like to sing. Many mammals have calls but few sing. The repertoire of an *aġviq* is rivaled by only a few songbirds. We've captured the gentle echoing cries, screeches, trumpets, and rubbery squeaks, sometimes bovine, sometimes human-sounding, sometimes like a bow scraping roughly across the strings of a double bass. Oceanographers put a hydrophone into the sea off the east coast of Greenland hoping to hear a few sounds.[2] They discovered a loud concert that continued twenty-four hours a day from November until April, with never the same melody between seasons. Kate Stafford led the listening project over three years of study. "If humpback whale song is like classical music, bowheads are jazz," she said. Even in the constant darkness of the polar winter, each aġviq finds plenty to sing about.

As the spring currents flow north and east, so does aġviq, into the summer's window of light at the top of the planet. The super-organism of krill that hatched in the Bering Sea is swept in a cloud to Alaska's northern coast. It's copepods, though, other tiny crustaceans that are the preferred calorific engines of aġviq growth and which draw the whales all the way east to the Canadian Beaufort Sea. They feast on these living globules of fat that swarm in the waters of Amundsen Gulf when microalgae bloom. Aġviq is said to feed two steps away from light. Leapfrogging to the bottom of the food chain eliminates steps where energy is lost and is why the whales can become so huge. It's also why they must spend so much time feeding. The thick blubber just below the skin stores energy and insulates the body. Its elasticity streamlines.

A male aġviq waits at the southern edge of the sea ice, resting his chin on the edge of the floe. The animals are straining against the final days of winter. Whales, seals, walrus, caribou. High above come geese, Arctic tern, ptarmigan, and snowbirds. All are pulled north as the freeze lifts off the land and water. When the sea ice opens up, the Bering Strait will funnel the sea mammals north. A pod of aġviġit doze at the edge of the polar ice pack. Only half their brains are actually asleep as like all whales they must make a conscious effort to breathe. One aġviq, a cow, is swollen. Her calf is growing, will be born in six weeks and swim alongside her. A gull lands on her back and she startles, thrashing the water. Around her whales do synchronized acrobatics. They tail-slap, mate, occasionally they breach and spy-hop, heads pointing vertically out of the water. The ice creaks and pops. A wind from the right direction will split the ice, open up a crack into a lead, a channel. They know it's not yet time, somehow sense the ice ahead is too densely packed. They are poised. They wait.

It was July 2005. Aġviġit were feeding in the Canadian Arctic, and scientists were tracking a "stunning" reduction in sea ice.[3] In the far north, chunks of thick, old ice were cracking, breaking away from the polar pack and drifting south. In London, four terrorists detonated suicide bombs on the London transport network at rush hour. Fifty-six people died. The city was in shock. I could tell from the back of my black cab, as it moved through the dark. There was more stillness, less scurrying. The few night workers I saw cast their eyes around them, looked up at the streetlights, as if checking for signs of which world they lived in, the one before or the one after. I'd spent a week on night shifts, reporting on the aftermath from locations across the city for an all-night breakfast news program that hit time zones across the globe as they woke. East Asia, South Asia, and finally Europe. On my last shift I interviewed a Salvation Army spokesperson at King's Cross. We stood next to a wall covered in posters of the missing. Dulled by exhaustion and adrenaline, I wasn't expecting to see a familiar face.

"How are you supporting emergency workers?" I asked. Then I saw her. The young woman at my bank. Just days before the bombings she'd helped me with a mundane inquiry about same-day payments, all the time beaming, as though I were giving her a gift. Her picture was on the wall. After work I took the bus home, blinking in the daylight. She'd been on that same bus route I later learned, traveling in the opposite direction. She'd sat next to the bomber. All the way home I kept seeing her face, framed by her blue hijab, smiling.

A nauseous sleep of unidentified length later and I was sitting opposite Alex in a café. I held a beer by its neck, concentrating on the cold of it, swiping the beads of moisture into nothing with my thumb. It always took awhile to get the hang of daytime after night shifts, and today of all glaring summer days it was helpful to be meeting Alex Kirby. Alex was rocklike, in opinions and build. He wore traditional clothes, proper coats, waxed jackets. His voice was deep and measured. He'd worked at the BBC for decades, had been environment correspondent, religious affairs correspondent, a bureau chief. It was reassuring just listening to him ask the waiter for potato pancakes and salmon. If anyone could put the world back in order for me, it was Alex.

"And two more Tyskies, please," he added, observing the speed with which I was drinking. I'd first met Alex a year before, after emailing him to ask for advice on pitching environment stories. I struggled in the planning meetings, when fifteen or so producers sat in a circle and took turns to sell their idea.

"What's new?" or "Too worthy, too World Service," an editor might say, or "We need a human angle, an eyewitness," or simply "Next."

I'd begun my career at BBC World Service radio as a business presenter. My editor had encouraged me, so much so that I'd written to the then director general, Greg Dyke. I'd told him the BBC needed a correspondent who covered environment and business together, I told him we were missing the whole story, and he'd even replied, politely pooh-poohing my idea. Now that I worked in news, it was even harder. Alex and I had met a couple of times to talk, but we hadn't solved my original problem, my Cassandra complex.

"I'm having more success with the Middle East, would you believe." I'd actually got a Hezbollah bigwig on the phone the other day, I told Alex. I was still trying to impress him, convince him, and myself, that I was not the idiot I so often felt at work.

"Doreen, you're a good journalist, everyone knows that," said Alex on cue. Even when multiple conflicts in the Middle East or London under attack weren't taking over the news agenda entirely, environment was a bloody hard beat. Sir Crispin Tickell, he said, had once explained to him exactly why that was.

Sir Crispin was a diplomat, whose first responsibility was the British Antarctic Territory and who counted among his ancestors an influential supporter of Darwin. When other politicians were ignoring climate, dismissing it as a purely scientific concern, he was already outspoken. He even performed a minor miracle by convincing

Margaret Thatcher to give a speech on it. In the early 1990s, during an interview, he'd offered Alex an explanation as to why the media didn't often cover science, specifically climate.

"It's because so few senior editors are science graduates," Sir Crispin said. Alex had offered the comments as a story to the editor of the *Six O'Clock News* on Radio 4. The editor had turned it down.

"He said it was interesting, but he wouldn't be running it," added Alex. "*He* was an arts graduate, he told me." The waiter brought the pancakes, topped by pyramids of sour cream, salmon, and dill. I realized how hungry I was, tried to eat slowly enough that I didn't make a mess.

At that time climate skeptics and deniers were all over the media. The right-wing tabloids shamelessly rubbished the science. "The claim of man-made global warming is a global fraud," wrote a *Daily Mail* columnist.[4] Skeptics presented themselves as courageous dissenters[5] against political correctness gone mad. Some would later be exposed as having financial links to the fossil fuel industry,[6] yet they were interviewed everywhere, in a warped distortion of journalistic balance. A *Guardian* piece giving the view of eight experts in the lead-up to the G8 summit quoted S. Fred Singer at the top: "The science of global warming is not settled."[7] An influential denier, he'd previously attacked the science on the harmful effects of tobacco smoke.[8] Even if unwittingly, the prominence given to his comments by the *Guardian* inevitably invited the reader to doubt the seven statements that appeared underneath his, all from people who took climate change seriously. Doubt was amplified by politicians who wanted to deny, delay, or distract from the issue. In broadcast media it was worse because there was only ever room for one or two speakers. The skeptics were usually effective orators, and on the radio program I worked for they were given half the airtime in debates because editors were told they needed an opposing view. The Intergovernmental Panel on Climate Change, the IPCC, had already found evidence that "most of the warming observed over the last fifty years" was due to "human activities"[9] and said the rate of warming was likely unprecedented in the past ten thousand years. But in discussions, skeptics presented uncertainties as more important than what was established and veered off into politics, economics, whatever.

A dogeared newspaper some days old lay on the table. "God, I hate that word," I said, enlivened by my second beer, jabbing my finger at the print on the page. Tony Blair was irritated with "environmentalists" criticizing the lack of political progress on climate, the paper reported.[10] *Environmentalists* was lazy shorthand for scientists, economists, diplomats, and political leaders, I complained. "It sounds so dismissive, so, so . . ."

Alex finished his mouthful and then my sentence: "It's just one up from *bunny hugger*."

I laughed, elated by the support.

Recently I'd attended a meeting on science coverage called by a senior World Service editor. The consensus in the room had been that scientists and engineers were boring to listen to. "I'm an engineer," I'd blurted. What was boring about people who could stop us blundering into disaster? "The engineers had very interesting things to say about the levees in New Orleans before Hurricane Katrina, about the likelihood of them failing," I pointed out. "I don't think we're putting them on air enough. We need to hear them out."

More widely, I didn't understand how climate science could be dismissed so easily and so often throughout the mainstream media. But then I didn't know about Exxon, didn't know about the oil companies' campaign of doubt. I didn't know that reputable journalists had been misled by the fossil fuel industry's misinformation.

"Doreen," Alex said, "you mustn't give up."

"I'm tired." I put my head in my hands, closed my eyes. I saw the beaming face of the beautiful girl in her hijab helping me at the bank. I saw the wrecked bus on the road. I saw my mom and me a few weeks earlier, looking over the city from the top of a hill at night, at the millions of tiny lights.

"Look," my mom had said with wonder. "Humanity." I'd noticed her repeating questions, losing her train of thought, had gently suggested that something might be up with her memory.

"Not at all," she'd said. People were so vulnerable, could be gone in an instant, and didn't recognize a disaster unless the wreckage was right in front of us. Climate felt as urgent to me as reporting on the horror of the terrorist attack.

Alex was still talking. I'd missed a whole chunk. He was wryly smiling. Did I know how a senior Radio 4 producer had congratulated him when he was made environment correspondent in 1987?

"Waste of a good reporter, they told me," said Alex. Being upright and facing the world suddenly felt too much of a challenge. I wanted to go home and lie down. Nearly two decades of scientific research later and what had changed? Humanity? What was humanity doing? Humanity was fucked.

The Arctic was the front line of climate change, I wrote in my application for the travel bursary. Anyone at the BBC who had an idea of how to spend the grant could apply for it. I did the interview down the phone from Jerusalem that December, in between trips to the Palestinian territories. After investigating, I told the interview panel, I would be able to give eyewitness accounts of what, if anything, was happening. I explained the plan, hatched with my mom's help. I would travel the northern Arctic coast, starting in the west, in Alaska, moving across Canada. I wouldn't prompt anyone, would just listen and, with their express permission, would record what Indigenous people and other locals thought about the warming, whether they considered it in the everyday. I had pitched as though my life depended on it, one interviewer told me afterward. They couldn't bear to say no.

Utqiaġvik, or Barrow as it was then known, would be my first stop. I wrote to the Barrow Whaling Captains Association, asking permission to spend time with the hunters, and called Glenn Sheehan, director of the Barrow Arctic Science Consortium, at the old Naval Arctic Research Laboratory base, NARL. He and his wife and daughter lived in one of the huts outside town. Glenn agreed that I could stay in an empty researcher's hut, but for one night only. After that I would need to find my own accommodation. I flew from London to Anchorage via Minneapolis. It felt as if I were taking my equipment on holiday. I carried two MiniDisc recorders in case the first broke, a video camera with an expensive Leica lens, a collapsible silver reflector for difficult light conditions, endless wires, spare tapes, numerous rechargeable batteries, and a folding tripod. I also had two bulky cases containing a satellite phone and portable sat dish I'd borrowed from work so I could call from anywhere in an emergency. I'd bought insulated canvas bags for everything, to try to prevent it freezing. I had no idea if anything would actually function in subzero temperatures, but carrying it all gave me a sense of purpose, kept me occupied, made me feel less scared.

On the bus in Anchorage, I met a Native Alaskan woman dressed in a tracksuit, her hair in a neat ponytail. She'd heard my accent when I spoke to the driver and asked me where I was from. She spoke with a rhythm and softness that I had not heard before.

"Cold up there," she said when I explained where I was going. "I've never been so far north. You got good clothes?" I told her I'd borrowed skiwear from a friend and was on my way to buy ex-military rubber "bunny boots" from an army-and-navy surplus store. They were recommended in the guidebooks. The bus meandered along stretched-out roads in between shopping malls and through parking lots. We passed a bird perched on top of a streetlight. "A raven," said the woman, pointing. She told me the story of Big Raven, who made the world, who was responsible for the dark and the light. When everything was water, Big Raven came and created the earth. He made the first heaven folk and the Inuit and the animals. "If you pray to Raven, he can bring fine weather for hunting." She wished me luck as she got off at her stop.

I found bulbous bright white bunny boots in my size and, in a department store, sunscreen that was all grease. The sun's reflection off the ice was fierce, I'd read, and if you wore a water-based cream, your skin would freeze. To prevent snow blindness, which sounded painful and frightening, I bought sunglasses with leather wings on the sides as well as ski goggles. Around the city, mountains reared up on all sides, giving me a feeling of trepidation and a new sense of scale. This landscape looked endless, powerful. If I went hunting, I thought, I would pray to Raven with all my might that I wouldn't simply be swallowed up in it.

Then I flew to Utqiaġvik. On the plane I sat next to a woman who introduced herself as Marie. She explained that she was waiting for her green card and couldn't leave the country. She was missing home in the Czech Republic, and her dad had suggested she travel to the top and the bottom of the United States to soothe her itchy feet. When we disembarked, the freeze outside pummeled us. I got a nosebleed instantly. The Korean American taxi driver who drove me from the airport to NARL told me that polar bears often hid behind mounds of snow around town. On one side of the road were buildings, on the other was the frozen Arctic Ocean, and bears could walk right on in. That evening Marie and I met for dinner at Arctic Pizza and walked around as much as we dared, running for it when we thought we saw a mound of snow move. People here left their doors unlocked, Glenn had told me, in case someone was being chased by a bear and needed to get inside quickly. I spent a comfortable but anxious night in the researcher's hut, a strange rounded metal capsule that hummed with the effort of the heaters. When I woke, I immediately got another taxi back into town. I followed my only lead. Glenn had suggested I go to the community workshop at the Iñupiat Heritage Center and talk to the locals, the whalers. The Iñupiat were subsistence hunters, dependent for centuries on bowhead whales, aġviġit, whose populations had been devastated by commercial whaling. Bowheads were massive, rotund icebreaker whales, who lived a long time and reproduced slowly. In the late seventies the International Whaling Commission, which was set up to protect the future of commercial whaling and included the major whaling nations that had decimated global whale populations, imposed a moratorium on the Iñupiat. The hunters challenged the IWC and, using a combination of rigorous science and cultural arguments, forced it to revise its stance. The Alaska Eskimo Whaling Commission was then established to self-manage the hunt in accordance with IWC rules.[11] A quota of about twenty whales per year was shared among approximately fifty family crews,[12] who hunted twice a year, in the spring and the autumn.

Arriving at the Heritage Center, I found a lone Iñupiaq man inside the workshop, wearing jeans and a backward baseball cap. He was slim, a little shorter than me, and was working quietly on the skeleton of a wooden boat, about seven yards long and covered with what looked like white hide. I said hello. He looked up, nodded slightly, and continued working. I checked the adjoining rooms. There was no one else in the entire place except the receptionist, a young man who was talking on his phone. I tried to make small talk with the boatbuilder.

"That's a nice boat."

"Uh-huh." He straightened up, then bent back down to rummage through his tools. I introduced myself, explained why I was there, that I was interested in climate change.

"Doreen from London, eh?" he summarized from down behind

his boat. There was no time to waste. I asked straight out if he was in a whaling crew and, if so, could I please join it? He stopped his work, circled the vessel, stood at the prow, and ran his hands lightly along the wood. I thought perhaps he hadn't heard me properly, but then he shrugged. "You'll have to ask the boss."

Okay, I said, where was he? Where could I find him?

"They'll be along sometime today." He was now smoothing the thick, pale fabric that covered the outside of the wood. Sometime today? I can't wait, I'm busy. Then it dawned on me that I wasn't busy at all and I had no option but to sit tight, chewing my nails.

The man eventually made a phone call, speaking in Iñupiaq. He looked me up and down while he was talking, as if describing me. After he hung up, I watched as he went back to the boat, checking the pull and push of the structure with his hands. He took occasional glances at me, and then I'd sit self-consciously still, examining the walls and the equipment in the room. When he stopped looking at me, I watched him again. He was slow, methodical, in his work. I began to feel calm.

The boss, it turned out, was Julia, the formidable and beautiful matriarch of Kaleak crew. High cheekbones presided over a stately face that regarded me with suspicion and interest in equal measure. She'd been in charge, she told me, since her beloved husband, Jeslie, a former mayor, had suffered an aneurysm while out hunting on the ice. Jeslie had made a miraculous recovery after being on life support, but his mind had lost some of its sharpness. Short-term memory loss would make whaling too dangerous, and Julia didn't hunt herself, so, until her children were old enough to take over, a respected hunter named Van had stepped in to help lead the Kaleak family's whaling crew.

"A vegetarian? From London?" Julia seemed skeptical I'd fit in, especially after she asked what I'd want in the way of food.

"I'll have whatever you're having," I followed up quickly. I'd sort out the details later. I just needed somewhere to sleep tonight. I would pay, of course, I explained hurriedly, in exchange for a room and for being allowed to join Kaleak crew on the sea ice and to talk to them about climate. I was interested in the science, nothing political, wasn't about to criticize the whaling. I didn't have much stuff, my camera was very small. The money would come out of a travel bursary I'd been lucky enough to win, so Julia needn't feel bad about charging me a reasonable rent. I'd help the whalers with whatever they needed, I was fit and strong, used to looking after myself, a good team worker. I didn't eat much anyway. It felt like a job interview, an important one, except Julia said nothing, didn't ask questions, just observed me carefully through her spectacles as I floundered, wondering what she wanted to know, what might reassure her.

"You can sleep in my sewing room," she said finally, and there in the Heritage Center a deal was struck. Kaleak crew included her nephew Billy, the man I'd first spoken to, who was still working on the boat; Julia's youngest son, Jeslie Junior, also known as JJ, who worked at the fire department; her middle son, Eli, an aspiring chef; several other members of the extended Kaleak family; and now me. Julia drove me to her home on North Star Street and showed me to a mattress among the parkas-in-progress, in the room next to Eli's. She eyed my clothes as I unpacked.

"The socks are good." She nodded approvingly at the inner, middle, and outer pairs I'd displayed but shook her head at my coat. She went to her room and reappeared with what looked like an entire animal in her arms. "Here, try this on top of your fleeces." It was a lambskin parka, heavy, and getting into it was like crawling into a tunnel that was only just big enough for my body. I had long enough in the dark to feel slight panic, and then I was out the other side, feeling much more substantial, and constrained. "Good," said Julia. It didn't matter that I couldn't move much and felt like a football, she told me, I'd get used to it. The main thing was that I was warm. Next I tried a white covering that fitted over the parka to make me the same color as the ice. As I was doing this, an extremely tall man strode through the door. "Honey, this is Doreen," said Julia.

"Jeslie," he said. I struggled to lift my now-giant arm to shake his hand. He laughed at me with the loose giggle of a child, only baritone, which offset his imposing presence. "Looks good. Fits you all right. You'll need that out there."

"You're all ready, ready to go out whaling," said Julia.

The bursary didn't require you to work, to do any journalism. It was a sabbatical. The idea was that you could immerse yourself in a place and absorb more than if you were questioning people as a reporter and narrowing the world down into stories. I was supposed to take thinking time away from the relentless news cycle, open my mind, and return bursting with creativity and new ideas.

Julia and Jeslie's house was made to relax in. The living room was comfortable, with a rich pink carpet. I sat down on the sofa, sank into the cushions.

"That's one of my favorite films," I said, seeing a copy of *Atanarjuat: The Fast Runner* on a shelf. Julia took it down and we watched it together that evening, both laughing loudly at the scene when Oki urinates on the pile of seaweed, not knowing that Atanarjuat is hiding from him underneath it. Jeslie sat with us for about twenty minutes before he got restless and said he was going to the Search & Rescue Base, where Julia said the hunters played cards and pool, and where the VHF radio was manned twenty-four hours a day in case of an emergency out on the ice or the tundra. If something happened, volunteers would go to help. After a few oatcakes, too overwhelmed to feel hungry, I went to bed, unsettled by its not being dark. I picked my way carefully around the piles of furs and collapsed onto the mattress, overcome with exhaustion and relief that I'd found such a hospitable family, just by chance.

Waking the following morning, safe from the cold and the bears,

I took in my surroundings more slowly. Jeslie was making coffee that smelled of hazelnuts. Eli was frying doughnuts, to sell at the bank later, he said. My breakfast was porridge, or oatmeal now that I was in the United States. Sun streamed in through a square window, gilding the kitchen surfaces with light. Looking out, I could see North Star Street, coated with powder snow, crystals visible on the surface. A wind was rippling the tarps on top of the boats just outside the house. Long icicles dripped from the eaves. Eli gave me a doughnut, soft and warm.

"When are we going hunting?" I asked.

"Gotta watch the sky." A lanky figure had appeared at the door.

"Hey, Van," said Eli, "meet our new crewmate." From the way Van looked at me and sighed, I could tell he was unimpressed. When the time was right, he dutifully explained, a gray line would appear in the clouds, reflecting the dark streak of open water and indicating an *uiñiq*, a split in the sea ice offshore. With the right weather conditions, this would widen into a channel along which the whales would migrate from the Chukchi Sea to the Beaufort Sea. I duly checked the sky every few minutes. I had a schedule, deadlines, needed to get on with it, so I could move on to Canada. After traveling so far, I was longing to get busy. I was also longing for another doughnut, eyeing the pile greedily, only just managing to hold back from asking for another.

"Out here." Julia wanted to show me something. She led the way through to the *qanitchaq*, or entrance hall. It was an air lock, keeping the cold out when people came in. It was also a useful storage space, full of footwear, parkas, equipment, and chest freezers full of meat. She lifted a lid. I could see huge cubes of pink topped with a layer of black. "This is dinner, this is the *best* dinner." It was *maktak*, whale skin and blubber, and was in high demand. Only the coastal people, whaling communities, could get it for themselves. "We share with everyone," said Julia. When Kaleak crew harvested a whale, she distributed the meat among the community and sent her relatives portions by air. She had family in Point Hope, a village farther southwest along the coast, and came from a long line of whalers. Her father, Jacob, and her uncle Amos were renowned as harpooner and captain. As the whaling captain's wife, Julia was arguably the most important person in the crew. The whales were said to come to her. The wife had to think peaceful thoughts and act generously because the old belief was that the whales might send a runner to listen in on what the women were saying. Everyone who contributed, by hunting, cooking, sewing, or lending equipment, was counted as crew. Elders gave advice when they were no longer physically able to hunt. Women could be hunters if they wanted to, Van said there were several, but it seemed to be mostly men.

Julia told me about growing up in Point Hope. One time she and her sister were out berry picking when they met an *akłaq*, a brown bear. They left their berries on the ground and walked away slowly, she said. Her dad had told her never to run from a bear. He'd also taught her how important it was to share and be hospitable. That's why she'd said I could join the crew. She'd thought of her dad, his generosity, what he would have done. "I just looked at you and thought, 'She seems nice, she can stay.'"

I kept myself busy sky watching, until Eli loaned me a book of old stories,[13] written first in Iñupiaq and then translated into English. The first was a creation story. When the big flood came, everything was covered by water and people could hunt whales. The hunters were out in their umiaq, their sealskin boat, and saw a grassy tussock surfacing. It was a creature, a whale. They failed to catch it, but Raven speared it from his kayak. It rose from the ocean and they saw flowers on it. The water began to recede and the worms and snakes wriggled away, leaving rivers behind them. The whale became the land.

The final story in the book was a historical account of a year of starvation among the Nunamiut, the Iñupiat living inland, when many people had already died of measles brought by a ship. During the autumn and winter of that year, there were no caribou, no ptarmigan, no sheep. The fish were not easy to catch. The black type became increasingly stark against the white of the page as I read the stories of families, adults, children, and dogs who died. The people and animals were named. The account had no emotion, just facts, until the narrator's father cried. The family traveled back and forth in search of food. In desperation, people ate everything possible, including caribou calf skins, leaving only the inedible skins of the boats.

I looked up the measles epidemic on Julia's computer. Outsiders had brought catastrophic waves of disease to the Arctic peoples. My hand became clammy on the mouse as I scrolled through an account of a meeting in 1834 between a Hudson's Bay Company trader and a group of families who'd never before encountered Europeans, near Kuujjuaq in Nunavik, Quebec, formerly known as Fort Chimo.[14] "We had been ill of a cold on their arrival," the trader had written, "and six of them died in the course of twenty-four hours. The poor people left us in a great hurry. They left their dead also exposed upon the rocks." In the summer of 1900, the Great Sickness struck. Influenza and measles killed thousands of Native Alaskans.[15] Outbreaks of disease, which also included diphtheria, typhoid, smallpox, TB, and polio, hit different groups at different times. Whole families died, orphans starved. Euro-Americans were largely unaffected or suffered only mild symptoms. The diseases were thought to have been brought by ships from Seattle or San Francisco and also spread by Inuit who had traveled to Siberia to trade with Koryak and Chukchi people, who'd likely been infected by Russian traders.[16] Ships between the goldfields in Nome and the Yukon River carried infections farther. In 1918, hearing of the deaths from Spanish influenza, the villagers of Shishmaref on the Seward Peninsula set up a barricade, manned day and night by armed guards, which prevented anyone from approaching and kept the flu out.[17] By the 1930s, many communities were estimated to have lost up to 90 percent of their numbers.[18]

As I absorbed the words, part of me wanted to stop, to look away from the horror. But how come I knew so little about what had happened here? It felt wrong. I continued, reading that Waldo Bodfish Sr., an Iñupiaq elder from Wainwright, had said survivors decided to have many children to build the population back up.[19] Harold Napoleon, the child of Alaskan Yup'ik survivors, a people who fished and hunted predominantly seals and walrus, wrote that the waves of death left behind a generation of orphans. Irreplaceable knowledge and stories were lost, he said. Yup'ik survivors refused to speak about shamanism. "Their ancient world had collapsed."[20] People were "without anchor . . . in shock, listless, confused, bewildered, heartbroken, and afraid."[21] Napoleon identified the suffering as post-traumatic stress disorder and linked it to subsequent alcohol use. He himself struggled with the consequences of alcohol abuse and addiction, and after observing fellow Native Alaskans during his prison term concluded "that the primary cause of alcoholism is not physical but spiritual."[22]

The snow piled up and the wind cut in around the house on North Star Street while I spent hours glued to Julia's computer. Outsiders, I learned, had used alcohol as a tool in their attempts to coerce and control, right from the start. In the early nineteenth century, trading companies and colonial governments used alcohol to "get them drunk and get their stuff,"[23] obtaining access to hides, food supplies, labor, sex, and land.[24] Whiskey was often used as payment. The people of Utqiaġvik were canny traders, and accounts from the end of that century recorded that Europeans often came off at a disadvantage.[25] Unscrupulous whites responded by getting people drunk before negotiations.[26] Scrolling and sifting through the history, I found research by anthropologist Barbara Bodenhorn, whose work with Iñupiat communities spanned decades. In the mid-1980s, she'd carried out an extensive study on alcohol use. Utqiaġvik resident Charlotte Brower told her that mild alcoholic beverages, such as fermented berries, were already used on some social occasions.[27] The ships brought stronger alcohol though, spirits, and with them binge drinking and violence among rank-and-file sailors, many of whom were reluctant Arctic voyagers, having been more or less kidnapped into crews. Early anecdotal reports from Alaska and Canada said Inuit peoples didn't easily acquire a taste for alcohol,[28] but heavy-drinking whalers, fur traders, fish processors, prospectors, and military developed a buyers' market for distilled spirits.[29] In 1834 it became illegal to sell alcohol to Native peoples.[30] For some, drinking was then partly an act of defiance against the outsiders, who thought they could make all the rules.[31]

In the latter half of the nineteenth century in Utqiaġvik, those who took up drinking and alcohol trafficking were mainly older men,[32] although a significant number of whaling captains shunned alcohol altogether.[33] During this period, people in Barrow told Captain C. L. Hooper how a trader had brought in a large amount of liquor and many had failed to catch seal for the winter, resulting in starvation.[34] After this, they had asked the traders and whalers not to bring alcohol again.[35] The younger generation drank far less. One man of that generation, called Kunagrak, told his son, Levi Griest, they'd found alcohol was "no help at all."[36] Iñupiat culture, with its highly organized whaling units and formal leadership structure, seemed to have empowered the people more than some others in their dealings with colonizers.

When the Yankee whalers departed, they left the technology to make alcohol, but many locals chose to quit or reduce drinking.[37] The withdrawal of the colonizing presence meant the Iñupiat relied again on traditional skills and reestablished their independence. For a time, social pressure not to drink was strong. Then those who served in the Second World War brought newly acquired drink and drug habits home. In the sixties and seventies more and more people went away to school and to the military.

Oil was discovered in Prudhoe Bay in 1968. This hastened the period of land claims legislation, when the impending Alaska Native Claims Settlement Act, ANCSA, essentially mandated that to negotiate successfully with the power brokers in Washington, DC, many Iñupiat had to engage in a deal-making culture where drinking was the norm, an expression of power. This period, when alcohol was reintroduced to several age groups and in a variety of contexts, is when some locals, who wanted to remain anonymous, told Barbara Bodenhorn it "started being a problem."[38] ANCSA was passed in 1971. From then on, business and political discussions involving huge amounts of money, vital natural resources, and intricate legal structures became never-ending.[39]

Young people talking to Barbara Bodenhorn in the mid-eighties said they might have a drink to lessen the impact of racism, of stereotyping and discrimination by non-Iñupiat, or to deal with work anxiety, money worries, and family stresses.[40] "It's hard to provide for families," a community member told her.[41] She concluded that chaotic heavy-drinking eras on the North Slope had coincided with periods of low political control and when autonomy over vital natural assets, such as animals and land, was threatened. Some people, speaking anonymously, told her that their partners, serious hunters, drank to escape rage at the imposition of new hunting rules and at feelings of individual powerlessness.[42]

I thought about my own drinking. I regularly used alcohol to let off steam on weekend binges with friends, to deal with anxiety and bond with colleagues at work drinks, and in attempts to prove whiskey-drinking prowess with favorite relatives. Some occasions, I knew, I would not have managed without being drunk. Julia had mentioned that she and Jeslie didn't drink. She hadn't made a big deal about it, just said they were better off without it. They'd quit years ago. I wouldn't drink here either, I decided.

I closed the browser and went to the kitchen, where Julia was sorting cutlery.

"Can I help?"

"You could put these on the table."

I arranged the knives and forks, contemplating her hospitality and openness toward me, the foreigner, and the tradition of generosity passed on from her father. Then I grimaced, thinking of the generations before, the people who'd lived, and died, when the first ships had arrived.

"You okay? Something hurting you?" Julia asked.

"I'm okay." I chewed my lip.

"Well, lunch is ready. Come and eat."

Julia, Jeslie, Eli, Van, and I took our seats around the table, a block of raw maktak in pride of place at the center. I put a piece of skin and blubber, about the size of a matchstick, on a cracker.

"That's how Ethel eats hers," said Julia. "The lady I work with."

I took a bite. My mouth and tongue burst with deep-sea flavors and smells. My throat rebelled. I fought for control, swallowed. Holy God, I had eaten whale.

"You want sardines? I don't want to make you sick," said Julia.

"No, I'm fine. Can I have some water, please?"

"You need chaser?" She laughed.

"It's just different from what I'm used to."

The house phone rang.

Julia answered. "Billy? Are you *imiqpiñ*? . . . They're working on the boat. Call when you're sober, then you can go help." She hung up.

"Was he high?" asked Eli.

"Yup. I said, 'You get sober, then you can help.'"

"We'll be done with the aluminum later today," said Van. The aluminum was a metal boat with an outboard motor.

"That's the chaser boat that goes after the whale once it's harpooned?" I said, trying to keep up.

"Yup, and when we're done with that, we load up, break trail," said Van. *Breaking trail* meant cutting a smooth path for the snowmobiles across the frozen ocean.

"Shake my hand, I'm being friends." Julia reached toward me. The rest of the table had paused and were watching carefully. I snatched my hand back sharply on seeing the shine of whale oil all over her outstretched palm. Eli and Jeslie roared with laughter. "It's the best, better than vitamin E oil," Julia said. "We need to put you back in that parka and take a picture of you, so your mom could see." She assumed my mom would be interested. Under Julia's approving gaze, I'd finished my maktak. "You just won your prize," she said, getting a bag of Eli's doughnuts out of the cupboard. "How many do you want, seven?"

"Did you find any in her room?" asked Eli. Everyone laughed. My reputation for liking doughnuts had already spread.

We'd been eating the whale that Kaleak crew caught last season, Van reminded us, keen to reminisce. What advice did they have for me when I was out there? I asked.

"Keep your eyes open in the front and the back and the sides," said Julia. I must stay out of their way, and if they asked me to do something, must do it with no questions asked. "Make sure there's no *nanuq*, no polar bear, around you. And no cracks. You see any cracks, you let them know."

"We're going to make you do a night shift," said Van. "Polar bear watch." Lots of polar bears were around, I'd been told. They'd shot one already that season. The bear had been eating a sealskin boat.

"They can run faster than the snow machines. They're big but they're fast," said Van.

"Right now it's feeding time for them," said Julia.

Were they trying to scare me, or was it scary without their even trying?

"Sometimes you can't see them until they're close because it's whiteout," said Eli.

"So if I'm on polar bear watch, how am I supposed to spot them?"

"Movement," said Eli. "Look for snow that is walking."

"Sometimes they can crawl up, sneak up on you, and you don't know," said Jeslie.

"Yeah, real low," added Van.

"It's important to be quiet," said Julia, "in case there are whales out there." She paused. "We normally don't take any outsiders because it's really serious when it's whaling season. You need to be ready to leave at any time. You never know what's going to happen, it's up to God."

It was true. I could never have predicted what happened.

LAGUNA OJO DE LIEBRE

Latitude: 27° 44' 59" N
Longitude: 114° 14' 60" W

"I need to see," says Max, peering over the side of the boat. The water rustles. Sun burns down on Baja, on the lagoon, on his little hooded head. We are nine passengers, including Ralph, the grandfatherly guide. Francisco, our Mexican driver, is steering the outboard motor at the back.

"Yes, you need to see," I say, putting my arms around Max's waist and hoisting him up to the side. He is tall for a two-year-old, heavy, and bulky in the orange life jacket. We peer over the edge, watch the crinkled water rising and falling away. There's a cold wind and a light fog. The sky is stuffed full of cotton-wool balls. Twenty yards away is another boat, packed like an egg box. We are watching a rock covered with barnacles about fifteen yards to starboard. The rock sighs.

Max is restless, bored of rock watching. "'Twinkle, twinkle, little star,'" I sing softly.

"Stop. No you singing." He takes up the song himself. "'How I wonder what you are!'"

"It's a solo performance," says Ralph.

The rock is moving. It's not a rock now, it's a giant slug, sliding into the sea. It disappears.

I see something under the boat, about a yard down. Something like a moon. Huge, gray, cratered. I brace my feet on the shifting wood. The moon rolls over. An eye the size of a tennis ball is staring straight at me from a few inches below the surface. The world goes silent.

There's a sharp *puh*, an explosion of spray in front of us and all over Max, who screams. Stinking bottom-of-the-ocean shrimp breath engulfs us. Tiny droplets catch a rainbow. Moon and water erupt into the air. Five feet of whale head is sticking straight up toward the sky. Gray whales are thought to see forward and down, which is useful when skimming prey off the ocean floor. It's angling its eyes to look at us. The downward-curved mouth is big as a slide, close enough to touch.

"Aaaah, go way, whale!" shouts Max. I don't know how to reassure him. It's his first sea monster.

"Incroyable!" a French voice shouts from my right.

"No teeth, right?" A hesitant American voice to the left.

I hold Max up. The dappled gray expanse sinks down. I dangle him over the side.

"Mummy, Mummy!"

"I've got you, I've got you," I gasp with effort.

Competing adult hands reach in from the side, under Max's, trying to touch the mottled back. His hand is batted away. Fuck off, this is Max's whale. I have lied and sweated and traveled more than five thousand miles to get us here. I grip him tightly, my hands under his arms, launch his upper body right out. He lands a pat. I yank him back in, then reach over the rim of the boat myself. The whale's skin is soft to the touch.

"Incroyable, incroyable. C'est hyper-doux," shouts the Frenchman.

The whale blows again and submerges.

Max screeches, "No me wet, no whale *puh*. Go now."

"It's holy water," says Ralph sagely.

"It's not going to *puh* again, it's already told me," I say to Max.

"It's a free spa," offers an American.

"C'est incroyable, eh?"

The gray whale mother lounges off to starboard again. Now she's checked us out, the calf appears, noses the air, bumps the boat. It back-flops on top of the adult, who rises up a couple of feet, lifting it and allowing it to roll off. Riding momentarily on her flukes, it tail-slaps the water. The splash reaches our grinning, cooing faces. The mother strokes the calf with her flippers. Now we've had our whale fix, the vessel seems to relax.

"Come here, baby whale, come here, gimme pat." Max's arms wave next to me. And, yes, you come to him. You answer his call.

Seven years ago, standing on the sea ice off the north coast of Alaska, I'd watched as Iñupiat whalers launched their skin boat and paddled across the black water. I'd wondered how it must feel to be that close, to be on the rocking sea, drawing up alongside a whale. Grays are a much smaller species than the bowheads they were hunting, and this is a sheltered Pacific lagoon, not the Arctic Ocean. If I fell in right now, I'd survive. Up there, I'd die, no question. The gray whales might even have seen the hunters when the grays were up north with the bowheads, feeding. It's where they and I are headed, all of us hungry in different ways.

Max rests his chin on the bright red lip of the boat. He's calm now, as though this is what we do every day. The white hull ripples below us. The water is infinite parts light and movement. The white above us is fractured with blue lines. The sun is a bright circle, doesn't quite make it through the cloud cover but shines a silky gray path across the water. A spout throws shards of light upward in the distance. Francisco stops the motor. The boat rocks. Water slaps on wood. There's sun and wind and spray on my skin, no land in sight. The salt water smells sharp. I breathe deeply and close my eyes.

"'Happy birthday to you . . . ,'" burbles Max eventually. There are irritated glances as he stands up and shuffles toward the side. Then a baby whale appears from nowhere next to him. He's hit a home run. There's a surge of adrenaline on board. Arms reach in from all around.

"He's a whale whisperer in training," says Ralph. Whales come like arrows. The boat lurches with excitement. It seems to me they come to us most. I can't believe it's coincidence, I want to feel blessed. I put my camera into the water, pointing the lens in the direction they seem to be coming from.

Gray whales are known as grunters rather than singers. The calls recorded in the lagoons are bursts of low rumbling knocks, drumming, and clicks. The eruptions sound conversational to me, conveying excitement and intrigue. It's a big annual party we've joined, adults mating, newborn babies playing. During the migration they vocalize most in the morning and evening. Out in the ocean there are predators to avoid, hundreds of miles to travel, and prey to seek out. Grays have excellent hearing. Close to the coast, where they often travel, it's noisy with human activity and they tend to stay quiet. Unfamiliar sounds could indicate a threat nearby. Researchers think sound waves are conducted and amplified through their skulls, and they can detect whether noise originates from above or below water. So although I can't speak whale, I know they heard Max's voice and instantly decided he wasn't a threat, were curious to find out more. The feeling's mutual.

"Where's that lovely big whale?" he chants.

"Can you translate?" says a man with white hair. He laughs when I do and introduces himself. Buddy, a grandfather from Atlanta, Georgia, he's military in his posture. Sandy, his wife, looks neat even though she's on a boat in the wind. The sea next to me gasps and sucks as the mother surfaces. Liquid swills down her curves, colors flash in the spray. I see her bulk hovering below the water and am calmer this time, can observe more. She's at least twice as long as the boat. She rolls onto her back and I consider pretending to fall in. You're not allowed to swim with the whales, but I'm so tempted. I rub her, sort of tickle her, on her chin I think, although it's hard to tell. The calf ducks under the boat. Does it whisper to her, little chirps and squeaks so predators don't hear, or do they call out freely to each other here in the safety of the lagoon? I wish I could read her thoughts. She rears up. I steal a rubbery, salty kiss. Max laughs. Buddy and Sandy high-five me.

Sandy leans in to stroke the head. "Buddy, Buddy," she gasps.

"Let me touch the hand that touched the whale," says Buddy. "When you say Buddy, Buddy, Buddy, you remind me of when we get it on." He giggles quietly. "You enjoyed it so much you needed a cigarette afterward."

Sandy pointedly ignores him.

We joke about how we'd tell partners we'd cheated on them with a whale. "She is enormous, round, with big rubbery lips, bristles on her face and fishy breath."

"Nothing will ever compare," says Sandy.

"The whale gave me tongue, I had to push it off," deadpans another man.

"Come here, come here, come here." Max waggles his hands over the side, fingers outstretched. I look around at the boat, at people who were strangers just an hour ago laughing together, playing together, like the whales.

"Why would a mother bring her baby to us? What's she trying to teach us?" says Ralph. "What's she trying to say?"

Max is sprawled in his pajamas on the swirling pink-and-blue-flowered duvet in our motel room. Fed, sleeping, and safe. The ceiling fan is pushing warm air around and I'm reading, trying to understand who it was we met in the lagoon today. *Eschrichtius robustus*, gray whale, you are the only living descendant of a species that lived thirty million years ago. Whales' common ancestor walked on land. Something like a tiny deer. You share your unique ear-bone structure with a forty-eight-million-year-old creature that fled to water in times of danger. Time imprinted its fossils in rocks found in the mountain ranges of India and Pakistan. Did the little hoofed animal ever look up as it ran through the ferns? Did it ever hear the chatter of the dry-nosed primates that would, so many lines and splinters on the family tree later, evolve into humans?

Devilfish is another name, given to the grays by the whalers in the nineteenth century. Yet you played so gently with us today. Why did you come to us? Why did you stop by me and let me put both my hands on you, while you rolled over and over, looking at me with one eye and then the other? Was it because we sang? You heard the voice of my son? Could you tell I was a mother like you? We are placental mammals, share a common ancestor ourselves. After the dinosaurs' reign ended eighty million years ago, we were siblings, small furry creatures scurrying sharp nosed and long tailed through the forest, climbing trees, crunching insects in our molars. Who could have known we would end up so different, so distanced?

My belongings are scattered all over the floor. Rucksack, car seat, buggy, clothes. I get up to organize things for the morning. There's the pile of layers I peeled off Max this evening. Black-and-white woolly hat to protect against the wind, sunglasses, a tube of waterproof sunscreen, the clay kind that doesn't rub in, makes us look like painted-up mime artists. I lay out the clothes in the order I'll put them on him. Swim diaper, wet suit, fleece, trousers, water shoes, red waterproof suit. I roll up the yellow safety line that attaches him to me, a clip at either end. As fast as I unsnarled the line today, he wound himself up in it again, just like he got entangled in his umbilical cord. In my head I'd rehearsed what to do if we cap-sized or, more precisely, if a whale got cross and flipped us over. I'd grab Max, kick down and out and away from the hull. I'd have to kick down hard because of the buoyancy of our life jackets. Then up to the surface I'd swim, holding him up in front like a trophy. The plan's success relied on the cord staying tangle-free, my holding it tight and short, no one and nothing getting between us. I stayed vigi-lant, kept him close. As I sort through it, the mountain of clothes and equipment exposes something I hadn't realized. I dressed my son not only to watch whales but also to ride them. He doesn't need a swim diaper and wet suit just to sit in a boat. I've evidently watched the film *Whale Rider* too many times, where Paikea, the Maori girl, rides the stranded whale away from land. Vivid imagination? I know that. Every school report said so. Stupid? I guess so. Desperate? Obviously.

The sea is where I've always run to, like the tiny deer did all those millions of years ago. It taught me my strengths and my weaknesses, taught me where I ended and where the world began. I learned about undertow when I couldn't get out during one strong tide, scrabbling frantically at the seething pebbles. I learned about the weight of water when a wave smacked me in the face. Mostly though, I learned that everything felt okay underwater. Submerged, I could scream out anger and fear, call out into the ocean for help. The sea absorbed everything and I became so pinprick small that anything inside me, any feelings, became inconsequential. I made sense, washing around, or rather there was no sense, I was just a collection of molecules. I'd come out full of endorphins, righted, reborn, every time.

From as early as I can remember, my mother veered from wild delight to despair. When she came down, she cast a shadow like a hawk descending. She could be happy, like a sun, and then, without warn-ing, raging against dirt, mess, silence, or for some other reason I didn't understand. When I was born, we lived in a village on a steep hillside in south Wales. I cried whenever she felt bad, she told me. She looked after three young children on her own, while Dad worked. I can see her face, set, as she pushed my brother and me, close in age, up the hill in a pram. I already know I am too heavy, too much of a burden.

When we moved to Jersey, there were neighbors, cousins, and family friends to explore with. A girl named Annabel, younger than my sister and older than me, lived close by. Our grandparents had been friends and our dads had known each other as children. Annabel was breathtaking in the manner of a lightning storm, and she was inescapable. Sometimes she was friendly toward me, protective even. Once when an older boy hit me, she chased him up the road and kicked him, her blond curls flying behind her. No one ever picked on me at school after that. But often she turned on me too. When my mom found bruises on my legs, I explained that Annabel had kicked me off my bike. Mom looked cross but said nothing. I wasn't sure I had her sympathy. She needed noise and laughter to keep her depression at bay, and Annabel was fiercely witty, could make any or all of us laugh helplessly. Sometimes, though, she would have puffy, bloodshot eyes. I learned to avoid her then. Once, walking past her house, I heard an adult shouting and the sound of Annabel crying, and I wanted to go in and tell whoever it was to stop. I stood there for a moment, took a few steps toward the front door, then turned and walked quickly away, head down, fists clenched.

My mother was a small firearm of a woman, with jet-black hair and blue eyes. "I'm a typical Celt," she'd say. My uncle Patrick, her younger brother, said that when she came home to Ireland to visit, he always knew she'd arrived because you could hear laughter from down the lane. When friends and acquaintances compared looks and wit within the family, as they often did, my mother was invariably at the top and I was at the bottom. Even the parish priest, who told me cheerfully that I resembled her, added, "But you're not as good-looking, of course."

I was the middle child, unremarkable, and I learned to stay out of the way. I liked to sit in my bedroom making animals, typically horses, out of Plasticine. Pintos were my favorite, although it was hard to make them because, after modeling the brown clay, my fingers left dark prints all over the white patches. I'd spend hours, bits of Plasticine littered around me, making up stories about wild mustangs who ended up winning all the show jumping competitions. Once my mother came in without my noticing and stormed out again.

"Why is she so *quiet*? It's not normal, and it's such a mess up there." Her conversation with Dad downstairs rose muffled through the floor. Her voice got louder. I fled outside.

Sometimes she fled too, like in the third year of primary school when my teacher, Mrs. McDermot, tried to lighten matters with a joke: "I hear your mum's gone on holiday. Ask her if she'll put me in her suitcase next time."

"She's not on holiday," I told her in front of the class, feeling a responsibility to correct the misunderstanding. Dad had sounded worried on the phone. "We don't know where she's gone." My mother was away for about a week before coming back with her smile recharged, saying she'd stayed with some nuns she'd met in Southampton. I asked her what I should do when I felt bad.

"Don't spread the misery," she said quickly, sharply. Crying silently under the duvet was the best solution, I decided. Sitting in trees was good, and pretending to be a runaway myself, like in *The Adventures of Tom Sawyer*, which my mom read to us at bedtime. While reading, she would smile and laugh, and her voice became a portal into different worlds that we traveled together. Sometimes I was Tom in *Tom in the Undersea World*, one of my storybooks from *The Water Babies* film, which I read to myself. When I was Tom, the made-up sea creatures didn't think something was wrong with me. I did not feel fear or shame in the underwater world.

We rarely touched in our family. Dad tickled me as a younger child, and I sometimes sat on his knee at night while we waited for painkillers to work on my recurring earaches. He carried me on his shoulders once during a cliff-path walk when I had a wheezing fit, and I faked wheezing for years afterward. But as I grew, touch was usually reserved for practical lifting onto rocks, pulling me up the steep inclines on the coastal paths, or out of a patch of quicksand I waded into one day. The sea, though, it embraced me, filling an unmet physical need. And I always knew it held another universe, that somewhere in all that vastness were other beings, gentle ones, like the whale.

Anecdotal history of the human-whale relationship was not as rosy as in my childhood imaginings. In Laguna San Ignacio, a few miles south down the Baja coast from Laguna Ojo de Liebre, the fishermen did everything they could to avoid the grays. They were said to attack boats and overturn kayaks. In 1956 at Laguna Ojo de Liebre, or Scammon's Lagoon, a famed Boston heart scientist had planned to hand-insert small darts to record whale heartbeats.[1] His boat inadvertently got between a mother and calf. The mother tail-swiped the propeller and rudder, swam back, raised her head as if to look at her handiwork, then took a deep breath and charged, smashing the side of the boat.[2] The men had to be rescued by another vessel. Then, in 1972, something extraordinary happened. Local fisherman Francisco Mayoral, known as Pachico, was out in his panga looking for grouper. An adult female surfaced alongside. Pachico was frightened and tried to maneuver away. But the whale came up repeatedly beside the little boat and for a time hovered directly underneath. There are different stories about what happened next. One says that after a time Pachico placed a hand in the water and the whale rubbed up against him. Another says she raised her head out of the water next to him and stayed there so long that he reached out and touched her with his finger, and then, when she did not react, his whole hand. An interspecies peace treaty had been brokered in the same lagoon where whalers hunted the grays a century before. This was the start of the phenomenon the tour groups call "friendlies." After that, Pachico took numerous ma-rine biologists to see this strange behavior. The whales came to him, and to Pachico they were more than friends.

"The whales, they are my family," he explained.

One behavioral biologist describes the encounters as "collabora-tive,"[3] showing intelligence at the least with a possibility of intentional communication. No food is involved, and the whales seem to want physical contact with people.[4] The initiation and spread of these in-teractions point to something called behavioral plasticity. The shift from ferociousness to friendliness in the lagoons shows the grays' ability to adapt, assess threats, take up new opportunities, and learn from others, perhaps even from other species.

Gray whales are the ultimate gurus of managing the unknown. Flexibility in finding new food sources is how they survived the ice ages. They live to at least seventy-seven years old, putting them in the top 1 percent in mammal longevity.[5] Researchers have found genetic similarities in long-living mammals, including in DNA maintenance and repair, immune responses, and other characteristics related to managing stress. These all help the grays tolerate new experiences, and what they do in Baja might indicate traits that could help them adapt and endure in a changed ocean, in extreme conditions. The paleontologist Nick Pyenson suspects gray whales might be "winners in the great climate change experiment."[6] I'm allowed to hope.

I've been learning from the grays to relax and let my guard down, to play. I feel a little braver, a little more future-proof already. Even if it was just for the length of a boat ride, we were accepted by them and, perhaps just as surprisingly to me after the past two years, by the humans too.

I've always sought out friends and teachers in the animal world, especially as a child. The grays' bristly chins, expressionless mouths, their watchful gaze and the dark eyes, with blue pools in the middle; of Bramble, the half-wild pony I fell in love with when I was nine. My friend Josie and I found her while exploring the lanes on our three-speed bikes. Small, round, and black, with soft, flapping velvet lips. We marveled at her, and visiting became my daily ritual after school. I named her after the bushes she stuck her head through when she heard my step on the lane. It took weeks, but she eventually allowed me to vault on and sit or lie on her back while she grazed, until the sky started to close in with sun fire and darkness, and I had to set off home.

I already had a head full of horses that had galloped out of the stories I read. Fiery steeds that transported people through magical quests. My grandfather in Ireland had been a skilled horseman, my mother told me, and way back the family had been Scottish horse thieves, so horses were in my blood. I knew I'd not a chance of ever having my own pony. We did not have that sort of money, but I mucked out at the local riding school every weekend.

Nearly a year after discovering Bramble, a smartly dressed woman who often walked her dog past the field told me the owner wanted the land back to graze cows on. "This pony was abandoned years ago," she said. "She bolted through a hedge, dragging her trainer behind her, nearly killing him!" She pointed out the rings on Bramble's hooves, which showed she'd been ill with laminitis, inflammation of the feet caused by overeating while alone in the field. "She's going to be put down."

I sprinted home. I remembered my uncle telling me of an old Jersey law, the *clameur de haro*, an injunction. If you stood in the road and shouted Norman French, no one could pass. If it came to it, I swore to myself, I'd stand there yelling, *Haro! Haro! Haro!*—and single-handedly stop the truck carrying Bramble to the abattoir.

But first I would talk to my dad. My aunt's unused, boggy field had plenty of grass. Bramble's coat shone like a billiard ball, showing she was hardy and could live outside. It was a wild and reckless hope, but Bramble had agency. She was a charmer, a beauty in the world of thickset ponies. She'd been shipped over from Wales, just like me. My parents came to meet her. I watched Bramble snuffle their fingers, with my own tightly crossed behind my back, all of them twisted together. While willing her not to throw me, I demonstrated how she now allowed me to ride her bareback around the field. My parents had a quiet discussion. Finally they agreed to take on ownership. I didn't dare believe it until the day a real, live pony was led into my aunt's field, in the brand-new red head-collar I'd bought with my pocket money. I loved my parents so much. They had saved Bramble's life and granted my impossible wish. I sat on the edge of the field that evening as she tore at the grass, not wanting to take my eyes off her. There was a rustle next to me. It was Annabel. I flinched involuntarily. I was level with her legs.

Annabel wasn't looking at me, though. She stuffed her hands deeper into her pockets. "She's beautiful," she said.

But we didn't yet know Bramble. She was headstrong and easily startled by tractors, dogs, a rustling leaf. Then, she was unstoppable, no matter how many people tried to hold her back. She would bolt straight into traffic, through fences, blind to anything in her way.

She was also an escape artist. "A little black pony has been seen going up the main road by itself." The centenier at the parish hall must have known our phone number by heart. That time, I retrieved her from a compound of racehorses, where she'd kicked and injured one of them. She'd been put in solitary, could barely see over the top of the stable door, and was nonchalantly eating hay. Another time, the centenier instructed me to go to a mansion owned by Miss Vivienne, who was heiress to her family's gin fortune. I walked slowly up the curved drive, past the Rolls-Royce and the guard-dog sign, toward the front door, which had white pillars on either side.

"I looked out the window and there was this most wonderful little pony, eating my flowers," sang Miss Vivienne, who was in her sixties and looked like she was famous, dressed in black with fair hair pulled back in a bun. Her laugh crackled like a firework around her giant house, and she invited me to stay for a boiled egg. After that, I visited her regularly. While teaching me to cook pasta, she'd reminisce about driving spies around during the war. And when I explained that, no, my mom wouldn't be worrying about where I was, that she liked me to be outside as much as possible actually, Miss Vivienne listened, with a gentle face.

Being with Bramble so much meant I saw less of Annabel. The neighborhood children were growing up and apart. In school, at thirteen, I was still nominally under her protection. Passing me in the corridors, she'd wave, and her cool goth friends would turn in my direction and smile. So when I saw her in a group near our house one evening, I couldn't help myself. I didn't clock that her silence was a warning sign, not even when the others left and she remained sitting on the wall staring at nothing. I started to tickle her.

"Stop."

Wildly excited, I took no notice.

"Stop it."

I came toward her again, hands outstretched, giggling. Then her arm was around my neck. I saw a rainbow-colored bruise as her sleeve fell back, and *thud*, the world swayed. My eyes and nose were silhouettes of pain. I struggled and shouted out, but Annabel was on the cusp of adulthood, stocky and powerful. She had me in a headlock. I glimpsed a dark bruise on her leg between her black boot and long black skirt as it rucked up before she punched again, and again. When she released me, I stood and saw my mom walking toward us, on her way back from putting out the bins. Blood flowed out of my nose, down my chin, glistened crimson on my fingertips as I put them to my face. I took a step toward my mother, but she walked smartly past, her face impassive. Annabel left unhurriedly in the other direction. After washing away the blood in the outside toilet, I went to find Bramble, buried my face in her mane, watched while the lights came on in the houses, until their shapes were swallowed by a black sky.

Here in Baja California, I am far away in time and space from all that I know, all that formed me as a child, all that took me down as an adult. Max and I wake up daily in a new landscape. I have set my clock to the grays and am borrowing their horizon for a while. We'll follow wherever they go, and they'll be leaving soon, out into the wild open ocean. What tells them it's time, what drives them? The calves perhaps, their ability, reserves of blubber and curiosity grown enough to explore. Their hunger? I know that somewhere along the line decisions were made, tickets booked, the yellow safety line ordered from an online chandlery, a route north planned. But it doesn't feel as if that was me. How did I get here? I admit it, I'm scared. I need to borrow some of the whales' courage too.

Before nestling up with Max in bed, I watch my camera footage from the lagoon. It's all gray-green and swirling motes underwater. A few minutes in, the swirls form shadows, the shadows strengthen until they are long shapes looming, bubbles rising from their sides as they twist. They eye me as they pass the lens. The camera takes the whale's-eye view, pointing toward the bottom of the boat. I hear Max singing from above, and then I appear, shrieking with delight, as they surface. Our hands reach for them. Water laps loud against the wooden hull. They blow kaleidoscopic spray into the air.

Max's song traveled across the species barrier. I wonder if the whales took anything of him into their own song, into the sea. We journeyed to see them. They came to meet us. They heard us.

UTQIAĠVIK: HOW TO WAIT

Latitude: 71° 17' 26" N
Longitude: 156° 47' 19" W

In the old days in Point Hope, Julia's hometown, I read that there was an *aŋatkuq*, or shaman, named Uqpik.[1] Uqpik used four sticks and lengths of hair as tools to tie the ice together and close the channel of open water. If the ice did not open, the whales would not come and people would starve, so the *umialiit*,[2] the whaling captains, killed him. They sent for an aŋatkuq who would aid the hunt, who would bring the wind from the right direction to open up the ice. This shaman brought his drum, left his body, and traveled to the seabed. The woman in the sea lives down there, the people said to one another, in the place of food down deep, *niġġivik*, keeping the souls of the animals in the bowl of her oil lamp. The aŋatkuq visited her and called at the home of the north-wind spirit. The wind turned around and the ice opened up. The people could go hunting.

"They're not supposed to do that." Julia was looking at the local newspaper as I came into the living room one morning. "They're not supposed to show any outsiders that." There was a full-page spread of photos. I glimpsed dolls, with faces that looked like masks. They were for a ceremony that took place in Point Hope, Julia explained, and were only meant to be shared in person, within the community. A taboo had been broken. She could not stop looking at the photos, shaking her head. I hoped she wasn't regretting her decision to let an outsider stay during whaling season. I was determined never to pry, only to listen. No one talked to me about shamans and I didn't ask, but Jeslie was generous with his explanations of the spirituality of the hunt.

"The whale gives itself to the whaling crew, gives itself up, if you are deserving." He held up an open palm. "Sometimes it comes right up to the boat." His arm curved through the air. He shook his head. "It's something spiritual"—he lifted his hand and brought it slowly down—"from the father in heaven." He moved his hands on either side of himself, like fins, as he traveled through the water. A crew had to behave well to deserve a whale, he said. An *umialik* had to be generous, had to open the meat store and feed the elders, the poorest, the orphans. The animal's spirit would recognize the generosity of its hosts and be pleased. Then more whales would come and lend their bodies to the people. The aġviq would share its body with those who shared with the people in turn. When the whale had been killed, its *iñua*, its soul, had to be treated correctly. It should be offered a drink of fresh water after death, through the blowhole. Ice cellars had to be cleaned out every spring so the whales knew their meat would be stored somewhere fresh. Every piece of equipment had to be scraped spotless. Harpoons, lances, paddles, and even the timbers of the boats had to be clean. Jeslie's intimate descriptions of the hunt and of the Iñupiat relationship with the whales were utterly unlike the practices of commercial whaling and far from the industrialized farming of livestock that led to my giving up meat as a child.

The ecology of humans on the Arctic coast has long been inextricably linked to whales. Archaeological digs have uncovered evidence of lifestyles that gradually came to be organized around whaling.[3] The bowhead hunt brought more people together around 400 CE, when they began successfully taking a whale almost every year.[4] The Thule, who succeeded the Birnirk people in about 900 CE and who were direct prehistoric ancestors of the Iñupiat, lived in semi-subterranean houses constructed of driftwood with whale rib and jawbone supports, then insulated with sod. They were whalers whose culture became dominant in the Arctic as they dispersed along the coast and settled large villages of hundreds of people, including Utqiaġvik, from 1200 to 1400 CE. Food was abundant and the communities thrived. Most surplus was owned and shared out by the umialiit, the whaling captains. Coastal groups traded with inland people, exchanging *uqsruq*, or whale oil, used for food and fuel, for caribou skins, furs, and jade. That way, the whalers could make clothes but didn't need to leave coastal areas for long periods of hunting. The relationships also helped inlanders avoid food shortages if hunting did not go well. I found a photo of a sod house in Utqiaġvik in the late 1800s, constructed using whale ribs at the entrance.[5] From the side, it resembled a bowhead, with the curve of the head dipping down to meet the slope of the back. A person emerged like a spout through the roof vent, often used as a lookout point, placed where the blowhole would have been and given the same name, *qiŋaq*.

After the epidemics and the wholesale slaughter of marine-mammal populations by commercial hunters, the communities were in crisis. There was no possibility of self-defense from outsiders, and that's when the missionaries arrived. They spoke of powerful spirits and brought medicines to treat the new diseases that had killed and weakened so many, and which the shamans couldn't cure.[6] The Iñupiat did not presume to know which spirits inhabited other lands, did not reject the Christian view. Anthropologist Hugh Brody, who spent decades in Canada, wrote that the Inuit spiritual belief left people open to a profound and intelligent uncertainty, allowing the brain to work at its fullest, widest potential, using both intuition and detailed information.[7] This uncertainty also left room for other beliefs. It was not binary and exclusive like Christianity, whose representatives said the Iñupiat were all going to hell if they didn't give up the shamans and convert.

Then came the schools. Across Alaska, from the early 1900s to the 1970s, the authorities compelled Native children as young as five who lived in villages without a school to be sent away.[8] Families were left bereft, communities lost entire age groups. Some children never came back.

Students in Utqiaġvik were luckier than many. It had an elementary school, one of the few where, initially, English was taught as a second language. Some families moved there from nearby settlements so their children could attend while still living at home. Hester Neakok, who was born in 1913, told Barbara Bodenhorn that students "went to school when they wanted to." She camped with her parents the rest of the time. Her teachers were both Iñupiat and white and did not punish children for speaking their own language.[9] Margaret Gray was pushed by her father, Bert Panigeo, both to learn hunting skills and to get a further education. "I am eager for you to get knowledge so we can catch on, so we Natives can keep up," he told her.[10] Like several others she left home and boarded at high school. Returning to teach in 1958, she found teachers and children were no longer allowed to speak their mother tongue in school, although she insisted on doing so if students were confused. By then, attendance was compulsory.[11] Marie Neakok said she'd liked school. Several of her teachers were Iñupiat, but "it was really hard because our teacher taught us not to speak Iñupiaq in our classrooms." Eben Hopson Sr., who became the first mayor of Barrow, remembered being hit with a ruler and made to stand facing the wall for speaking Iñupiaq.[12] Iñupiat children would never before have experienced corporal punishment, he said.

The experience of Native children across the Arctic was often much worse than this. The schools, run by the federal Bureau of Indian Affairs, by private churches, and later by Alaska's state government, were institutionally part of an assimilationist project, which became increasingly aggressive and ruthless. Hugh Brody wrote that across Alaska and Canada "the residential school was part of a process of ethnocide"[13] that emerged from agriculturalist settlers' need to obliterate rival claims to land, an attempt to "stop people being who they were, to ensure they could no longer live and think and occupy the land as hunter-gatherers." Students from other parts of the state sent to elementary or high school told researchers from the University of Alaska of sexual and physical abuse, dormitories full of small children crying through the night, and having been so badly beaten for speaking Native languages that they became unable to speak them ever again.[14] Those sent away had no opportunity to learn about their culture from their parents. The Yup'ik Alaskan author Harold Napoleon said church and state had aimed to destroy Native culture and language, and his own experience was that "it was not an attempt, it worked."[15] It wasn't until 2017 that representatives of the Presbyterian Church traveled to Utqiaġvik to apologize to the "stolen generations."[16]

Utqiaġvik got a high school in 1975, a year before the Molly Hootch case, in which two young Native Alaskan women sued the state[17] and secured a commitment that resulted in 105 new village high schools, so children no longer had to travel away. By then, Julia and Jeslie had already left to board at high school. This took them away from home at the age they would have been learning about the responsibilities of adulthood and Iñupiat social values. With a focus on sharing, on leadership as a responsibility rather than a privilege, and valuing the different roles of both men and women alike, these principles were more expressly equitable than the mainstream US values taught at the time.[18]

Julia had gone to the best school, Mt. Edgecumbe in Sitka. North Slope pupils were known for being academic stars and were often accepted there,[19] where they excelled and were able to prepare competitively for further education.[20] I asked nervously how she'd found it.

She said it was good, that she'd learned discipline. "I was so lazy before I went, didn't even know how to make my own bed." Before school, she said, her parents just let her play. The play, though, had included learning. I knew that from her story of berry picking as a child. She'd known how to forage food, how to deal with a bear. Ultimately Julia and others, as elders like Bert Panigeo had hoped, found themselves politically empowered by the education they'd received. Friendships were forged across cultures. Interregional alliances took root and helped generate statewide action. When he was mayor, Jeslie had written about his time at Chemawa Indian School in Oregon, crediting it with leaving him better prepared to defend Iñupiat sovereignty. "I remember well a certain day in the late summer of 1967. I was pulled from my family and community, put on an airplane, and sent to a place three thousand miles away from my Barrow home."[21] He described the homesickness he felt in the first three months: "As my relatives and friends back in Barrow gathered together over shares of whale, caribou, geese, and frozen fish, I would sit down to a table to eat cafeteria food. I would miss the winter Eskimo games, and the spring festival. . . . Our parents and grandparents knew that many changes were coming to our land, and that we needed education if we ever hoped to deal with these changes. . . . Self-government has given us the power we need to protect our culture, and our priceless animals and land from threats which could have taken them from us."

The knowledge and beliefs that Jeslie was sharing with me now had survived concerted colonial efforts at cultural destruction and forced assimilation across the Arctic. Iñupiat culture, with the cohesive power of the whale at its center, had endured. When Jeslie, Julia, or one of the crew spoke, I listened.

"No one can catch a whale on their own," said Jeslie. Sharing was the glue that had kept the Iñupiat together throughout centuries of change. "If someone asks, you can't say no. If there's extra, there it goes. The peace you feel, it's something special." The role of the umialik was unchanged, I realized. Jeslie and Julia now lived in a prefab house on stilts, they had snow machines instead of dog teams. Alongside the harpoons, the whalers used Yankee whaling equipment such as the darting gun, shoulder gun, and bombs. Commercial fishing floats were used instead of inflated sealskins, and they had a chaser boat with a motor as well as the traditional umiaq. Much of the technology was different, but the way the hunt maintained connections between people and with whales was largely the same. The place seemed somehow to be living, populated with dreams, thoughts, and histories. Animals were ever present in the clothing and in the whalebone and baleen visible in and around people's dwellings, as well as in people's awareness and conversation. To be here was to be held up by whales. To speak to residents, with their deep knowledge of both the whales and their ecology, was, I felt, as close as it was possible to get to hearing from the whales themselves. The harpoons though, the time it took whales to die once they'd been struck, the number that were lost and died under the ice—I tried not to think about it.

Jeslie suggested I talk to some elders. He took me to the house of Warren Matumeak, then waved as he drove away. Warren was seventy-nine, with downy white hair and large glasses. He had a hearing aid that he never bothered to put in, he told me. On the mantelpiece was a picture of him, wearing his furs, speaking to Bill Clinton. Climate change was coming, said Warren, and there was no way of stopping it. In fact, it had already arrived.

"Out at my fish camp the land has changed." Warren's landing strip, for small planes, wasn't smooth anymore because the ice underneath had melted. He could no longer use it. Freeze-up was later than it used to be, and the river breakup was earlier. As he talked, Warren built the landscape with his hands, flew the plane. When he was young, he'd heard an elder talking about the weather. It was so good, so calm, in that elder's description. In his final years, the elder had said the weather was angry. Warren described a storm that hit suddenly once when he was out hunting. His father had noticed a black speck on the horizon and urged them to work fast, faster, cutting up the walrus they'd caught. It was a close call. "We had to throw away some of the meat to stay afloat, to lighten up the boat, to make it home."

Warren laughed easily, even when he spoke about what he called "the change." He was Christian. "The Bible tells us we'll be hearing more of wars and famines and other things that make life hard." He got up to make coffee. "So you're British?"

"Well, Irish really." When I detected colonial history around me, I automatically took refuge in my Irish passport. Though here it made no difference, in terms of the historical trauma, what sort of Europeans my ancestors were.

"Oh, the British and Irish don't get along. They getting on better? What causes that?"

"Differences over land," I said as vaguely as possible.

"Land? Got lots of land here, here in Alaska." Warren poured condensed milk into his coffee and settled himself at his table. "The world is changing," he said to his coffee, to himself, "you never know what's going to happen next. The weather is very angry."

Jeslie picked me up. He told me that when he was young, the elders had told him the ocean would one day be ice-free and ships would be going past, east and west.

He saw that it was slowly coming true. "It's scary," he said.

"Questions, questions. You just have to wait," growled Van in response to my third query about ice and weather in the space of half an hour. I couldn't help the questions coming every time I saw him. I went for a walk to stay out of his way. People walked up the middle of the road, which was shiny with packed snow and sliced with snowmobile tracks. I was still getting used to the cold, so I didn't stay out long and instead offered Julia help with the shopping. She played Johnny Cash in the car, and we both sang along. We bought silicone for the whaleboat and camping supplies in Stuaqpak, the supermarket or "big store." I was alarmed by the amount of meat on the shopping list. Pork chops, bacon, hamburger, sausage, Spam, ham, oxtail, and chicken. I put several extra boxes of oatmeal in the cart and bought myself a couple of giant blocks of cheese.

On the way home Julia danced in the driver's seat when "Jackson" came on. "I like Johnny Cash, I like June Carter Cash. We saw them in Anchorage in the seventies."

My walks outside lengthened as I acclimatized. I talked to everyone I met. People spoke thoughtfully, with a soft musicality. I could tell another language was behind the English. Yards were full of machines, whaling gear, whalebone, walrus bones, and tusks. There were restaurants but no bars. The city was "damp," which meant the sale of alcohol was forbidden. It could be flown in, but only if you had a permit approved by the police department.

A liquor store had opened in the early 1970s, I learned, when an influx of outsiders came, along with all the oil money. The oil wealth paid for health care, education facilities, and improved infrastructure. Jobs were created, people built new homes. The rate of change was phenomenal, and hunters juggled their subsistence lifestyle with paid work.[22] Native and non-Native residents struggled with alcohol use. The liquor store shut after a few years, but throughout the eighties rates of alcohol-related deaths, abuse, and illness climbed to horrifying levels. The city had voted to become "dry," "wet," "dry" again, and then "damp." Deaths linked to alcohol use outnumbered, several times over, those from natural causes.[23] And the suicide rate across the North Slope Borough was roughly twice the state average, four times the national average.[24] But in Jeslie and Julia's house, where no one drank, I saw nothing of the problems alcohol caused.

I revisited the Heritage Center, where I'd first met Billy. The crew worked on the boats with unrecognizable pieces of equipment. A radio blasted out music as Van, Billy, and another crew member wrestled with the ends of a rope, twisting them over and over each other to create a secure loop through a circular metal catch on a harpoon.

"Really warming up, up here," said Billy when he saw me. "The polar bears are swimming long distance. Some of them drown without reaching shore." He smiled into my camera. "It's been getting so warm in the past ten years. It's different, the weather. Seas are rougher too." He went back to burning the end of the rope, examining it through thin-rimmed glasses. Walrus were also affected, the crew said. Loss of sea ice forced them to swim greater distances to find ice to haul out and rest on. In the summer, the sea ice was receding so far north that the water was too deep for them to dive to the seabed for food such as clams and snails.

"Pretty tough stuff, uh," said Van, struggling with the stringy strands. "What's going on," wondered Marvin Gaye. The crew discussed their work in Iñupiaq. Chatter. Laughter. I stayed longer than I needed to, watching and filming, long enough that I disappeared into the background and they ignored me, Otis Redding crooning, "Sittin' on the dock of the bay . . ."

I discovered a huge oil painting up on a wall, showing a whale hunt. The boat was alongside, almost on top of, the black back. A hunter was poised on the prow, holding the harpoon up, ready to throw. They aimed to spear the brain through a soft spot in the skull. The sea in the picture was stormy, dark. I couldn't understand how anyone could attempt that without falling in and dying. Sometimes, still, there were awful accidents, people dragged under to their deaths, boats capsizing, ice platforms breaking away from the land-fast ice and taking whole crews out to sea. I had the satellite phone I'd borrowed from work, a complex bit of kit. I tested it every week on the beach, but apart from that, all I could do was feel deeply uneasy, and at the same time excited beyond belief, about what I had let myself in for.

By the Heritage Center reception desk where he worked, twenty-three-year-old Robert Kaleak posed for the camera in black jeans and hoodie, underneath a thirty-five-foot model of a bowhead. Although giant, this was a replica of a small one. Its enormous downturned mouth looked very serious. When I asked Robert if he was going to go out whaling, he looked serious too.

"I'm thinking about it. I'm working two jobs, but I'd like to get out there." Robert had been out on the ice when it broke off from shore in 1997. He described, in a gentle voice, how he'd thought they were going to make it back, but the trail had ended abruptly in the water. The other side of the ice was already about thirty yards away. The snow machines were useless. While they watched, the gap widened to more than a hundred yards. Robert glanced from side to side, remembering. He and the rest of his crew had waited four hours before being picked up by helicopter. "Sometimes I think I'm going to go out, but then I think of that experience and it changes my mind." I switched off my camera, thinking about the rougher seas Billy had mentioned, the increasingly unpredictable weather Warren had described. The dangers Robert would face if he did go out were only going to grow.

Browsing books in the Heritage Center shop, I read a story of a hunter, Aaŋa,[25] who got caught between moving boulders of ice and was unable to free himself.[26] The scene was described to villagers by Vincent Nageak, an elder, in 1978. The crew was trying to help Aaŋa when he said, "I don't think you can take me off from here with those little penknives, do you?" He had a pipe in his mouth. As soon as he'd spoken, the ice began to move, taking him down. Just before he disappeared out of sight, he smiled at the others. I could not stop seeing Aaŋa, smiling, as he vanished into the ice. What kind of person must he have been, able to face death with such serenity? I bought the book, along with a pile of others, and a white whale carved from walrus tusk for my dad.

Still we waited for the right weather conditions for our own hunt. I visited Eugene Brower, president of the Whaling Captains Association, who lived a short walk from Julia's house. He told me proudly that he was third in a line of captains. His father, the late Harry Brower, had been a respected and knowledgeable community leader. His grandfather Charles Brower was the first white settler in Utqiaġvik. Eugene's frustration with the outside world was evident. His home was changing and no one had asked his permission.

"Different people with different ideas come up, they don't understand our way of life, our way of sharing. They want to impose their rules and regulations on us. Sometimes that's very hard to understand. And now we have to lock up our homes. We never used to have to do that." Eugene said he opposed oil exploration. No one had the expertise or equipment to clear up an oil spill, he said. Companies had tried to do a test run, but even with ideal conditions they failed. "They think they have the technology to withstand Mother Nature, but they don't. The force of the polar pack ice is very strong." Seismic activity to explore for oil? Also a strong no from Eugene. "With that amount of noise being emitted into the ocean, what's that going to do to the game?" He said studies were needed to examine possible impacts of noise from the seismic boats themselves as well as the long lines of air guns. He felt outnumbered. Alaska was huge, he said, the Iñupiat were just one small group of people. Other regions had their own problems and interests. "We're being boxed in." If oil was found out in the wild and a pipeline built, it would deflect the migration route of the caribou the Iñupiat hunted. "Once you block their way, they can't cross it."

"The village of Nuiqsut is a good example," he said. "They got gas lines and pipelines going all around their village." The ConocoPhillips Alpine field was about eight miles from Nuiqsut's houses and schools and could produce more than a hundred thousand barrels of oil in a single day.[27] The village sits on the Colville River delta, a prime hunting site used for generations, right along the caribou migration route, and at the mouth of a river teeming with fish.

Researching Nuiqsut afterward, I found hunters saying oil industry activities were disturbing the caribou and making it "harder to put food on the table,"[28] as resident and tribal administrator Martha Itta put it. Health issues were also coming to the fore. Some locals had reported increasing respiratory illnesses, and seizures, particularly among their children, which they believed were linked to the surrounding drilling boom. ConocoPhillips said it had been working with the community to investigate concerns, and its monitoring showed high ambient air quality,[29] better than national standards, although winter extremes made taking some measurements challenging.[30]

Rosemary Ahtuangaruak, a former mayor of Nuiqsut and longtime community health aide, argued that self-reporting by oil companies was insufficient, that air quality should be monitored by an independent body. On her night shifts, while helping residents with their breathing problems, she'd watched the flaring, when the natural gas associated with oil extraction was burned off aboveground. "As the development got closer to the village, problems increased, more people were having trouble," she told US interior secretary Ken Salazar at a meeting in Anchorage in 2009.[31] In 1986, levels of flaring were low, but by 1989 there could be twenty in twenty-four hours, Rosemary said. Over winter 2020 and spring 2021, she reported seeing thirty flares in a twenty-four-hour period from multiple sites, on more than one occasion.[32] US Environmental Protection Agency emissions estimates from oil industry activities in North Slope Borough[33] show nitrogen oxides as the top air pollutant, with sulfur dioxide, volatile organic compounds (VOCs), and particulates also emitted. Nitrogen dioxide is associated with cognitive impairment and neurodegenerative diseases[34] and is linked, along with sulfur dioxide, with epilepsy.[35] Ozone, formed when VOCs from gas flares are hit by sunlight, is known to trigger asthma in children.[36] Some VOCs cause cancer. Particulates affect breathing and contribute to heart disease.[37]

In February 2012, there was a blowout at a well owned by the Spanish company Repsol. Rosemary said the smoke plume took two hours to hit the village, and many residents got short of breath. "We had nowhere to run. It was forty below."[38] The air-quality monitor was out of operation for routine maintenance. A state study put the high incidence of respiratory illnesses after the blowout down to a bad flu season.[39] Rosemary dismissed the alternative contributing factors put forward, including a general lack of air circulation indoors, as attempts to deflect attention from the main issue. Later in 2012, Nancy Wainwright, a lawyer with the environmental law firm Trustees for Alaska, contacted the state authorities, saying a number of locals were having trouble breathing after seeing smoke from the Alpine oil field. She'd learned that Nuiqsut residents and health aides were "afraid of retribution" if they reported this, so, she added, she was doing it for them.[40] Many villagers worked for the landowning corporation that contracted with oil companies[41] and were dependent on the industry for jobs.

Eugene Brower's biggest worry, though, was the warming of the ocean. "How's that going to impact the animals we live off?" Every year, an icebreaker carrying scientists would come through, but their analyses and experiments weren't helping his community. "The people who are doing the research are not coming back to share their results with us, to help us prepare. By the same token scientists are using the knowledge of the local people. Those scientists sometimes become world-famous. Ours is local knowledge, not written down in history." His voice remained soft. "There are alternative energy sources you can look at. If they can send someone to the moon, they can make different types of equipment that don't use oil." He sighed and looked around. It was lunchtime and I could smell something delicious cooking. "I'm grilling some salmon," said Eugene. "Want some?" I said thank you but no, Julia was expecting me back.

"Now that you're going to go out whaling, I'm going to miss you, honey, miss my man about the house," said Charlotte, Eugene's wife, seeing the interview was over. Alongside her day job and studying for a degree in HR management, Charlotte sewed in the evening, did the fine hand-stitching on Eugene's caribou-skin parka. He picked it up to show me, pointed out the wolverine ruff, which didn't absorb moisture, wouldn't freeze to his face.

"You fall in the water in this, you float. Mouton fills up with water and makes you sink. This here"—he stroked the pelt—"the hairs are hollow, hold you up." He could sleep outside and not feel the cold in the clothes that Charlotte made for him. He wouldn't even need a tent.

Back inside the living room at North Star Street, the VHF radio crackled to life. "From Rescue Base, good afternoon." Via the radio whalers shared information on ice conditions with other crews camped along the edge of the lead. Their channel was monitored by volunteers at all times during spring whaling. People on land didn't speak unless it was an emergency.

"You have to be ready to move as fast as you can, otherwise you're in great danger out there," said Jeslie. If a whale was struck, I had to be quiet, he instructed, and listen to understand what was happening. Was it dead? Had it gone under the ice? If a whale was struck and lost under the ice, it was counted the same as if it had been landed and butchered. Once a whale was caught, they would pray over the radio, thanking God for the gift. "People get on the VHF hollering, 'Amen, amen.'"

In the mornings, the local channel was a chorus of leisurely greetings. "Top of the morning . . . Good top of the morning . . . Good morning . . . Good morning, *arigaa*. Good morning, Charlie Brower, good morning . . . Good morning, Martha Neakok, good morning . . ." Someone asked for a lift and found one. "Five bags of cinnamon rolls, ten dollars a bag," called someone else. A reply, "Cinnamon roll, I come pick up after eleven. One dozen."

A regular weather forecast came over the radio with information on the wind and any leads opening up. "Peak wind seventeen miles per hour from the south. Winds from south nine miles per hour. No open leads visible from Point Barrow southwestward. There's a big lead near Cape Lisburne area. . . ." We were waiting for an east wind, to open up a crack offshore.

I found a sanding machine at the Heritage Center, where carvers worked alongside the hunters. Billy was often around, fixing up the umiaq, and an elderly carver called Perry showed me how to use the equipment. I spent my days learning to grind and sand and shape odd scraps of whalebone into whales. One morning I walked past a pair of freshly skinned polar bear paws, poking out of a sack outside the door like giant skeleton hands. They reminded me of the origin of the skins for the boats, and the pieces of bone I was working on.

Perry was approving of my carving. I had the knack. This was how I'd whiled away a lot of my childhood, fashioning creatures out of Plasticine. Except whalebone is magical to hold when you think about where it's been, how deep in the ocean. Some pieces were like volcanic stone, with lots of little holes. Some were denser, harder to handle, but the whales still seemed to emerge with little encouragement from me. The first one I made, the tail was upright like that of a fish, rather than horizontal like a whale's. Van said it looked like a salmon. The second one was small. It was clearly a bowhead. I'd caught the likeness.

Billy came over to see what I was doing. He examined the tiny whale closely as he turned it in his fingers. "It's a little *iŋutuq*," he said. An iŋutuq was a very round whale, the most tender and delicious by all accounts, the best catch.

I gave it to him.

SCAMMON'S LAGOON

Latitude: 27° 44' 59" N
Longitude: 114° 14' 60" W

Max's toy boat bobs off over the lagoon, pushed along by a giant bristled chin.

"My boat," he says. "Gimme boat, whale." Francisco, the driver, retrieves it, laughing. I almost feel that the whale might be laughing too. Max clutches the whale-toy boat, affronted. It's red and white like our real one and now it's treasure. A mackerel sky sweeps overhead. Then the whales are gone. The mood on the boat dips. There's brief excitement when we see a white back curve out of the water in the distance. It's an albino and has been spotted here before, Francisco says.

"It's Moby-Dick," says Sandy. The sky is smeared with just a few clouds now. It's our second day on the lagoon, nearly noon, and the sun seems more scorching, the wind more intrusive. It's a relief when we scrape up onto the sand for our lunch break on the beach. I tip Francisco ten dollars. I can't tell if it's too much, but it won't ever feel enough for what we're getting.

"Thank you, men who driving the boats," sings Max.

"Stay here with us," says one of the drivers standing in a group next to the beach hut. With them is a little boy about five years old. I'm relieved to see another child and grateful the drivers are so playful. We take a break from the whale-watching frenzy and arrange shells on the yellow sand as the others board, mainly gray heads bobbing off on a now navy-blue sea.

There's a smell of something fishy, something off. I check Max's diaper. It's not him. Walking a little farther down the tide line, we discover a dead baby whale decomposing. Close up, the stench is unbearable. Little whale, what happened? I wonder if the mother tried to support it at the surface, to keep it alive, or if it was born dead. Perhaps things can get complicated during birth for whales too, although I doubt an umbilical cord could get wrapped around a whale's neck in the same way as with Max, given they're so streamlined.

I've seen curled whale fetuses in the Natural History Museum in London. At the earliest stages, they look similar to humans. Strange things happen during gestation, which is up to sixteen months for a sperm whale and twelve months for a gray. It's like seeing evolution on fast-forward. Baleen whales initially grow tooth buds, which are reabsorbed. There's a reminder that whales once walked when hind-limb buds appear fleetingly and then disappear into the body. Only at around seven months can you recognize the different whale species. The tiny specimens in the museum were cut out of pregnant females that were harpooned when scientists joined the whaling fleets in Antarctica at the beginning of the twentieth century.[1] It's consoling to remember that their data consolidated the argument for a moratorium on whaling. It's also a reminder of the human capacity for brutality.

"You are making a decision," the psychotherapist said. I sat on a comfortable chair next to a low table that held a box of tissues, examining the stitching on the rug between us. "Somewhere inside, the decision is being made." I had booked an appointment for a termination. The date was approaching. I did not know what to do. There was the bean I had seen on the ultrasound, wriggling its limb buds enthusiastically, and there was Pavel. It did not feel as if a decision was being made inside. It felt like that scene in *Star Wars* where they are in the garbage compactor and the walls are closing in.

"Sort it out," Pavel said when I told him I was pregnant. "I don't want a child, with you, now. We can have one later." We had stopped meeting. "I don't want you to experience being a single parent," he emailed. "It'll be so difficult, financially, emotionally, practically. . . . Will you even be able to work?"

"Will you come to the appointment with me?" I typed.

Pavel avoided my question. "You did it once before. It's the same thing. You'll be fine."

I hated myself for having told him of the first time. That time I was barely twenty and it wasn't the same thing at all. That time had been after a night out dancing, celebrating my first in engineering, a bent head of short dreadlocks meeting mine. The boy, Chidi, was a history postgrad. I was besotted with him. He called me Freckles. It was a dream come true, we told each other. His family, though, were not pleased. Neither was my mother. She tried to book me an appointment for a termination. I refused. But eventually he and I went to the GP and, in monosyllables, booked one ourselves.

We walked to the hospital together early one morning. I was sedated. The nurses could not have been kinder. Chidi walked me home. There was no pain. I didn't know that after the abortion I would still have a child, even if I didn't. I had dreamed of her face. She was always there, my ghost child, growing a year older with me, every year.

This time, more than fifteen years later, I had a job and more friends with children than without. I was just back from a stint in

Washington, DC, going to press conferences with Barack Obama, watching his helicopter flying over my apartment, chasing senators in the US Capitol for a comment, boarding the first flight to LA at rumors of Michael Jackson's death. A couple of times I'd spent weekends with Pavel, when he visited the United States for work. Soon, I would be offered the environment-correspondent job for World Service radio, a six-month gig, a chance to prove my mettle.

On the morning of the appointment, I left my flat share with the letter from the hospital folded in my pocket. I locked the door behind me. My friend Jo, who lived nearby, had agreed to come with me.

"I might not go," I'd said to her.

"Whatever you decide, let me know where to meet you."

I walked up the street toward the main road, toward the bus stop. I remembered the first time around, going into the hospital, the automatic doors. Chidi had held my hand. I thought of a tree in the park, an old chestnut with wide limbs.

The decision is being made, I repeated in my head. I got on a bus. I texted Jo.

The chestnut's limbs start low and thick on the trunk and reach laterally through the air, unimpressed by gravity. Huge tentacles, spreading, searching. Jo was walking down the path, looking around. I waved at her from under the tree, then gestured to the lowest branch.

"I can't get up there, Doreen, I'm too short. And anyway, I don't climb trees."

"Oh, come on." I gave her a leg up, then put my hands on the branch to launch myself up. My body was already different, ripening, and my arms were too weak to propel me high enough. She tried to pull me.

"Can't fucking do it." I glared resentfully up at Jo.

She was now swinging her legs and grinning. "Quite nice view actually."

"Do you want a leg up?" A jogger was passing.

"Yes, please."

He cupped his hands.

I'd lived near the park years before and this was a favorite spot. If you climbed the tree, onto the highest branches, you were hidden in the foliage, concealed and at the same time out in the wide-open air.

"What if I'm a shit mum, Jo?" I was only half joking. We sat side by side on the branch. "What if I mess them up and they end up delinquent?"

"What if they find a cure for cancer or invent calorie-free chocolate?" She reached for a branch above us and pulled it down so it tapped me on the head.

I searched in my pockets for something to throw at her, found the hospital letter, crushed it into a ball. It bounced off her shoulder and fell to the ground.

"Or, Doreen, what if they're just kind?"

I watched the time pass as the tree held us in its generous great arms, until I knew I'd missed the appointment and it was safe to leave. Retrieving the crumpled-up letter, I dropped it into a bin as we left the park to find breakfast. The decision had been made a long time ago.

Every day I went to the local pool, submerging myself and all my emotions. I thought of my child floating too, safe in the amniotic fluid inside me as I hauled myself, my belly, my vagina, my vulva, out onto the tiles. On all fours, I was animal, palms splayed sideways like flippers. I like to dive, each little escape from dry land, the feeling as my full weight plummets and the water envelops me. I was heavy, though, with my growing bump. I misjudged and belly flopped into the pool with a frightening slap. The swimming inside me stopped. The baby. Oh my God, have I killed it? An electric shock through my heart. Each day in periods when there was no inner movement, I felt this fear, convinced I had done something to harm my unborn child.

Even in the pool, my sanctuary, I'd find myself overcome with blind panic. I felt pressure from the water underneath, pushing me up as I stretched out along the bottom, bubbles leaving my sides. Then, a reassuring wriggle inside. Buoyed to the surface, I wondered for a moment why people drowned at sea with all that weight of water beneath them.

Water does not reject. Forty lengths, enough swimming to exhaust me of adrenaline, all feelings, before going to work. When my manager had come over and asked if I'd like to be environment correspondent for six months, I'd gasped and smiled. Then I'd remembered my situation and said I needed to think about it. I'd been unable to sleep that night, and the boiler in my rented room seemed to growl louder than usual. The next day I'd told my manager thank you but no and gone to the toilet to cry. Then I'd gone back to my desk and cried. A colleague sitting opposite me sent a message saying I could go home if I needed to, if there was something wrong. I went home and cried. How could I be saying no to the chance of a lifetime? But the job would be a challenge, and I'd read that anxiety during pregnancy could cause preterm birth and even affect a child in later life. I needed to stay calm for the baby. Flying in the first trimester was also controversial. I couldn't possibly do that job and bear a child, not knowing where I would end up living, what would happen with Pavel. Something would go wrong, I knew it. I needed to protect the child at all costs. Looking back at that fear-filled woman, who believed she could not do her dream job and be pregnant at the same time, I wish her just a little more strength, a little more self-belief. I try not to judge her.

Only when I swam did I not think about the job, the future, Pavel, didn't wonder whether our having had sex last week might mean my child would have a dad. I thought about whales. I thought about their breath, rhythmic and slow, hissing across the sea ice toward me. And I thought about the particles of water flowing past me, length after length.

I'd learned about water, how it moves, while studying engineering at university. I'd never heard of computational fluid dynamics, or CFD. In the first lecture I'd doodled, while the chalk chattered on the blackboard.

"Everything is finite in the physical world," said Dr. Anderson. That, I heard. *Everything is finite?* Decades later, I still turn this sentence over in my head, probing it with wonder and suspicion. CFD is used to describe how particles move in a flow. A quickening heartbeat, blood pulsing through the body's vessels. A whisper, the air is disturbed. In CFD, you look at behavior of flow in miniature. You learn to deal with unknowns, putting them in equations with Greek letters such as ϕ, α, β. This makes the unknowns look small, manageable, makes them solvable. My unknowns were not small. I could not get them into an equation.

Swimming, I was surrounded by definitions. Water obeys laws, the law of the wall, the law of the wake. There are two types of flow, laminar and turbulent. Laminar flow is when layers of fluid slide, or shear, past each other in an orderly fashion. Whale shape is streamlined to encourage it. I pushed off from the wall at the shallow end, hands together like an arrow, head tucked down. When gliding, my body was surrounded by a thin aquatic cocoon called the boundary layer, and the water right next to my skin moved slowly, in laminar flow. On whales, barnacles like living in this layer. Their larvae can get a foothold on the skin, they can find more plankton to eat, and they can mate, releasing sperm into the slow-flowing stream for the females to catch. Farther out into the world, and behind the contours of my body, the flow got faster, more unpredictable, chaotic, turbulent. There were eddies, vortices, stretching and distorting, taking energy from my movements, cascading into smaller and smaller disturbances in my far wake, all the way to nothing. Turbulent flow is a waste of energy. But if you look at it another way, it's the reason water can absorb so much, any frantic movement, my forty lengths a day, the vibrations every time I'd screamed into the pool or the sea. I've always found it difficult to make myself heard on land.

Taking a breath for front crawl, I got a mouthful of swimming pool instead of air, choked. It tasted of chlorine and something else. The water was full of bits of other people. Skin, food, saliva, snot, shit, blood. My skin was the boundary between all this and me. As I flipped over to start a new length, I imagined that I inverted. My insides, the amniotic sac, my growing child, this was now my universe. Everything outside was now inside my skin. Within me, I held the pool, the other swimmers, every stinking puddle, stream of dog piss, drop of thunderstorm. Even when I was the right way out, it all met and mingled in the water cycle that I learned in primary school. Evaporation, convection, precipitation. Water flows around the planet and through all living things constantly. Any other person might have water molecules inside them that were once inside me. Water carries messages across borders and boundaries. Water in the air is flavored by the water on the ground. Clouds move across continents. They deliver rain with radioactive particles, sulfur dioxide. The Gulf Stream ocean current delivers warmth from Mexico to Britain and northwest Europe, gives us our mild winters. Water speaks to water. Blue whales communicate across entire ocean basins. At least they did, until we broke the sea.

Three weeks after my belly flop in the pool, I was doing paperwork in my room. I went for a wee. The trickle into the toilet did not stop. After a few minutes I rang Bridget, a doula whose childbirth classes I'd planned to join soon.

"Sounds like something's happening," she said. It was Sunday morning. My roommate and my best friend were out of town. Pavel was on his way to a wedding and did not care to turn around. He might leave the reception early, he said. I was on my own.

I had so much admin to get through, the baby wasn't due for nearly a month, and I hadn't even planned to have it in London. Pavel and I had argued about that just the day before. I shuffled paperwork around urgently, then slept, but I woke needing water, more water, water in me and on my skin. I was so thirsty. I drank glass after glass, spent hours in the shower. Then I vomited, panicked, and called Bridget. She and her husband came to collect me. He dropped us at the hospital. Fully dilated, said the nurse. They rushed to fill a pool.

Two hours later, 11:00 p.m. The final twenty minutes. Pain hits. I cannot speak to the midwife. The only voice I hear is Bridget's. I hold her wrist in my mouth, scream when she retrieves it momentarily to remove her watch. I am afraid for the life of my child, who isn't coming out, is tangled up in the umbilical cord. I release Bridget's wrist, submerge, and blow into the pool. Facedown, I call for the whales, cry out into the water for their help. I summon them with all I have. Then I feel them there, their movement, their bulk, blowing and breathing with me in the bloody amniotic water, feel I am no longer alone.

Perhaps, somewhere in the ocean, there was a memory of my voice, its vibrations, from all the times I'd yelled *Help!* into its depths. From all the times I'd been on boats and sung out to wherever I thought whales might be.

Perhaps they've got a message back to me. Perhaps a water particle still resonates, remembers the whale it was part of, when she dived down deep, came up to breathe, called out to the world.

Perhaps the water has brought the whale's song, to help my son journey safely into our watery world, and my arms.

The whale-watching boats have disappeared over the horizon. Max and I build a giant sand whale on the beach. He positions shell eyes on the head while I look across the water. This lagoon used to be called Scammon's Lagoon, named after Charles Melville Scammon.

The town we're staying in, Guerrero Negro, means "black warrior," which is the name of a whaling ship that wrecked nearby. Scammon was born in 1825 and first sailed here in 1857. He hadn't planned to be a whaler. He captained trading vessels, but jobs were scarce, so rather than give up the sea altogether, he went whaling.[2]

The crew of the *Boston* had left San Francisco set on boiling up the creatures of the sea into oil, in the name of human enlightenment, literally as well as metaphorically. Whales lit up the nights and oiled the wheels of early industrial societies. But by late summer 1857 the *Boston* had been voyaging for eight months and hadn't a single barrel of oil or sealskin to show for it. The crew would get no bonuses if they returned with nothing to sell. Captain Scammon convinced his hesitant and fearful men to follow the migrating grays to the coast of Baja California. Seeing the "monsters" and their heart-shaped spouts apparently disappear into the desert, he sent a schooner to search the coastline. After two days, an entrance to the lagoon was discovered. They found it peaceful, teeming with turtles, birds, fish, porpoises, and just a few whales. While the men waited for more whales to arrive and made preparations to hunt them, Charles Scammon watched them play.

"One in particular lay for a half hour in the breakers . . . at times making a playful spring with its bending flukes." He admired how the mother gray, by seeking out the warm lagoons to give birth, "manifests the greatest affection for its young."[3]

The gray was not commercially prized. Sperm and bowhead whales yielded twice as much oil. Baleen from gray whales wasn't suitable for corsets or for whips for horse-drawn carriages, and lagoon whaling was known to be horribly dangerous. Whales attacked and broke the boats. "When the first boat arrived with her freight of crippled passengers, it could only be compared to a floating ambulance. . . . Men have been instantly killed, or received mortal injury."

The whalers gave the grays the name *devilfish* and considered them a cross between a sea serpent and an alligator. When calves got in the way of the whalers' sights and were struck, their mothers showed desperate ferocity, charging and overturning boats: "The parent animal, in her frenzy, will chase the boats, and, overtaking them, will overturn them with her head, or dash them in pieces with a stroke of her ponderous flukes."

Babies were used to lure the mothers into shallow waters, where they could not fight. I think of the whales in these same waters, their gentleness, the baby whale jostling the light, trying our outstretched fingers. As they searched the lagoon for their mothers, the calves made a noise that was audible to the whalers. I move closer to Max on the sand, so I can feel him near me. Thinking about what happened here, the quiet of the lagoon feels eerie.

Charles Scammon drew beautiful pictures of the whales, including of embryos, with heads that look like birds. The drawings are almost photographic and show severed umbilical cords trailing from the stomachs.

The whalers targeted both pregnant and nursing females: "A whale which had a calf perhaps a month old was killed close to a ship. When the mother was taken to the ship to be cut in, the young one followed, and remained playing about for two weeks; but whether it lived to come to maturity is a matter of conjecture."

The attacks continued through the night. "The scene of slaughter was exceedingly picturesque and unusually exciting." Boat crews knitted the whales' giant lips shut[4] and towed the bodies to the ships. Blubber was heated in try-pots and spewed thick, stinking smoke into the desert sky. The ships returned to San Francisco low in the water, heavy with barrels of oil. Bread casks, deck pots, coolers, mincing tubs, and finally the try-pots. They filled every container they had. The stench was said to be so strong that a ship could be smelled before it could be seen on the horizon.[5]

The impact reached far and deep. The naturalist Roy Chapman Andrews wrote, "For over twenty years [preceding 1910] the species had been lost to science," with some believing it to be extinct.[6] In the water, the change wrought was an emptiness, a lack of sound and motion as grays no longer dived and surfaced, a dip in nutrient movement through the water columns and a resulting fall in diversity. The seabed lay undisturbed. As much as twelve Yukon Rivers, 916 million cubic yards of sediment, was not stirred up by the grays, did not provide food to a million screaming seabird beaks.[7] I imagine the sudden absence, the calls of the remaining grays going unanswered.

In my mind, I can see the form of the mother whale as she turns on the boats, trying to get to her calf. The water is full of blood. I cannot unsee her eye.

What is worse, though, is that I can understand something of what drove Charles Scammon. The lure of the sea, his quest to understand everything, his desire to provide for his family and to contribute to human progress. I imagine him as an older man, leaning over his desk in 1874, completing his book about sea mammals. He acknowledged, seemed to understand then, the scale of destruction in Baja: "The large bays and lagoons, where these animals once congregated, brought forth and nurtured their young, are already nearly deserted. The mammoth bones of the California Gray lie bleaching on the shores of those silvery waters, and are scattered along the broken coast, from Siberia to the Gulf of California; and ere long it may be questioned whether this mammal will not be numbered among the extinct species of the Pacific."

The bones of the giant are bleached white by the sun. The skeleton is surrounded by tall palms, suspended above the tarmac as if it were swimming. After two and a half days with the gray whale families in the lagoons, we're looking at the remains of an adult. The backbone is supported on a metal arc. Thick struts underneath are splayed out as though struggling to hold the weight. I walk along under the sagging line of tail, hunched so as not to hit my head. Ribs dangle from white wire threaded through holes drilled in the vertebrae. From the tip of the tailbone to the end of the jawbone is about nine yards. This was a whale that died nearby, I suppose. The spine and shoulder blades don't look so different from those of a human. The fins too, the bones look like fingers.

"Careful," I warn Max as he runs behind me. Judi, a youthful, red-haired granny from the group, follows him, eyes crinkled with a smile.

"No one can say he isn't yours," she says. I hadn't noticed we were dressed the same. Jeans, blue hoodies, beige baseball caps. It was foggy, cold, this morning. Now the sky is heatstroke blue, the sun has clear sight of us. Max starts to unzip his top.

"You need to keep that on or you'll burn," I say. He has only a short-sleeved T-shirt underneath.

"I not cold, I lovely warm, I fine, Mummy." We have the same pale skin that burns in seconds, large blue eyes, freckled noses. It's as if a piece of me split off and is running around, arguing back. He sees me produce sunblock and swivels to escape.

"No cream, Mummy. Not on me. Nooo." I grab an arm, negotiate. He agrees grudgingly to put his top back on if it means avoiding being slathered in sunscreen, then he runs off, looking over his shoulder to make sure Judi is following. I have my whole body to myself.

Standing where the whale's heart would have been, I imagine it pumping, once every six seconds, and half that rate during a dive. It would have weighed about two and a half times as much as me, around 360 pounds. I count the beats, hold my breath between them, look up along the spine, out through the skull, the rostrum extending forward like a nose, jawbone curving up from below. I wonder when this whale lived, how it died. I imagine it moving through the water.

As if in answer, the ground and the skeleton lunge forward. I stagger, as though on a roller coaster hurtling downward, my stomach left behind. The chatter of the group disappears and I hear rushing. There's pressure on my head, on my chest. I can't feel my feet. I stick my arms out to steady myself against the ribs. Cold fingers reach straight through me. I edge back carefully out of the skeleton, sit down abruptly on the roadside grass.

Max appears. "Sit on knee." He catapults himself backward into my lap.

"You okay? You look a bit pale," says Judi.

I nod, concentrate on my breathing, the heat of the sun on my back, the warmth of my son's fingers, until the ground steadies and I'm sure I'm not going to faint or throw up. I stand slowly, don't look back at the skeleton. I'm worried that if I do, I might see it move.

It's called a whale fall. The final dive. The sand opens in a haze of slow awe as the body settles in the abyssal zone, meets the sea floor thousands of yards down. It is not alone for long.

If the carcass has come to rest in shallower waters or floats bloated by gases as it rots, the process is quicker. Predators work faster, higher temperatures help the decay. Down where it's colder, where the water pressure is greater, a community gathers. A hagfish uncurls, a wrinkled sleeve of slime. It hasn't eaten for months, flicks through the water to scissor the flesh. This is an island of food in an impoverished region. Four yards of sleeper shark does not need its stealth here. Sea fleas and crabs dig in. Researchers say these dark deaths created an evolutionary stepping-stone for mussels. The giant caters at every scale, expands life in every dimension.

When the eyes, skin, muscles, brain—all that pulsed with life— are gone, they come to occupy the bones. Thick yellow and white bacteria mats, clams in the sediment, bone-eating worms, snails, limpets. A clamor of spineless creatures crawling, gliding, streaming from the black ocean floor toward the fat-rich skeleton. As it decays, sulfides and chemical reactions fuel more microbe life. The energy that was bound together as whale supports a web of life for up to a hundred years.

We are carbon life-forms. All of us. And when we die, we take our carbon with us, wherever we go. The ocean has a natural biological carbon pump, as the water moves the detritus of life from the surface to the deep. The death of a great whale grounds two thousand years' worth of background carbon into the sediment where the body lies. Two tons of carbon stored in a forty-four-ton whale. How to imagine that? I'm twenty-nine pounds of carbon. It doesn't help much with comprehending the scale. The large baleen whales roaming the ocean form a repository of carbon that has shrunk as we decimated the species. If we let great whale populations recover fully, scientists estimate 160,000 tons of carbon would be sequestered each year through their carbon-grounding deaths.[8] Others say we are living in a world with a depressed ecological function,[9] an ocean less able to cope with the changes humans have wrought. Whales keep the oceans alive, circulating nutrients, their feces stimulating the growth of phytoplankton, which fix more carbon and produce oxygen. Economists have even weighed in, saying protecting whales would help counter anthropogenic effects, help protect us from ourselves.[10]

If only you were allowed to live, and die, in peace.

UTQIAĠVIK: WHALE SNOW

Latitude: 71° 17' 26" N
Longitude: 156° 47' 19" W

Big fat flakes of snow drifted past the kitchen window. I watched them fall, while stirring honey into my oatmeal.

"Whale snow." Julia sighed. "That's the kind of snow you get when whales are around. They're out there. Just we can't get to them."

Van came in, gave me a terse nod.

"Is an east wind coming?" I asked him. "Is the ice opening up?"

"Just wait." Van was holding in his own frustration at the weather. Giant blocks of ice that had broken off the northern pack during the previous summer melt had made their way to Utqiaġvik and were now grounded off the coast. Thick ice meant a safe platform to travel on, but it would need a strong and steady east wind to push the pack offshore, to form the lead, and a current that worked with the wind to keep the lead open. The wind blew this way, that way, didn't settle for long enough. It was becoming clear that I wasn't going to be able to travel the route I'd planned across northern Alaska and Canada. I'd used up so much time waiting, I'd be lucky if I managed just one more stop. My money was disappearing fast on rent and on food from the supermarket, which was expensive because it was flown in.

The hunt I would be joining was one of five subsistence hunts recognized by the International Whaling Commission, which met annually and reviewed quotas every five years. To satisfy the criteria, groups needed to prove a nutritional and cultural need for whale meat, and the whale population needed to be sufficiently robust. The Arctic hunts had become a political football in power plays between the United States and whaling nations such as Japan. In 2002, Tokyo orchestrated a block of the Iñupiat quota. Approval needed a three-quarters majority of the forty-eight member countries. Japan's influence was strengthened by their overseas development aid budget, and the vote fell one short. The opposition included the Solomon Islands, landlocked Mongolia, and several Caribbean nations.

"Our coastal whaling bid has been rejected for fifteen years. The United States ought to feel the same pain," said Masayuki Komatsu from Japan's Fisheries Agency.[1] The issue precipitated a special meeting of the IWC, and Japan eventually backed down. For the Iñupiat, outsiders judging the hunt could create real problems. Van said they'd been criticized for adopting technologies that made the hunt safer and more efficient. The guns and bombs, snow machines, outboard motors, the front-end-loader tractors for carrying whales from the beach to a butchering site that had moved inland due to coastal erosion. Van had no intention of being defined by outsiders' stereotypes. As the world changed, so did hunting methods. Van as an Iñupiat claimed the right, like any other human being, to choose whatever blend of tradition and modernity he wanted in his life.

"Expected we'd all be living in igloos, did you?" Van seemed suspicious of me. I supposed I had no real business there, as a *tanik*, a white person, and a woman on top of that, except Julia had said I was coming and no one argued with Julia.

I knew he was uncomfortable with my constant questions, but I just couldn't stop. I was relentlessly curious, openly admiring, lacking in preconceptions, and, ultimately, totally helpless. For a family so generous, for whom sharing was such a central part of their culture, I was impossible to turn away, even eventually for Van.

An inflatable globe the size of a beach ball hung from the ceiling of the lab. On yet another day of waiting, I was being given a tour of the city's climate-monitoring site. My guide was Dan Endres, who'd been chief of the National Oceanic and Atmospheric Administration Observatory for the past twenty-two years.

"It's interesting, it's a challenge." Dan's tone suggested tying a shoelace rather than overseeing a gigantic data-collection operation in a place where the temperature was above freezing for only two and a half months of each year and winter was twenty-four-hour darkness. "Show me where you think the atmosphere ends."

"There." I held my hand out about an inch from the surface of the inflatable globe.

"No." He slapped his hand right onto the ball. Then he exhaled on it. "The moisture from my breath is thicker than the atmosphere. The entire ecosphere is thinner than a sheet of paper." Everything Dan studied was there, all the gases, the greenhouse effect, climate, was contained there, in that nothing space he was showing me. Dan did analysis for government agencies and universities, shipped samples back and forth. When he talked about his day-to-day tasks, I became lost in a cloud of chemicals and processes.

F11, F12, methyl chloroform, sulfur hexafluoride, the strongest greenhouse gas known. When Dan started, they were measuring 4 somethings of sulfur hexafluoride, and now it was up to 5.5 or 6 somethings, in just six to eight years, he said. Sulfur, man-made and from volcanoes. The tundra, was it a CO_2 source or a sink?

"The Arctic's been called a mirror to the world. People are be-

ginning to realize more and more just how critical it is, what's coming out of Barrow."

"What are you seeing?"

"A huge increase in CO_2." The lab was one of five major sites.
The others were at Mauna Loa in Hawaii, Trinidad Head in California, American Samoa, and the South Pole. The lab was several rooms
full of instruments humming furiously, vibrating. Pumps brought in
air samples from outside. There were two employees. Teresa was the
technician, but it was her day off. Dan joked they split the workload
fifty-fifty, he broke things and Teresa mended them.

The walls were covered in the celebrity graphs of climate change.

"This is the most famous data ever to come out of the Arctic." Dan pointed to the chart of CO_2 levels on the wall. The line
climbed steadily up the y axis as it traveled from left to right. He
rattled off his observations. "I've seen CO_2 levels increase almost
one hundred parts per million. Temperature changes, it's lots
milder. Different plants are growing outside. Spring—earlier melt
by seven to ten days. Fall—the freeze is a lot later. When I first
came up, we could be out on the sea ice in mid-October. Now
you wouldn't dare go out until November or December." He talked
about the thinning of the ice, which wasn't visible on the satellite
images because they only showed the extent of cover. The longer period of sun would affect plankton chemistry, create changes
in feeding habits for migratory animals such as whales and seals.
The whales liked to pass under the ice as a protection, but as it
receded, they'd be farther and farther out. Any subsistence hunt
would have to be farther out too. There would be a danger of
being trapped by storms.

"Is there anything else you want the world to hear?" I asked.

Dan laughed.

I'd have liked to have given him a megaphone that reached everyone on the globe. "Like if you were king of the BBC?"

He thought for a while. "Whatever happens here will happen to the rest of the world. It's the early-warning bell."

I remembered how fiercely I had argued in the interview for the bursary. I'd pitched the Arctic as the front line of climate change, and the evidence was all so clear, so incontrovertible. When Dan stopped talking, I felt scared. I worked for a news organization that represented truth and accuracy. How were we not telling this story properly? What was going on?

What was going on was that media all over the world had regularly been allowing skeptics to misrepresent science without adequately challenging them, and presenting them as though they carried equal scientific weight to mainstream climate researchers. Sadly, at times, the BBC was no different.[2]

An independent review of BBC science coverage four years after my trip to Utqiaġvik found the corporation was so determined to be impartial that it sometimes put opinion on a par with well-established fact. This "insistence on bringing in dissident voices into what are in effect settled debates" created what the report called "false balance."[3] The review was led by Steve Jones, an emeritus professor at University College London. He compared it to inviting a mathematician and a maverick biologist to debate what 2 plus 2 equaled.[4] The mathematician would say 4, but with the maverick saying 5, the audience would come away believing the answer was somewhere in between. Jones also noted that BBC Science was "head and shoulders above other broadcasters." Clearly the media as a whole, not just the BBC, wasn't doing a good enough job. Dan could make as many thousands of measurements as he liked, could make this his life's work, but the media would ultimately determine how many people ended up believing, in climate terms, that 2 plus 2 did not equal 4.

———

I felt a tremor under my feet and looked nervously at Craig George, who stood next to me on the sea ice. Craig had been resident biologist in Utqiaġvik for more than thirty years, and while the hunters waited, he'd offered to take me out to the flaw zone, an area of unconsolidated ice where the pack ice that rumbles around the top of the planet scraped by, building ridges and cracking the ice along the floe. Craig was a reassuringly expert presence, even out on an ice floe.

"Take a good look at that multiyear because you may never see it again." His white mustache was dusted in frost. Multiyear ice, he explained, was an ice floe that had experienced a good cold winter, survived the summer, melting at the top, then frozen the next year, again and again. Slowly it developed a gentle, rolling relief and might also be fractured and deformed, revealing startling colors, blues and greens. During the summers, the salt leached out of the ice and it became a good supply of fresh water. We were standing on some of the old ice that had broken off in the north and floated south. I was seeing a now-rare phenomenon, the Arctic as it used to be, before the melting and thinning. "Polar bears and scientists like it too." The last time Craig had seen multiyear in the shore-fast ice such as this was 2001, and since then, because of the warming winters, it had been generally "flat, first-year, without the big old blocks." Multiyear ice had character, he said, carried some of its history with it. "That's probably what's going to go first. It's sad, in a way."

A craggy white mountain was sliding past about ten yards in front of where we were standing, giant chunks toppling off the top.

"Whoa, look at that. We have to be very careful. The problem is, if we take some pressure from over there, this whole thing is going to shatter." Craig pointed to the ice at our feet. I could hear cracking. It sounded gentle. The ice looked so solid under its powder-snow coating. The mountain was slowing down. "We're taking some pressure here. Let's retreat, let's get outta here." Craig laughed, but he was moving quickly to the snow machine. I followed and lumbered onto the sledge. We were watching plate tectonics in real time, he explained. You could see mountain building, thrust faults, fracturing. Floes were banging into each other. "It's like how the earth's crust was made. All the same processes." He started the motor and we roared off.

He'd pushed it to the last minute, perhaps for the thrill or perhaps so I could feel the force of plate against plate, so I understood the pressure that could make the ice we were standing on break up and open beneath our feet, swallow us or detach, break off the landfast ice, carry us out to sea. I imagined us from above, as if seen by a rescue helicopter, dark dots in a seemingly infinite, shifting ocean of white.

The ocean may be vast, but we are filling it up. It absorbs as much as one-third of all human carbon emissions, which has helped slow the rate of climate change on land but comes at a cost. CO_2 reacts with seawater to form carbonic acid, and the more acidic the ocean becomes, the less CO_2 it can absorb.

Experiments show that acidification—decreasing ocean pH— damages coral reefs and causes reproductive problems in fish. Animals such as corals, oysters, starfish, sea urchins, and mussels are less able to fix carbonate from the water to build shells. When CO_2 dissolves in seawater, it causes an increase in hydrogen ions, which bond with carbonate, making it unavailable for creatures that need it to form skeletons. Animals then have to use more energy to calcify, leaving less energy for other life processes such as breeding. Species in trouble if coral continues to decline include fin fish as well as shellfish. Scientists say the clown fish, *Nemo*, has little chance of genetically adapting quickly enough to a dramatically changed environment.[5]

All life depends on the great body of water that swirls and splashes around our planet. When we damage the ocean, we damage ourselves.[6] Phytoplankton populations, which provide at least 50 percent of the oxygen we breathe, are reducing. Cold water holds more oxygen, so the warming waters have lower oxygen levels. Fish are already suffering from hypoxia.

The drifts of shelled zooplankton are bigger players than their size suggests. Almost all larger marine life eats zooplankton or other animals that do. It roots the food chain, right from the bottom, and deposits carbon as sediment on the seabed when it dies, where it's stored for decades or centuries. In the Southern Ocean the shells of pteropods are already dissolving.[7] Like corals, these tiny sea snails have shells made of aragonite, a delicate form of calcium carbonate that's easily corroded when seawater absorbs CO_2. Experiments have shown foraminifera zooplankton can't manage higher acidity. It becomes difficult for them to build up their shells. One study predicts that if we continue as we are, benthic foraminifera are likely to be extinct in tropical areas by the end of the century.[8] Long term, levels of acidity predicted by 2300 have been found to dissolve not only sharks' denticles or scales but also their teeth. There are winners though. The outlook for jellyfish is rosy.

The radio in the living room on North Star Street was holding forth on the weather. Jeslie and I sat at the table, rapt. "From Point Franklin. May sixth. Five to ten degrees tonight. Sunday, east winds fifteen mph. Monday and Monday night east winds too." Oh, God, I thought, east winds, we'll be going out soon. The forecast was interactive and you could ask questions. Someone did but I couldn't understand a thing.

"He's too close to the mic," said Jeslie.

There were about five questions, unintelligible to me, that the forecaster evidently understood. "Let me check my map real quick. . . . Let me check the satellite for you real quick. . . . Hold on just a second and I'll check for you. . . ."

I fielded a question too, from the radio program I worked on in London. A producer asked if I could get a polar bear hunter for a comment. The International Union for Conservation of Nature's Red List had officially upgraded the bears' status from conservation-dependent to vulnerable. I could just imagine Van's reaction if I asked him for an interview. I offered to get a local biologist, but the program wanted someone who actually shot and ate bears. One man had already put on his polar bear suit to show me, and there were those polar bear feet in the sack outside the Heritage Center, but I didn't feel my usual journalistic bravado. Would they blame the hunters? I didn't think climate change, polar bear ecology, and the cultural context of the hunt would fit into two minutes of radio. If a hunter was interviewed and felt misrepresented, the community would blame me. I was on sabbatical, not on duty. I said no one was available, hunters were busy getting ready to go out on the ice. Well, said my colleague, would *I* talk about the polar bear hunters instead? No, I said, I was so sorry but I was also too busy. In fact, I had to go straightaway, bye. I went back to the sofa with several of Eli's doughnuts and more hazelnut coffee, thinking of what I'd heard before coming, about locals refusing to talk to journalists, being suspicious of them, closing ranks.

Van stomped in at just after ten the following morning while Julia and Jeslie were at work.

"There's an east wind," he said happily. "Might open up. It depends on the current, if it's coming this way. The current is stronger than the wind."

"What does it look like out there?"

"Don't know, it's whiteout. So we just gotta wait, I guess." He winked, my questions and his answers now a well-rehearsed script.

"I find it difficult waiting." I was proving a slow learner.

"It's how we do it, anyway. Wait, wait, wait. We're used to waiting this long." He sat back on the sofa.

"What are you going to do while you're waiting?"

"Just wait. Clean out the garage for my sister." He told me about growing up in Utqiaġvik with seven sisters and four brothers. Learning to hunt whales, walrus, bears, bearded seals, and fish from his father. Now that Van was warming toward me, he was the best company.

"Just imagine," he said, "long time ago our ancestors used to use seal oil for lamps, for heat. Now *that's* cold. We're spoiled with natural gas, National Weather Service. We can't read the weather now. My grandpa used to go out the door and say, 'It's going to blow about twenty-five miles an hour.' How the heck did he know that?" Van sat back on the sofa, sighed. "Those people down in the lower forty-eight, they go turkey hunting, they get so excited. It's nothing like it, not even close. The ocean is our table. It's awesome."

Around town, crews were getting their kit together, preparing to camp out on the ice and wait for the bowheads. The crews would be dotted along the edge of the lead, sharing information on the radio. Each chose its own spot, hoping whales would surface there so they could paddle out and throw or thrust in the darting gun, loaded with harpoon and projectile. The shoulder gun would be fired within seconds. When a whale was taken, it would be announced on the radio, which would erupt in cheers, signaling that people should come and help. A heavy rope tied around the tail allowed the umiaqs and motorized boats to tow it. A block-and-tackle pulley would be anchored into the ice to pull it up, with many hands on the rope. Over the next day and night, the whale would be butchered and divided among the crew who harpooned it and those who helped tow it to shore, land it, and cut it up. The hunters allowed scientists to take samples for research on the health of the bowhead population. Women from the successful whaling crew worked continuously, cooking and preparing the meat, others lent a hand, and the next day a flag would be flown from the house, an invitation for all to come and share the food.

The crew members did several recce trips onto the ice. I rode pillion on their snowmobiles. We examined *quppaich*,[9] or cracks, and took guesses on which would be the one to yield. I felt intrepid.

"Don't get too close," Billy said. We passed polar bear tracks and stopped to look more closely. He showed me the fox tracks winding behind, as the scavenger followed the apex predator. It was a female bear, he explained, the tracks were small, as bears went. "She's gone this way about seven hours ago." The outline of the prints had softened, were not as sharp as when they were new.

The sky was blue with soft clouds streaked through. Out on the frozen ocean the snow was thick and smooth, concealing ice boulders, ice walls, impassable terrain. As the pancake ice disks, or pans, shifted, broken ice was pushed up. There were low fields of ice rocks and sometimes ragged ice castles with turrets that towered above my head. I helped to break trail, getting a lift with another crew member, Riley.

Billy came too, carrying a rifle over his shoulder. "Never know when you might meet a bear."

We needed to break through to the next pan. It was a joint effort, the path was etched with tracks of multiple snow machines, meandering lines rippling wide at the edges on the flat parts of the trail. I joined six men wielding pickaxes but my hands blistered after a couple of flings. The group made short work of a shoulder-high stack. The blows caused little ice avalanches. Tinkling shards scattered off and the powder snow on top slid onto the ground. Chunks were thrown to the side. I climbed up onto a small block, and the landscape opened up, snow-covered boulders as far as I could see.

I found that my equipment worked, though the place screeched with so much light that I struggled to see what was happening down the camera viewfinder. I pointed it and hoped I was capturing something. The crew joked into the lens, "We'd like some of that global warming around here." It took a while to get used to wearing two pairs of gloves. Initially I fumbled so badly I dropped my shiny new MiniDisc recorder down a crack in the ice. It disappeared from view. I got down on my hands and knees and peered into the fissure, wondering where my piece of equipment had gone and where it would end up.

"Stay away from that crack!" Billy shouted. "You might just go the same way." It was easy to forget the danger, in all the beauty. I had a spare machine back at North Star Street, but if the ice wanted that one too, I wouldn't be arguing, wasn't feeling quite so intrepid anymore.

The men advanced steadily, leaving a smooth path that undulated up and down. Others hacked at the ice to each side. The trail needed to be wide enough for the boat and sleds to pass through. The ice was a maze that the whalers navigated every year to find a route to the whales. In spring, aġviġit typically swam past in a northeasterly direction. Ice conditions forced the migratory path close to land. Utqiaġvik didn't always yield much food for whales, but with favorable conditions it could become a feeding hot spot in autumn. Sometimes krill were swept across the Chukchi Sea and then, with east winds and the Alaska Coastal Current, were pushed into the shallow shelf regions. Either way, it was an ideal location for the hunt.

In 1977, the International Whaling Commission became concerned about low bowhead population estimates. It wasn't sure they could ever recover from commercial whaling. Long-living, slow-reproducing animals are vulnerable because they don't rebound quickly, even when a threat or danger is removed. The IWC decided numbers were too low to allow hunting and gave the Iñupiat a quota of zero. The hunters argued that official population estimates were too low and hired lawyers to fight on their behalf.[10] At a special December meeting of the commission, the United States negotiated a small quota in recognition of the subsistence and cultural needs of the Iñupiat and committed to carrying out substantial research.

The North Slope Borough created a scientific program to count the population. Scientists and hunters put their heads together[11] in a collaboration driven in part by a friendship between whaling captain Harry Brower Sr. and Tom Albert, a veterinary scientist hired by the borough to lead the study. Until then the count had been visual, with people spotting passing whales from the shore-fast ice and some being spied from the air. The hunters explained aġviġit could also travel under the ice[12] or swim too far offshore to be seen. The hunters objected to planes flying overhead, and researchers hadn't found aerial surveys very helpful. Sonar would also have disturbed the hunt, so hydrophones were lowered into the water to listen for the voices of whales passing by. Sound, crucial for all marine animals, is especially critical to survival in that cold, dark world of constant travel. Aġviġit rely on their voices, the echoes of some calls, and their keen hearing abilities to communicate, avoid predators, and forage.

The count began. In one instance when only three whales were seen, hydrophones tracked 130 swimming under the ice.[13] The combination of traditional knowledge and the census, including complex statistics, revealed many more bowheads than the numbers the IWC was quoting. Population estimates were revised upward, and the IWC backed down. Tom Albert said the bowhead fell from the moon, in terms of how unusual it was to science. Generations of Iñupiat, though, had watched the whales. They *knew* them, they had to, being so dependent on them for survival. The hunters understood aġviġit resilience, had watched their recovery. After establishing that their traditional knowledge was right, the Iñupiat became stronger, more organized, more politically resilient themselves.

One evening after breaking trail, Billy brought a 1970 Disney film to Julia's. It was titled *Track of the Giant Snow Bear* and starred one of his brothers as a teenager. We watched it in the cozy living room. Julia and I sank deeply into the sofa while Billy perched on the edge of one of her big chairs. The film was narrated and the characters' Iñupiaq speech was not translated. The boy, Timko, made a pet of a baby *nanuq* that got caught in a trap and called her Paka. While we watched, Billy kept getting up and looking out the window at the sky. He didn't seem comfortable indoors. The nanuq cub was exploited to full furry cuteness as she slid around together with Timko, and when he taught her to pull a sled. When she got bigger, she broke into the meat store, eating everything, and he was hauled up in front of the village council. Paka was banished. Timko decided to leave the village too. At this point Billy got up and went out the door.

As I watched Timko struggling to navigate his allegiances, split between the village and his disruptive nonhuman friend, I remembered Bramble escaping from her field and kicking the racehorses.

Billy came back in, smelling of cigarette smoke. "They used seven *nannut*[14] for the film, six tame and one wild." The bears were kept in cages, and he said his brother, playing Timko, was scared at first. He trained with them for weeks before filming, and a trainer stayed close by throughout the shoot.

The best scenes were when the bear and boy met again during Timko's year of self-imposed exile from the village. He shared his catch with Paka, throwing flashes of silver toward her across the frozen sea from where he'd been fishing through a hole. We got to see the bear stomach-slide across treacherously thin ice, and I wished myself into Timko's mukluks when he and a fully grown Paka snuggled up to sleep together.

Bramble had been my companion when I also couldn't seem to find my place among people. One time, my mom was hosting a barbecue for the neighbors. My brother and sister had friends over and were busy outside. My friend Josie was off-island, and I watched listlessly through the kitchen window as people arrived. Annabel and her younger brother came into the garden, followed by their mother. Her dad and mine were obscured by smoke as they tended the coals.

My mom put her head around the door. "Make yourself useful, Doreen. Wash up those bowls, will you?" She went back out, continued directing. "Annabel, you fetch me a jug, please. Top shelf in the kitchen." Annabel came in, surveyed the room. My mom followed behind her. "Doreen, are those bowls ready?"

"Your lower lip sticks out, Doreen. It's ugly," said Annabel. She'd been surveying me too, sizing me up. As I'd got older and taller, she'd become more wary of attacking me physically, but our dynamic had never changed. I stared into the suds, washed the bowls quickly, stacking them on the drainboard. "I'm telling you this for your own good," Annabel continued. I tried to speak to my mom, but an animal howl came out. I ran past both of them, out of the kitchen, and sought refuge with Bramble. As she lay dozing, I'd sat on the grass beside her, resting against her back. I never made it to the barbecue and nobody bothered asking why.

"Good friends, huh?" said Billy from his chair, as Timko and Paka slept together in a picture of peace.

I smiled and nodded. I liked to think I understood Timko and Paka. The boy who loved the bear, and the bear who quietly accepted him for what he was.

When they went hunting together, the bear swam alongside the kayak, chin-first, a V-shaped wake of bright blue water trailing behind her head, and I remembered taking Bramble into the sea. We'd usually go via the woods. There, the dappled light made her into an undersea creature. Blacks, blues, and browns swam all over her body and in her eyes. The woods were said to be part of a historic *perquage* path, a sanctuary path of Jersey legend. There was one in each of the twelve parishes. They led from the parish church to the beach by the shortest, quickest route. Those accused of crimes could claim sanctuary in the church and had a chance to escape prosecution by going down the perquage to a waiting boat that would carry them to France, never to return.

When we got to the beach, Bramble was reluctant, but I used the full force of my arms to keep her head turned toward the swash and kicked her with my heels. The tide must have been coming in that day, and I underestimated the depth. It took me a moment to realize that she was swimming. She'd become a whole new being with an unfamiliar gait, surging as if she were a single muscle. With the thick yellow-green water of low tide up around my legs, I was somehow more afraid of being thrown here than on land. I could feel there was nothing solid underneath us as her hooves thrashed. It seemed a long way to fall, into a viscous, bottomless ocean.

Then Bramble called time, twisted her head. We were back on the sand, smashing through the rivulets, clattering out of control up the cobbled slip and careering straight onto the road, which was thankfully free of cars. She ran up the hill until she couldn't run any more. Sliding off, I led her home slowly, inhaling the sharp, musty smell of her sweat. Both of us out of fight and tired, her sides heaving.

I wondered what a polar bear smelled like, close up. Billy said it wasn't unusual for a *nanuq* cub to have been made a pet if its mother was killed. They could be fed with evaporated milk and would follow the person who took care of them around out on the tundra, sleeping in the house. I asked Billy what happened to them when they grew up.

"Zoo, maybe. That big Paka, she went to a zoo in San Diego."

At the end of the film, the untamed bear had its moment when we saw Paka gone wild. Timko returned to his village as a skilled hunter and carver. The human and nanuq had grown up side by side, had accompanied each other into the lives they were meant to live, back with their own species. Seeing the bear amble off into the white expanse, I wished again, as I had many times as child, that I could have set Bramble free.

"I had a pony once," I began, wanting to share the memories, the similarity of the bond.

Billy nodded, raised his eyebrows with interest.

"She . . . she . . ." But I couldn't finish the sentence.

Bramble was never really tamed. Although she could be persuaded to tolerate people on her back, even sometimes to pull a small cart, like Paka pulling the sled, perhaps I didn't really want her to do what I asked. One summer, aged eleven, I was riding bareback with a head-collar and rope in the field when some impulse possessed her. She broke into a flat-out run. She was headed for the fence, but I knew she'd stop. The wire was too high to jump.

Bramble did not stop. She took the fence. I was flung back and then forward as she soared, landed, and jackknifed up the track. The fields thudded past, one, two, round the bend, three. One more and we would be at the road. I could hear traffic. As the vehicles got louder, I imagined her with a broken leg, blood on the tarmac. I was not wearing a riding helmet. I let go of the rope and her mane and launched myself sideways off her back. I landed in the grass, curled against the hooves that were sure to catch my body or head. There was nothing. Just the zip of cars close by. Opening my eyes, I found Bramble staring into me, her neck lowered. She snuffled me roughly, shoved my arm. I got up, hugged her solid neck, and stood holding on to her for a long time while she grazed.

I only understood it later. She did not want to go without me. We needed to leave together. And being with her, I was learning to choose my moment and run.

Outside the house on North Star Street the snow was packed hard, tinged yellow, and the crew were loading up sleds, ready for when the ice opened up. I watched uselessly.

"Propane canisters," said Leif, a towering XXL Carhartt-clad giant of a man, as he tied them into place. "To keep you warm. So we don't have cold butts."

"Won't it melt the ice?"

"You won't melt a hole in *that* ice." He laughed. He contemplated the stove, tents, boxes of food and cigarettes. "With this load you could sleep anywhere in the world."

Van was directing the crew and checking on them as they worked.

Julia stood outside the front door. "This is the best time, when they're getting ready to go out. It's a good feeling."

Jeslie and Van went back inside to listen to the VHF. I followed, not wanting to miss anything.

"Ten-four, okay. Six miles from here," said Jeslie. "Okay, standing by." He didn't need to translate, I understood. The ice had opened up, six miles out. It was time to go. The bottom dropped out of my stomach. I retreated to the sewing room and put on as many clothes as I could. The house bulged with people of all ages. I could hear Leif telling stories about the time they were rescued by helicopters. I couldn't bear to listen, went for a walk, trying not to think of what I was about to do. The streets were busy with snow machines. The crews had all heard the forecast, were making last-minute preparations. I didn't dare stay away for long.

When I got back Julia was wearing her best parka, rich with fur and careful stitching, a skill passed down the generations. I was just in time. Jeslie led a ceremonial prayer, said in Iñupiaq, in a circle around the umiaq. Julia, Jeslie, and I watched as the crew, all men, mounted their machines, hitched up the sledges, and zoomed off one by one down the road, which was brown and white with snow and sludge. The snow machine engines had a warm rumble. I listened to each cycle as I stood there, not knowing what to do. As the final few machines roared into life, I felt panic. In all the days, the weeks, of waiting, we'd had no discussion about where I, the hanger-on, would go. And now it was too late. Only one crew member was left, Billy.

"*Kiita*," he said, or "let's go" in Iñupiaq. He jerked his chin toward the back of his machine. I waddled over, so bundled up I couldn't climb on. I made a huge effort, launched myself off one leg and toppled onto the seat, awkwardly grabbing hold of him. A sound of unease came up from my stomach, moaned out of my mouth as we sped away down the road.

"You okay?" shouted Billy over his shoulder.

"I'm still here." I didn't know if I was okay. The buildings and approximately four thousand inhabitants of Utqiaġvik disappeared behind the snow-covered bluffs on the beach. The recce trips had prepared me a little, but they had been for a few hours only. This was the real thing. We were saying goodbye to the land for as long as it took. When we moved beyond the beginning of the trail, which I'd helped smash into being, the ice bristled. Pale blue, translucent green-blue, crackled deep blue, jeweled emerald towers high as houses shot past. We were aiming for the lead, that I knew. A crack had finally opened up, creating a passage along which whales would migrate from the Chukchi Sea to the Beaufort Sea, across the top of the planet. We passed an animal trail, looked like Arctic fox to me. Billy didn't stop to explain this time. We were making good progress across the white desert, a pan. I tried to think of how to describe it. Icing, cake. I did not have the words. My attempts were so inadequate and embarrassing, even though only in my head, that I stopped thinking, let go of language, just let the world be.

"Where are we going?" I yelled.

"To the edge."

THE SEA OF CORTÉS

Latitude: 26° 0' 53" N
Longitude: 111° 20' 20" W

"I'm surprised you've brought the toddler, even though he's a good little traveler," Judi says. Mike and Mary, a British couple in their forties, frown and turn to look out of the window. Mountains lollop past. Don, the tour leader, is driving us across the Baja Peninsula. The rest of the group have left, and in the second part of the whale-watching tour we will look for blue and fin whales on the Sea of Cortés, as well as visit more lagoons where the grays gather. Max and I are in our element, on the road. He's calm in his car seat, engrossed in watching the scenery fly by.

"Well, we like being on the move," I say.

Judi and Don seem to hit it off, talking together throughout lunch.

Back in the Jeep, Mike asks Don about his life in the Philippines, where he lived during his thirties. "You're not one of those Americans who ended up with a teenage Filipino girl on your arm, are you?"

Don doesn't answer the question but instead replies that he's taken care of having more babies and can't think of anything worse than having a two-year-old around. A busload of children goes past.

"What are they doing?" asks Mary.

"A desert trip or a whale trip," says Don.

"As long as they're not going where we're going," says Mary.

I look at Max sleeping. Have they forgotten he's here?

We arrive at our motel in Loreto, tucked behind the main street. A giant picture of Frida Kahlo surrounded by flowers and birds is on the wall of my room. She looks composed and knowing. Wind rustles in the palms outside as Max plays with a little Mexican boy. Before turning in, we shower, then lie wet-haired on the bed, overlapping, making the most of the space after being cooped up in the car. My face is burning from the sun. The lampshade, dotted with multicolored glass beads, rocks gently in the breeze. The carved leaves on the headboard mirror the foliage around Frida. There's a filament-thin spider making its way delicately across the ceiling, a gecko in the corner. Max's small leg and arm are hooked over me, owning me. I'd like to live in this room forever, with Frida, the spider, the gecko, and Max, knowing whales are nearby.

When we get out on the water the next day, a pair of gray whales surface right next to us. The mother is supporting the baby on her side. I'm doing the same as Max leans on me while we peer over the edge. We stroke them both as they sigh, spy-hop, and eventually submerge. After an hour or so without any more sightings, we turn back toward land. The boat is quiet. We see a spout and the driver stops, but the whale passes us without coming close. I try to strike up conversation, but the others' faces are stony. In the silence a cold realization settles and I understand what Judi was saying at lunch yesterday, that Mike and Mary didn't realize Max and I were coming on the second leg of the trip. I remember the comments in the car.

Perhaps they thought it would be an edgy adventure, but a two-year-old is happily toddling along. They don't want us here.

I quietly sing to block it all out. "'My young love said to me, my mother won't mind . . .'" It's my Irish granny's song, that my mom often sang in the kitchen or when driving the car. A few phrases in, the shape that passed us stops and slowly turns in front of the boat. It comes back, hovers next to me and Max. I lose myself in splashing, in the strange kinship. A couple more whales come. I wish we could be in the water, could swim away with them.

"There won't be any life jackets on the boat tomorrow," I over-hear Don telling Mike at dinner. I strain my ears to catch more, but it's carnival night and the restaurant we're in is heaving. It's already been a tense afternoon. After the first boat trip, the wind whipped up and Don called off the afternoon's outing. On the drive back to Loreto, he answered Mike's question from earlier in the day, telling the car about his Asian girlfriends and complaining about the Western stigma attached to age differences in relationships.

Judi leaned over in the Jeep. "Don's disgusting," she whispered in my ear. "The others are pissed off that you're getting to touch the whales so much." She hiked her eyebrows.

"Is that why they're being so unfriendly?" I mouthed back.

Judi shrugged.

In the restaurant I make my voice as pleasant as possible and ask Don if there will be child life jackets tomorrow. Two giant, brightly painted birds stare at us from a mural on the opposite wall. Don doesn't know. Perhaps I could rig Max up in an adult one if there are any, he says.

"And watch him slip through," snickers Mike.

I tell Don I can't take Max out on a boat without a proper life jacket because he can't swim.

Don goes bright red. He looks at me as though it's the first time he's seen me. "Listen, Doreen, you signed up to the trip." His voice is loud. He asks me to step outside.

"I need you to listen to *me*." I match his volume. I'm hot and my heart is revving like a motor. This is why I do all I can to avoid confrontation. Judi tells me to take a deep breath. "I am not going outside with you while you are being aggressive," I tell Don.

He pauses. "I'm a slow thinker, so if someone gets aggressive with me, then I don't react well."

"We should both calm down for a few minutes," I say. Don goes outside.

I've seen Max go underwater, when he was a year old. He was with some friends and their children by a lake, and I was swimming in chest-high water. He walked across the shore and into the shallows. When I saw him coming, he smiled at me.

"Stop, wait there, darling," I called, heaving through the weight of water as quickly as I could. My feet sought traction on the slope of slimy pebbles. Max continued walking out into the lake. I got to a depth where I could run. I saw him lose his balance and go underwater just as one of the women on shore splashed into the lake behind him and picked him up, then put him in my outstretched arms.

"What was wrong with her?" I heard the woman say to her husband afterward. "Why didn't she react more quickly?"

I tried to explain that moving across the stones had been difficult, adding how horrified I'd been to see Max coming toward me in the lake.

"Oh, but he was doing so well," she said. "It was such fun watching him try."

I kept seeing Max's face underwater, hadn't let him near water without a life jacket since.

"Do you think I'm being unreasonable?" I ask Judi, Mary, and Mike.

"Look," says Mike, "the boat's not going to sink. No one's going to let him go down." Judi says no, he needs to be in a life jacket. Mary says it's my choice, I don't have to go out, I can ask for a refund.

"Give yourself some credit, you're exhausted from dragging a two-year-old around," says Judi.

"Don't get yourself upset," says Mike.

I wonder how different this conversation would be if I were a man traveling with a child. I wonder how different the entire trip would be if I were a man, or if I had a male partner alongside. For a gratifying moment I imagine my traveling companion is the Hulk, envision him picking up Mike and throwing him about.

Don returns and says he will find a life jacket for the next day. He tells us to meet at Loreto harbor in the morning.

Max and I walk sleepily to the dock as the town is waking up. We watch the pelicans preening. They look as if they're trimming their tummy feathers with giant beak shears. The others arrive all together in a taxi. Don appears with a pile of life jackets.

"Universal size," Don says as he passes me Max's life jacket. It's universal adult size, like mine.

Judi offers to help, takes the straps and ties them around Max's waist so tight he screams and the jacket still moves around anyway. "There we are," she says.

Don suggests we sit at the back if Max is going to be noisy. I loosen the life jacket straps so they are not hurting him, hold him close the whole time. He breastfeeds and sleeps. Out on the water we see a blue whale, so big it's like a runway appearing out of the sea. When we can't see spouts, Mary complains to the boat driver. I start to hate what we're doing, wonder if our engine is annoying the whales. They come here to mate and give birth. Nothing could be more private. And here we are chasing them every time they come up to breathe. We are so loud. Ships crashing through the sea, propellers, engines roaring. Baleen whales communicate with low-frequency signals, and large ships create noise in the same frequency band, so we drown them out. The freedom of the seas is a joke. It just means it's a free-for-all.

I try to imagine the ocean depths quiet, teeming with life and secrets. Max wakes, stretches, and brushes Mike's life jacket with his foot. Mike whips around and glares. This is the last boat I get on with him. I hate him. He turns away but I can't relax, so I continue glaring at his back. You were little once, weren't you? What's wrong with taking a child traveling, teaching them to get lost, rather than staying put, stuck inside the same four walls? Why the fuck are women expected to give up the world when they give birth?

When I was about ten, Dad built me a room at the far end of the loft above the adjoining barn. Farmworkers had once lived in the roof space, and even getting there was an adventure. Access was through a large, hinged picture at the top of our stairs, which swung out to make a door when you hooked your fingers behind it and pulled. In my room, I could identify whoever had climbed into the attic by their footsteps on the wooden floorboards, which were unvarnished and dull brown from more than a century of farm dirt. My dad's tread was heavy, ponderous. He spent hours at his worktable, the space lit by a single hanging bulb. He'd bang things, paint, polish, scrape off rust, and wrestle with metal jammed in the jaws of a huge vise. Every weekend he went to the shooting range, and every Friday he'd be up late, making bullets for his vintage rifles. The noises and smells were comforting. Gunpowder, paint, mineral spirits, WD-40, grease, and Swarfega. Tap, tap, tap.

My mother's footsteps were lighter and faster. She might be happy, announcing that we were going night swimming or that David Attenborough or *The Young Ones* was on TV. But often she climbed the stairs driven by rage, sometimes when I was already in bed. If she wanted the dishes washed, that was at least doable, but she might just want to point out my faults. Hoping, I suppose, to shape me into a lovelier child. In my room I was cornered. I'd try hiding under the bed, but that just brought scorn.

"Life doesn't give you second chances, you know," she'd say.

During a tirade I'd keep still, look straight ahead, my expression as blank as possible. That way, there was nothing for her to catch hold of. My withdrawal made her even angrier, but once I had retreated into myself, I was stuck there, couldn't get out again even if I wanted to. I did not move until distant thumps marked my mother's feet going down the stairs.

When other children came over, she seemed happy and often sang. She would bake for us then, until the kitchen overflowed with iced buns, apple tarts, scones, and bread.

And the books. The sitting room was full of unsteady towers of the volumes she devoured. Books spoke to her. She recited poems as part of her everyday speech. As she knocked on the door, she might say, "'Is there anybody there?' said the Traveler. . . ." When going to the shops, she'd sometimes launch into "'I will arise and go now. . . .'" Her early education with nuns in Ireland had been literary, rich.

"We memorized Yeats, Frost, Gerard Manley Hopkins, the *greats*," she said. "It's like having very expensive furniture in your head," and she tried to furnish my head in the same way.

My mother was the second youngest of eight and often recalled her childhood when we found ourselves alone in the car. She was close to her younger brother, Patrick, and had a favorite big brother, Sean, who read her his *Dandy* comics and carried her on the handlebars of his bike. By the time I was about twelve, though, I was also party to darker memories. She'd been "interfered with" throughout childhood. When my mother talked about this, her voice and eyes would dull. One older brother, Jack, and another boy would climb through her bedroom window at night, she said. And sometimes she'd find a man, a family friend, waiting for her as she walked home from school. Jack, who died when I was small, was schizophrenic, she told me, and had in later life suffered terrible leg injuries, requiring amputation, when he threw himself under a train.

I don't know if Granny ever knew, but when my mother found the words to describe it, she eventually confided in another of her male relatives, who told her she was crazy, imagining things. When she spoke about that, her voice was barely audible.

Knowing that my mom had suffered as a child put me on her side, and I tried to be good. I would come down in the night and clean the kitchen, the way it said to in the *Girl Guide* books. This infuriated her. "Trying to be a saint, are you?" If I was quiet, that was not okay either. My mother hated silence, she said it reminded her of the men in her past.

One day a tall stranger came to visit. I remember him standing in the yard. My mom would not let him into the house. She told me later that they had known each other as children, that he had come all the way across the sea, to apologize.

I met my Irish granny only once. She was in her eighties and going deaf but was still hard at work around the farm. We'd gone to Ireland for a big reunion. There were around twenty cousins, some from as far afield as Canada. Granny was everywhere, seeing to the stove, towering over the table with a pot of stew. She had counted the grandchildren carefully, so even though I was shy and last to the table, I found a place set especially for me. I loved her immediately, even though when my cousin Sally spilled orange juice into her stew, Granny told her to eat it up, not to waste food, and that it all got mixed up in our stomachs anyway. I nodded in agreement while Sally cried into her plate.

The myths and legends current in the mountains that overlooked the valley where her farmhouse nestled held little interest for me. Granny was legend enough. Her father was a fisherman and she had traveled the ocean. Before getting married, she'd gone to America, got a job as a housekeeper, then made, lost, and once again made her fortune, my mother said. I watched Granny moving around the house in her tweed skirt and tried to imagine myself into her world, to understand what it was like to be so strong.

Granny had not had it easy. She'd been sent to America by her mother, after failing a secretarial exam, my mom told me. Great-Granny was apparently tough. When she was three, her father died in a farm accident, and her mother, my great-great-grandmother, now alone with six children, was evicted because she could not pay the rent on time. Mothers, over the generations, struggling to keep their children safe.

I have a memory of being in the bath, aged about seven. I am playing with a city of limpet shells on which I have drawn smiley faces with my special metallic-silver felt-tip pen. My mother sits next to the bath. She is telling me, in a quiet voice, that she got rid of the baby before me. I imagine an older girl but I can't see her face. My mother is saying something about the bath, the bath didn't work. I like the sound of her voice when she talks quietly. Is it my bath she is talking about? I wonder, as I plop a limpet shell into the water. My bath is working, it's warm, full of bubbles and friendly faces, it's cleaning me and my mother's hands as she wrings the sponge. She says *knitting needle* and I think about knitting needles in the bath, imagine using one to pop the bubbles. The memory is hazy and sometimes I wonder if all of it is real, though I can still feel the bath, its temperature, the water getting colder. Words are still coming out of my mother. You stayed, she says, you didn't let go. I know I took a long time to be born. Is that what she's talking about? She smiles at me, a big smile. I shepherd my limpet people to the end of the bath, away from the taps, as my mother pulls out the plug.

"You are the first person I ever loved," she told me when I was fifteen. "Before you came along, I was too damaged." My dad said she was different, calm, whenever she had a baby, and I liked thinking of her loving me as a newborn, although over time it had become clear she loved my siblings equally, if not more. She often couldn't tolerate the dreamy tomboy who "looked like a gorilla." She bought me pink dungarees, which I ripped on barbed wire when falling out of a tree, and a white suit with Snoopy on it, which I refused to wear. I was woven into her, though, determined to make the world right for her. Not being what she wanted was painful.

A row of disused pigsties was next to the house, and a chest freezer was in one of them. I was in my first year of A Levels, sixteen. I'd bought a tub of strawberry ice cream on the way home from school, eaten half of it, and was putting the rest in the freezer. I took hold of the handle to open the lid. My hand involuntarily gripped the metal as if it would never let go, and I was instantaneously pulled, or thrown, on top. The freezer was live and I stuck to the lid like a magnet, could not move. I screamed and screamed, but in my aunt's barn next door a potato sorter was rumbling and it drowned me out. I slowly juddered along the length of the freezer until I reached the end and fell off, my hand wrenched free. Though shaky, I was able to stand and walk slowly. I found my mother in the house, dressed up to go out, with colorful beads around her neck. She was going to see a friend.

"I just got stuck to the freezer. I couldn't get off," I stammered. She was preoccupied, clearly running late, listened briefly, then said she had to go. She got in the car and drove away down the road.

That evening, she told my father about the freezer, and he mended it. The next day I recounted what had happened to my physics teacher, Mr. Porter. He explained that when I had touched the metal, 240 volts of alternating current had pulsed through me, overpowering the electrical impulses from my brain, causing my fist and whole body to clench and unclench fifty times a second. That's why I had vibrated and moved along the freezer. I was lucky, he said, that I was young and fit and had fallen off so soon.

I liked Mr. Porter. He'd said that my experiment to determine the entropy of ice was genius, the best design he'd ever seen. He also said he was concerned that I never smiled.

Max and I walk out of our motel as it is getting light, leaving the rest of the group sleeping. The sky is pink and orange and the water soft silver below. At the harbor an easy sky meets a crumbled jetty of rocks coated with black snake-necked cormorants and snug brown pelicans. The surface of the water is in lively conversation with the wind. I feel the day expanding. But I am uneasy, remembering what my friend Elena said to me before the trip. Elena is Italian, a polyglot, and infiltrates Mexican drug cartels to make documentaries. We met at journalism school.

"Whatever you do, you mustn't get lost in Mexico, darling. You don't speak Spanish. You need a guide. You can't even *look* lost. If you do, Max will be kidnapped." I remember the training from work about reporting from situations that risk turning nasty. Always have an escape route planned, the instructor said. I scan the harbor, look around for people I could shout over to for help.

The evening before, Judi had come into my room. Don had told the group he wasn't a babysitter, she said, and was going to suggest I get one. At dinner, Max needed a diaper change, and since the restaurant's bathroom was broken, the staff arranged for me to go next door, to an ecotour center. Two smiling men behind the desk waved us in. On our way out they introduced themselves as Hector and Jesus. I saw my chance. Yes, said Hector, they had child life jackets. Yes, I could go out on their whale-watching boat the next day.

"I've got a boat," Max said proudly. "My boat is red."

"Will you bring it along tomorrow, to show me?" Hector asked, then said to me, "Be at the dock at seven." I'd already told the others we would take a break from the group trips. No one had said anything and Don had shrugged, so I didn't give details of my new plans. I'd felt relieved, but now I wonder if I'm taking a stupid risk by switching tours. Perhaps we should have just stayed on land.

At seven o'clock sharp Hector comes along, waving out of the window of a truck that has a boat on the back. Fears of kidnapping vanish. Riding with him are Ellie and Diane, fit, gray-haired friends from Montana. Diane asks if they can carry Max's toy boat, and Ellie asks to hold his hand. Hector lifts him up for a better view of the dolphins that flank us as we cruise slowly out of the harbor. They are blue and gray and liquid light, streaming under the stern, turning on their sides to look up at us. I point to where we saw whales yesterday. Hector's on the radio, speaking Spanish. As we approach the blue whale feeding grounds, I see our group in their boat. I wave enthusiastically. Hector draws up alongside to speak to the driver.

"What are you doing over there?" yells Mary.

"Having a wonderful time," I shout back.

Judi waves and calls to Max. Mike doesn't look at us.

The sea seems convex, as if it were going to spill out over the world. Blue whales and fin whales are all around, with the double spout of the humpback. One blue whale is named Calabaza, which means "pumpkin" in Spanish, because of the shape of the white marking on its tail. It's been coming for thirty years, and they think it's a male because they've never seen it with a calf. Calabaza breathes seven times, then sticks up his tail and dives. I watch the bulk and muscle slip away.

"Have a little swim, Mummy, like a whale," says Max.

I laugh, but Hector hears him and nods at me.

"Really?" I ask.

"We'll watch Max," says Diane. "No problem."

I look around. No sharks. Ellie and Diane have been talking about Diane's grown-up daughter in such a way that I'd trust them with Max all week. I will regret it forever if I don't do this. I quickly undress until I'm wearing just T-shirt and knickers, dive off the side of the boat before I can change my mind, breaststroke down as far as I can, and shout, "Love!" with all the power in my lungs, down to where Calabaza might be. All I hear is a far-off burble through the tremors in my skull.

Unlike Calabaza's ears, the human eardrum can detect vibrations efficiently in the air but not in water. My hearing's patchy anyway. When I was five, I was partially deaf for a year, until I had grommets put in. I have vague memories of a muffled, soft world, with voices intruding at the edges, like spikes. My mother used to like telling the story. I had passed all the beeping hearing tests, but when she stood behind me in the GP's office and said my name, I did not react. When she shouted, I responded. Only then did the doctor believe her. Part of me finds this underwater silence familiar, comforting.

Hearing is everything to whales. Humans are visual but whales inhabit a world that is often without light. Tactile when close together, when they are traveling and hunting, they are essentially their voices and ears. An oceanic layer called the deep sound channel best carries whales' calls. Here, conversations can bounce between layers defined by ocean temperature and pressure and travel for thousands of miles. Upcalls, downcalls, screams, grunts, roars, growls, belches, pulses, perhaps babies squeaking at their mothers.

The first recordings of whales in the wild were made in the 1950s by William Schevill.[1] He was working on submarine sonar for the US Navy. When the military suspected the low-frequency blips they were hearing were Soviets trying to locate American submarines, he reassured them the sounds were from fin whales. In 1970 whale song became an unlikely smash hit on land, with the release of bioacoustician Roger Payne's *Songs of the Humpback Whale*. Scientists have recorded a North Pacific right whale singing in the Bering Sea, a gunshot sound, moaning, warbling. So few right whales are left that it's not known if it was singing to another of its species or calling out to find one. Some whales have regional dialects.[2] Sperm whales live in clans and recognize one another by their calls as they traverse thousands of miles of sea, the young learning their specific vocalization from the adults. According to Hal Whitehead, a marine biologist and sperm whale expert, sperm whales are living in massive, multicultural undersea societies. One analogy would be elephants,[3] another would be us.

I imagine Calabaza moving somewhere far below me as I swim. Our bodies, whale and human, swell the sea. He will have inhaled truckloads of air in those seven breaths and with a flip of his flukes descended into darkness. Might he have heard me? He could be calling, a low tone that can echo off submarine canyons, spreading for hundreds of miles. He might have damaged hearing too, could have been subjected to an air-gun barrage during seismic exploration for fossil fuels. The sonic shots penetrate the seafloor, sometimes to a depth of hundreds of miles. Testing can go on for months, several times a minute. It's difficult to prove how whales are affected because they're so hard to study, but air guns are believed to have pulverized internal organs in giant squid, discovered after they washed up onshore.[4] Observations of western gray whales, during seismic surveys in their summer foraging grounds off Sakhalin Island, found avoidance at ranges of up to fifteen miles as well as disrupted breathing patterns[5] Air guns kill zooplankton and their larvae from three-quarters of a mile away.[6] In simulations, scallops suffered increased mortality and were seen recoiling from the sound.[7] Once oil or gas reserves are found, more ships come, pipes are laid, the drilling starts. Both bowhead and gray whales have altered their migratory course to avoid industrial noise.[8] When ships and boats are nearby, grays vocalize more frequently, and their calls are louder when noisy outboard motors are around.[9] In other words, they have to shout.

Naval exercises involving midfrequency anti-submarine-warfare sonar are associated with mass strandings of beaked whales.[10] The whales seemed to die within about four hours of exposure to sonar exercises, with massive hemorrhages in vital organs such as the brain and heart. The US government acknowledged that the "tactical mid-range frequency sonars aboard US Navy ships" were the "most plausible source of this acoustic or impulse trauma."[11] Low-frequency sound technology is also used to monitor ocean warming. The thermometry experiments use the deep sound channel, the whales' communication hotline.[12] We make noise even when we're trying to assess the damage we're doing. It's not going to get any quieter for you, whales.

I hang suspended, part of the Sea of Cortés, enveloped in silence. Then I notice a shadow below. It's whale-shaped. Terror sweeps up and through me. I kick frantically toward the light, thrash through the water in the direction of the boat, clamber onto the deck. I hear Max chattering to Diane.

"Yes," she says, "I prefer trains to buses too."

Looking overboard on unsteady legs, I realize there is no whale and what I saw was the shadow of the boat, carried under by the sun into bottomless green.

"You look radiant," says Diane. I certainly feel alive. My body thrums with adrenaline. It's always been a wish of mine to swim with whales, but all my romantic notions are gone. What if one found me annoying or flicked me with its tail by accident? My speech is the chatter of a monkey, not the song library of whales. Whatever connection I might like to imagine, my ancestors made different decisions. Here, in the whales' world, I am out of my depth.

———

The rope ladder upgraded my bedroom into an adventurer's paradise. Dad got it as part of a lot at an auction.

"Might be good for your tree houses, Doreen," he said. We had a shortage of bedrooms, which meant my parents slept on a sofa bed in the living room and it was impossible to enter or leave the house undetected. The rope ladder was a game changer. It had thick wooden rungs knotted through with strong pale blue rope and was easy to loop around the cast-iron bedstead. Hung out the window, it reached most of the way down the granite wall. I could scale down like Spider-Man and jump the last bit onto the path at the back of the house. Then I would creep away, trying not to crunch on the gravel.

Josie and I spent most of our time wandering or at my house. I wasn't often invited back to hers. Josie's mother said I was lower-class, Josie had reported. Her mother disapproved of my running around wild in bare feet and said Josie came home having forgotten her manners, although Josie was just as wild, if not wilder. We sometimes called our parents from a pay phone to say we were staying over at the other's home. Then we'd be free to spend the night outside. Together we climbed, literally, the walls of the island, the cliffs and outer limits of "the Rock," as Jersey is affectionately known by its inhabitants. One windy day we found ourselves slipping down the cliff-top grass at Grosnez, the site of the ruined medieval fortress in the far northwest, toward a drop of three or four stories. Choppy sea slurped over pointed rocks below. We were silent then, each for herself, flat against the cliffside. Slowly, slowly wriggling sideways, scrabbling urgently if we lost a finger- or foothold again, inching up little by little, gripping but not so hard as to dislodge a precarious stone anchor.

"That was too close," I said when we were safely on top of the cliff.

When my mom drove my friends home, we'd stand up on the rear seat of the green Citroën Dyane with the roof rolled back, leaning in as we took a corner. The car would roar and reverberate as she led us in singing Irish ballads at the tops of our voices. Sometimes Dad took us in his motorbike and sidecar, which fitted two children squashed up together and occasionally tipped thrillingly when we went around a bend. He brought home yellow and blue mopeds from an auction, and we rode them over ramps and around the fields until they broke. My friends and I once crawled all the way to the sea along several miles of muddy stream through gardens, fields, and woods, high on Lucozade tablets, singing all the way. It took us the whole day, and by the end of it we had shed the human world, become shrieking, glittering amoebas of mud. It was pointless and wonderful.

One summer's night during my midteens, when friends of my parents were babysitting, Josie and I climbed out of my bedroom window and down the rope ladder. A chill was in the air so we wore our coats. We walked to the sea and then along the coast, chatting and skimming stones, clambering over rocks, ending up at a promontory called Le Hocq.

It was too cold to swim, we agreed. The hiss and heave of high tide was soothing. We shaped pebble pillows on the lip of stones by the seawall and lay down, then spent a long time shuffling around.

"No matter what I do, there's a pebble in my back," I said.

"They're too big, too lumpy," said Josie. "And the sand's too wet to sleep on."

We walked back home, singing Suzanne Vega, Bob Marley, and trying to imitate a Tom Waits growl. It was past midnight when we arrived.

The rope ladder was gone, my bedroom window shut. Had the babysitters discovered my escape route? Or was it my mom, teaching me a lesson? We checked the outside toilet to see if the key was in the green Wellington, its usual hiding place. No key. So with some musty blankets from the barn, we curled up in our coats, side by side on the damp grass in Bramble's field. She grazed up so close that it sounded as if she were eating our hair, then snorted off again.

"Did you see that?" said Josie.

"What?"

"Over there, near Orion's Belt."

"I can't see anything."

"Look! A shooting star."

I stared. Wishing was my specialty. "It was probably just a satellite." But seconds later there was another. They gathered pace, more and more. Startled, staring stars, falling out of the black nothing, down toward us as we lay in our now-perfect spot on the grass. There were so many that we stopped wishing, stopped counting. Our eyes brimmed with points of light, and I felt my mind expanding into a limitless universe, into dark matter and into light. It was all one, I realized, the stars, the earth, Bramble, Josie and me, all of us were made of the same stuff, just somehow organized differently.

"Josie! We're made of stars."

"Cosmic, man."

I picked a handful of grass and threw it at her as she laughed.

We must have slept, but the storm continued in my head all night. Thanks to the rope ladder, thanks to being locked out. Enough wishes to last a lifetime.

I can't stomach getting in a car with Mike for the three-day drive back to the United States. First thing in the morning I tell Don that Max and I will stay on in Loreto when the group leaves. I smile and try to sound casual. I walk to breakfast with Judi, who reaches for Max's hand.

"I got the full picture last night at dinner," she says. "Mike told me he can't stand the sight of children, and Max being here has ruined his trip."

"What about his own kids?"

"I said that, and he just said, 'Well, they're all grown up now.' I thought you were making it up. It's kind of hateful."

"I didn't mean to wreck anyone's holiday."

In the queue for breakfast at the café I tell the others we will say goodbye to them here. Mary asks what I'm going to do. I'm ambiguous in my reply because I haven't a clue. Don talks to the table about a friend of his who mysteriously disappeared in the area. I don't show it's working, that I'm getting scared. I tickle Max on my knee, make him wriggle and shriek. He was well behaved all this time, and Mike hated us anyway. Don clears his throat, asks me what made me decide to stay.

"It seems nice here." I sound ridiculous. I don't say I feel uncomfortable and unsafe because we're so clearly unwelcome.

"Are you with someone?" he asks.

"No."

"Since you're vague about your plans, I feel compelled to tell you that a woman traveling on her own in Baja is in danger." He continues his story about his friend, who left from Guerrero Negro in a van. The van was found later, burned by the side of the road, with a charred body inside. I say that's terrible but that Don doesn't need to worry about us, I'm an experienced traveler. My voice is shrill. As they reverse out of the motel parking lot in the Jeep, I still wave and smile with genuine pleasure. Max blows a kiss to Judi.

Back in our room I open my laptop and, with shaking hands, immediately book the next available flight to LA. It's in two and a half hours. The motel manager helps me order a taxi. Then it's a frantic pack. Max copies me, opens his mini-rucksack. He crams in Flash and a jigsaw of the whale migration I bought in Guerrero Negro. I can't find my talisman sperm whale carving, or all the whale key rings I bought as presents.

"Where are the whales?" I ask Frida's portrait desperately.

"In *mine* bag," says Max.

We are ready just as the taxi arrives outside. The drive to the airport is breathtaking. The rocks and the sky and the mottled brown earth speeding past. We pass cacti grouped like marathon runners on the side of the road. As we draw up outside departures, I hand a bunch of notes to the driver, don't wait for the change. I run into the airport with Max under one arm, bags and car seat balanced on the buggy.

The Sea of Cortés is shining bright blue below as we take off. The plane banks. One wing dipped toward ocean, one flooded in sky. I feel the whole world turn upside down and the beauty of the water breaks over me. I say a silent goodbye to Calabaza, imagine him down there, and breathe a thank-you. I think about the gray whale mothers and calves. They must be leaving the lagoons. The fear for them, as they move out into the deep waters, is as overwhelming as the love.

UTQIAĠVIK: BELONGING

Latitude: 71° 17' 26" N
Longitude: 156° 47' 19" W

From the back of Billy's snow machine, moving across the sea ice, I saw the light change, dim a little. The air was white, almost opaque, and the going was bumpy. The convoy that was Kaleak crew appeared and disappeared ahead of us, dotted along the trail like musical notes on a stave. The umiaq paddle boat and the aluminum chaser boat looked waterborne already, buoyed along by the sledges. The wind had clear sight of us and roared as it swept through our party. I was grateful for my borrowed down-filled mittens and the bunny boots, good for temperatures as low as −50°C. I guessed we were probably close to that point in this gale. I wore three pairs of socks, three pairs of gloves, and thermals, fleece trousers, and ski pants. What stopped me from freezing to death, though, was the lambskin parka Julia had lent me, and of course Billy, whose back hid my face from the cold, which cut straight through my balaclava and ski goggles if I peered around him. The sun sank to as low an angle as it ever would in spring, turning the world blue. My body was warm but I went cold right through at the thought of the ocean that sat, dark and deep, below the ice we were traveling on.

"Watch out for cracks," Billy shouted over his shoulder. The crew was on constant alert for signs I was oblivious to. They'd all hunted since they were children, understood ice in all its forms. In the company of these experts, unable to fend for myself on any level or even speak the language that described the landscape, I was reduced to the status of a small child.

The *tuvaqtaq*, shore-fast ice stuck to the seabed, and the idea of land were well behind us. My face and hands were numb so it was as if they were not there when Billy turned our machine around, shouting and waving. The crew circled back. One man had stopped and was examining the fully loaded sled he'd been pulling. A runner had broken coming over a particularly steep rise on the trail. The boats had been set almost on end as they climbed and fell over each *ivuniq*, or pressure ridge. It was surely someone's fault for not checking the sled, and as we were forced to stop, it made us vulnerable to the cold, polar bears, and whatever else might be out there. My travel companions did not look for anyone to blame. They formed a single unit, working together to fix the runner in the deafening wind. They set up a tent, off-loaded the sled, and examined the break. I watched. Van gestured to me that I should go inside.

"I can help," I shouted, indignant. The air screamed louder than me. No one could hear what I was saying so I stretched an open hand toward Ira, who held the saw. He hesitated before passing it to me. Several of the crew watched skeptically. I gave my best efforts to sawing the splintered runner for a few minutes, then returned the tool. The expressions of some crew members, who had been wary or downright hostile, opened up. Van, who'd ignored me since we'd heard the announcement on the radio, who had sped off without checking I had someone to ride with, gave me a nod. When the sled was mended, the crew returned to their snow machines.

"Riley, follow me with the umiaq," shouted Van, who was towing the sled carrying the aluminum boat. "Doreen, stay with Billy."

"Okay there? You cold?" shouted Billy before starting the motor.

"All good," I yelled back.

"Hold on tight."

I held on, but I did not clutch at Billy's parka quite as tightly as before.

After hours of traveling we reached the lead, where the water cut through the sea ice. A harsh white merged the world, below and above. There was no brown, no yellow, nothing of the land. The lead, a streak of gray, was the only thing of a different color. The surface water was solidifying before our eyes. Farther out, the water shifted, was still liquid, but overall the ice was winning. We worked quickly to set up camp as the snow blew horizontally. The channel was about half a mile wide, I guessed. You could see the other side. I followed the crew around, trying to be useful, copying them. They hacked at the ice at the edge of the lead to make it smooth, so as to provide an inviting place for bowheads to come up and breathe. I was allowed to help—shoving blocks of ice away with a pole to be taken off by the current—but not for long because Van was too afraid I'd slip and stumble in. If I fell in, I'd drown, be swept under the ice or freeze to death in minutes. I stayed close to the crew.

White world, white tent, white parkas on top of our furs. It was hypnotic. The white was for camouflage, to prevent the whales from seeing the hunters. A blind had been made from slices of ice, stuck up like a row of incisors. They would hide the crew, and the harpoons, from any animal that looked up over the ice edge. You could see people clearly on the ice, their actions, their intentions, how they held their space. There was no room for artifice. I felt pared down to my bones and concentrated hard on each moment as it came. The snow did not turn mushy or melt. It stayed soft and feathery. We scraped a path with spades to ease walking between the tent and the hide-covered bench—behind the white ice wall—which was set back six yards from the lead and out of sight of the whales. Everyone moved slowly, energy was conserved. It was not good to sweat because then you would be wet inside your layers, would get cold. Feet especially had to stay dry.

Alappaa?—"Are you cold?"—was a frequent question. *Ii* was "yes." *Naumi* was "no." *Utuguu*, "a little bit."

The crew laughed at me filming them, did little dances at the lead's edge, pretended they were going to dive in. Van knelt on a caribou hide, holding the harpoon at an upward angle, pointed toward the water.

"Propane heater, propane stove, melting ice for water." Leif was in typical jovial form, making coffee inside the cooking tent. Five people were lying in the sleeping tent. The routine was that there was no routine, given how day and night were no longer useful distinctions. One long day dimmed and then brightened, repeatedly. I had no idea what time it was. We were on hunting time. Clocks were meaningless. At any hour there were people awake, alert and ready, observing the weather and the ice, every movement, every change. "It's glacier ice out here," said Leif. "Old ice from back in the day, fresh water, not salt water." I could go get some ice, he suggested, make myself useful.

"Find a smooth-looking bump. Like a big old bump on the head," said Van. The snow was deep. I sank half a yard, hoped there were no cracks or holes. Taking a pickax from the sled, I found a smooth hill, climbed to the top, and looked out over the dark lead. I attacked the top of the hill with the pick. The metal skirted off to the side, tiny bits tinkling off. I smacked the pick down harder, encouraging myself with a running commentary. The pickax bounced off. Nothing. I had a few more goes, finally loosened a chunk. Under the snow, a sudden blue. I'd found the old ice. I lifted the pick right above my head and brought it down with all possible force. A few splinters. "Quit talking to the ice," shouted Van. I eventually accumulated a bucketful of giant ice cubes to take back to the tent. Leif handed me a pork-chop sandwich ringed by thick fat. He and Eli shared cooking duties. Vegetarian? Leif mouthed the word. Nauseated at the sight and smell, I hesitated a moment, but seeing his expression, I took the sandwich, said thank-you, and chewed, concentrating on the salty taste and trying to ignore the crunch of the fat and the juice of the meat. I breathed through my nose and swallowed mouthfuls as quickly as possible, sipping scalding instant coffee in between bites.

Van had set a compass down on the ice. Any change in the direction of the needle would tell us if our campsite had broken off and we were floating out to sea. I checked the compass obsessively. I also tested my satellite phone, calling London, then put it away in the tent and forgot about it. Everything required thought and planning when I was outside. Being, watch for bears, cracks, and any change in the compass. Looking, careful if it's bright or you'll get snow blindness. Breathing, best facing away from the wind. Going to the bathroom or, more accurately, going behind the small ice hill to relieve myself. To do this in freezing cold without flashing or wetting my furs needed care and precision. Wet clothes would freeze, so I squatted cautiously and lifted my parka wide but not wide enough to let in the vicious Arctic wind. Sleeping also took careful consideration. The crew were allowed to sleep on the hide-covered bench, but I wasn't. When I dozed off, they ordered me straight inside.

"You'll freeze to death," said Van. "You're not Iñupiaq." Finding a place to sleep in the communal tent took getting used to. Van's snoring was comically loud, though he joked that Ira's was the loudest.

"She's lying next to Jeffrey," someone giggled, not realizing I'd woken. Jeffrey and another crew member each made a journey from camp back to town to attend court for some alcohol-related offense. But out here there was no alcohol. It was a sanctuary from drink and drugs.

The crew spoke in staccato Iñupiaq syllables over the VHF, swapping information on what was happening with the weather and any sightings. They described the ever-changing weather conditions, had words for all thicknesses and ages of ice. Most of the words seemed to stay at the back of the throat or be made with the tongue safe in the mouth, away from the cold. The hard sounds such as *q* traveled well. There was no need to shout on a day like this, a waiting day.

"Good afternoon, everyone," announced the VHF. A chorus of *good afternoon*s came in reply. The whole community was out here in spirit, everyone vicariously part of a crew. "Good afternoon, come and get candy from Leavitt base. . . . Good luck Leavitt crew, good luck everybody, from W-W base. . . . *Quyanaqpak,*[1] Auntie Alice, good luck to your crew too." Walrus were mentioned briefly. Van shouldered a gun, looked down the sight to the west, balancing it on the stern of the umiaq.

"Do I look like a tanik?" asked Leif, who had just returned from a trip to town to see his girlfriend after we'd been on the ice for about a week. "A white man," he translated for my benefit. "Someone said I look like a tanik today. Must have been my brown duck bibs." He pulled the flaps of his hat. "A real squarehead."

"How will we know when a whale comes?" I asked.

Leif funneled breath through spit at the back of his throat, a low rasping. "You hear that, then you see black. Then these guys get excited."

"The big old ones, they sound like a motor. The ice vibrates," said Van.

I couldn't imagine it, wasn't sure I believed any whales would actually come.

It's been suggested, by Craig George and a collaboration of scientists and Indigenous whalers, that the bowhead is likely the longest-living mammal on earth. The female calves every three to four years, with pregnancy lasting three months longer than a human's. Aġviq might live for more than two hundred years, making it a sort of time machine. In 1981 an ivory harpoon head with a metal point[2] was found in the blubber of a whale caught off Wainwright, a village farther west from Utqiaġvik along Alaska's north coast. After that, more traditional harpoon heads, made of stone and ivory, were found in landed whales. Comparing the heads with harpoons collected by anthropologists allowed the dates of their use to be narrowed down to between 130 and 200 years earlier, before contact with Europeans. By studying eyeballs from freshly landed whales, Craig and his colleagues were also able to age individuals. The lens in the eyeball contains proteins that change over the whale's lifetime. One whale, a forty-eight-foot-long male killed in 1995, was estimated to be 211 years old. The Iñupiat already knew the bowheads were long-lived, put their age in the order of "two human lifetimes."[3] The hunters weren't surprised.

A two-hundred-year life span means a big, old aġviq would have seen a lot. It had escaped the little umiaqs and the whaling ships. It had heard the ocean becoming progressively noisier and was lucky enough to have avoided ship strikes. Perhaps it noticed the recovery of the bowhead population after commercial whaling stopped, which according to Craig is without doubt one of the great conservation success stories of the past century.

"They're tough, resilient animals," he says, "but they are headed into an uncertain future." Although the Arctic Ocean is becoming more productive, nobody knows to what extent bowheads or their prey will be able to adjust to ice-free waters in the warming, acidifying waters. Among experts, concern and optimism jostle side by side.[4] Bowheads evolved as ice whales, and statistical models suggest the Arctic could become ice-free in summer in the decade 2030–40.[5] As crabbing and fishing activities move north, some say entanglement is the greatest threat to baleen whales worldwide. So many factors could weaken the whales. To endanger or even exterminate aġviġit, we wouldn't even have to deliver the final blow ourselves. Today's whales will be pioneers for as long as they live.

I sat behind the white ice wall on the hide-covered bench and waited. Billy went and stood on a pile of ice about six yards high, a sentinel. Looking across to the other side of the lead, where the white stretched up toward the north pole, I tried to spot polar bears. Billy had met one on the trail during a run to town. It had blocked his way and then approached him. He'd run around the other side of his snow machine, he said, and shot into the air to scare it off.

"There, there's one," Riley said.

"See the tall ice? There!" said Billy.

I could only see ice.

"Over there. Follow the ice up past that hill, past the blue ice," said Van. I scrutinized his face, for signs he might be teasing. "There's another one. Look for the black nose."

Riley made it his job to educate me on hierarchy. I was at the bottom, obviously. That meant I needed to keep the coffeepot filled and ensure a constant supply of ice for water. There was always something to watch, even if it was just hunters watching the lead, the ice, or the sky. I'd look where they were looking and try to see what they were seeing. I'd been given a book for young whalers[6] by a kind woman in the school district office. In both Iñupiaq and English the little spiral-bound guide explained weather terminology, bow-head morphology, whaling equipment, and butchering. The captain could grade student whalers on different exercises, including drawing a map of the trail to the whaling camp, keeping a daily whaler log, recording weather and lead conditions, and completing a whale observation form. In that way, whaling could be incorporated into the school curriculum. I approached Van and tried pointing out an area of ice with what I thought was the correct term. He raised an eyebrow at my mangled effort and declined to comment on my scribbles on the trail map. I put my book away and went back to watching and listening, collecting multiyear ice, and making coffee.

The wind was brisk, the surface of the lead writhing in a blue-tinted night. Then, the whales came.

I heard them before I saw them, their breath hissing through the air. Punctuating the silence. The sound was so startling, so alien, it broke the world open. We were no longer the only beings on this spinning sphere of rock. They appeared in the lead, belugas, each breath a triumph of endurance, of stealth, of intelligence, of community, of evolution, of luck. Rhythmic wheels rolling through the water. The mothers huge and white, moving along the lead like ghosts. The babies small gray cogs next to them. They gave little time to the air, just a hoarse backward gasp, a roll of the back. Their aim lay far ahead. I recorded their breathing from the edge of the lead, filmed them for hours. Here was another mind at work, one I could glimpse only the surface of. Still we waited.

I was on the most enjoyable night shift I'd ever known. The tent murmured as the crew played cards. I lost every time. Billy told me about the time a grizzly bear bit his boat in half.

"What a pain. I hate grizzlies," I replied, and continued melting ice for water. Then I stopped. What had I just said? Who was I again?

Outside, the moon-dragged tide moved on, surging up onto the ice. It made a deep sound, echoing, booming with the weight and disturbance of air and water meeting, the force of planetary bodies brought to bear on the spot of ice where we camped. Crunching, swallowing, heaving, popping, sighing. The lead was loud, but we were quiet at the edge because whales' hearing is so sensitive. Billy and I had moved to the bench, were watching belugas passing.

"Sometimes," he murmured into the night, "we see a gray,

aġviġluaq." This is the strangest memory, hardly a memory at all. The words bided their time for years before I really heard them, as if for the first time.

The profile of a seal floated past, as though disembodied. The radio whispered Iñupiaq. Billy smoked and coughed. A pile of cigarette butts was gathering next to the blind. He stood, poured his coffee dregs on top of them. In the tent the others rested, lying in full outdoor gear, a similar landscape of white mounds to what was outside. Van mumbled into the radio and I heard Julia's voice. I didn't hear the signal, but suddenly everyone was outside next to the boat. Billy took hold of the *aqu*, the stern, ready to push it off. The crew watched to the west. A lot was going on, on the radio.

"First whale, seven-one, good morning," said a woman's voice.

"Kaleak crew, seven-four," Julia was calling.

Billy left the boat, went to answer. "They're up there," he said.

"Everything's up there," said Van softly, with frustration. But as he spoke, a slowly curving black back slipped into view, far out in the lead. It looked to be the length of a bus or two. The crew's movements became silent, fluid, coordinated. Van glanced back at me. I was not moving, and he nodded his approval. I was not allowed in the boat or even near it, would be a danger to myself and others. The whale sighed into the distance, and Van returned to the bench. The camp settled back to watching. Though aching for sleep, I couldn't bear to miss anything. Walking off a little way from camp I stared out over the lead, singing my granny's song softly to the water. It was to distract myself from tiredness and to offer up the only gift I could think of to this most ancient of hunts, and to the hunted.

"'And then she went homeward with one star awake, as the swan in the evening moves over the lake.'"

Billy was watching me. Realizing the crew might be able to hear, I wandered self-consciously back, hoping no one was cross I'd made a noise. I crept into the tent. I would sleep, stay out of trouble. Once inside, I turned and lifted the entrance flap to look out. Van was right by the umiaq. I could see the round black back of a whale, yards away from where I'd been standing and singing. The whale circled and surfaced again, gave a sharp blow.

"Inutuq," murmured Billy. "It's looking for someone."

The hunters climbed into the boat.

"There's a rifle over there"—Van pointed to the sled—"in case a polar bear shows up." He wasn't joking now.

The men pushed off from the ice. The whale came up to breathe again, a perfectly round wave, dark as the ocean, only discernible by the unbroken shine of its back. I could not see the bulk underneath. It was blanketed by a sea that absorbed every speck of light. The whale circled back toward the camp. The men paddled silently, the harpoon roving the air, the point at the end of the spear like an eye on a stalk. The umiaq suddenly struck me as flimsy. I could do nothing, so I worried about everything at once. The cover might have a hole, the boat might capsize, and if they got the whale, it might pull them under or smack the umiaq with its huge flukes. I did not move but my heart beat wildly, as if I were the hunter—or the quarry. One more slip of black back above the surface. Then the whale was gone before the crew had got close enough to take a shot.

Later that day a huge adult about fifty feet long came up, blowing like a geyser, again where I'd just been quietly singing. I felt that if I reached for it with a paddle from the edge of the ice, I could have touched it. I wondered if the whales had liked the song, which was slow and gently haunting. Perhaps the vocal runs meandered in a similar way to some of the whale calls. The crew clambered for the boat, but this time they did not even have time to launch before the whale was under the ice, already away.

"You're our whale caller," Van said.

When I next came into the tent, a space had been made for me on the skin floor. I was handed an enamel mug of coffee, me, who had made it for the others every single day up until now. I couldn't stop grinning. They laughed and I hid my face in the fur of my hood. One whale came from beneath the ice, directly under our camp. Perhaps it had heard us already because it swam in a straight line, away from the edge. From that angle, I could see a hint of the colossal bulk underneath, ripples around its back as it came into sight briefly and then disappeared.

Just a little way up the lead another crew was doing the same as ours, pushing off in a white umiaq, all dressed in white, outlined by the gray ruffs of their hoods and the dark gray water. This scene had been the same for hundreds of years. As I watched them, the seconds felt unstable, indeterminate.

Archaeological evidence shows that as the climate cooled around 1300 CE, whaling communities concentrated in areas of the Arctic coast where it was still possible to reliably access leads. Boats needed to be hauled for miles across the frozen sea to the leads, and the catch had to be transported back to the villages. People learned to live together more densely, cooperatively, rather than moving autonomously wherever they pleased.

The world pulled focus to the present. Van was at the ice edge. Other crew members waited by the blind, Billy by the boat. Everything was the same, except me. I scuffed my bunny boots around on the ice to break the spell. At the edge of the lead, not too close, I looked down into what could have been outer space, except here we'd already met other intelligent life. I imagined the voices of seals and walrus moaning, crackling, booming, yelping, trilling. And of course the bellowing and harmonics of aġviq. I wished I could hear it all and wondered if the conversations had evolved over the centuries. *Let's get lunch* probably hadn't changed much.

Aġviġit are on the move, gliding through channels and under the puzzle of ice. Their backs leave a trail along the roof of the frozen ocean. Using the pockets and holes where they've broken through, they can breathe using tiny gaps because of the blowhole on the summit of their mountainous cranium.

Aġviq is a swimming head. Its mouth, proportionally larger than that of any other animal, gapes like a moving crater in the plankton-dusted streaks of light from above. Whales skim-feeding look serene, but the torque on their jaw when they close it is immense. To maintain body weight an adult swallows up to two tons of food a day, synthesizing the tiny creatures sieved through the baleen into blubber and muscle.

Baleen is the evolutionary invention that allows the great whales to reach their enormous size while they filter-feed and travel vast distances. Bowheads are from the Mysticeti suborder, which lost their teeth and grew rigid plates, made from keratin like our hair and nails, around twenty-five to thirty million years ago. The giant polar whale, aġviq, has approximately 320 plates of baleen in each of two racks on either side of the upper jaw. They grow longer than in any other species, in some cases to more than thirteen feet. Sometimes aġviġit move through surface waters feeding together in an arrow formation like a *V*. In this way prey may spill from the mouth of the leading whale and be caught by those behind. The whales are extravagant, with white chin and belly markings, beautiful black skin, and blubber that can be half a yard thick. With aġviġit, all the vital statistics are high. Their population is slimmed down though. The lowest pre-whaling estimate put worldwide numbers of bowheads at fifty thousand.[7] By the time commercial whaling effectively ended in 1921, fewer than three thousand were left worldwide. The depletion of bowheads and walrus caused horrific famine on St. Lawrence Island in the Bering Sea in the late 1870s.[8]

The bowheads number approximately twenty-three thousand today.[9] Calves grow rapidly while they're nursing, and the Iñupiat typically used ribs of one-year-old bowheads as fishing net weights because they were so hard and heavy. After the supply of rich milk stops, it's impossible to sustain the same rate of growth with their short baleen. Until they are five years old, fat and bone from the skeleton are withdrawn to build up their enormous heads and the forests in their mouths. During this time, the ribs can lose 40 percent of their mass. Orcas in the western Okhotsk Sea have profited from this weakness. A drone filmed a pod attacking a juvenile whale three times their size, too big to drown. The matriarch battered its side, crushing the ribs, while others blocked its escape. Juvenile carcasses had been seen with wounds thought to be from orcas, but their tactics were mysterious until the ramming attack was captured on camera. Scars heal white on the black skin of aġviq. More marks consistent with killer-whale attacks are being seen every decade, with increased human observation, higher numbers of orcas, and longer open-water seasons all thought to be reasons why.

Once a whale is four or five years old, the size of the baleen rack means it can feed enough for the body to grow again. Adult length is up to twenty-one yards, and weight can be 110 tons. Indigenous hunters have seen bowheads smash their huge skulls through ice nearly half a yard thick. Their intelligence and sensitivity are also stunning. In *Arctic Dreams*, Barry Lopez wrote of an English whaler, the *Cumbrian*, which in 1823 came upon an eighteen-yard female bowhead sleeping in light ice in the Davis Strait, between Greenland and Nunavut.[10] The whale woke, swam slowly once around the ship, then put her head to the bow and began to push the vessel backward. The crew was spooked, transfixed. Several minutes went by before they took up their harpoons and killed her. Lopez also describes one bowhead's reaction to the sensation of being struck by a harpoon. It "dived so furiously it took out 1200 yards of line in three and a half minutes before crashing into the ocean floor, breaking its neck and burying its head eight feet deep in blue-black mud."[11]

The wind had picked up. The water in the lead was perturbed, ripples in some places rolled by waves. This sea held moving beings, seemed to be conscious, to desire more movement. The elements were aiding the bowheads. It became harder to see them when they rose above water. The harpoon pierced the air, held in readiness at the *sivu*, the bow of the boat. Was I imagining it or did the other side of the lead seem closer? The radio and the camp became busy with Iñupiaq being spoken. The crew members were suddenly everywhere. I was not imagining it. The pack ice was coming in, approaching our camp. The water looked as if it were boiling. The lead was closing up fast. The tent came down in minutes, supplies were packed up. I snapped a photo of the umiaq, the boat that Billy had made, perched on the edge of the ice in the blue night, before it was hauled back onto the sled. Then I got my video camera out, spurred into journalistic action by the drama.

"Put that thing away." Van was next to me in an instant. "Help pack up!" I moved around urgently, looking for a job, took an edge of a tent as if to start folding.

"Hey, leave that," someone shouted. Snow machines were buzzing off every which way. Billy was towing the umiaq off already. "Doreen, go with Leif," Van yelled. I ran to Leif on his machine, but the combined weight of the two of us and the sledge we were pulling was too much for the motor. The snow machine did not budge. We were being left behind. The lead was closing up even faster. Leif jumped off. Oh my God, was I being abandoned?

"Go! Get the fuck out of here!" Leif roared. I couldn't see any path through the choppy ice hills and had no idea how to drive the thing. I'd only ever been a passenger. But I needed to get away from giant, shouting Leif and the advancing ice. He ran to jump on someone else's sledge as I twisted the handle grip and shot forward, wrestling with the steering as the machine surged up an incline. I glimpsed limitless white, and the other snowmobiles on a path to my right. Then the wind smacked my head as if it were angry, and the machine plunged suddenly downward. I drove so fast, and so far, making for where I thought land might be, that the crew, who had been watching my progress carefully the whole time, laughed about it for weeks afterward.

"You're tough," said Van, back in the kitchen at North Star Street, with all the crew around the table. We hadn't caught a whale, but other crews had, and everyone was safe. Julia had made caribou stew from a cut stored in the freezer since the last hunt. She handed me a bowl. I watched the steam rising from it, thinking of the peanut butter and Sailor Boy crackers in the cupboard. I had no moral objection to the stew, after being out hunting in that cold, and after learning the history of this place. My body might still object though. I took a tiny sip of the liquid from my spoon, worried I'd retch. But my time on the ice had wrought unseen changes. The stew tasted rich and delicious.

Billy nodded at me. "You did good out there."

"We'll miss you when you go," Van added.

Looking at him, I remembered the early weeks when I'd been full of questions and his stock response had been a gruff "Just wait," accompanied by exasperated sighs. That time, that woman, felt a world away.

Jeslie enlisted me in a plan to trick his brother Harry, who was coming to visit. I was to pretend to be a taxi driver and stand in the airport when the plane arrived, with a sign saying KALEAK. We giggled as we drove over. The passengers filed into the small arrivals building, most of them immediately enveloped in hugs. I noticed a man with white hair and mustache, standing still, looking around the hall.

"Harry Kaleak?" I called out. "This way. North Star Street, yes?" I kept a businesslike tone.

Harry nodded slowly and followed me wordlessly toward the

door. We passed a pillar, and Jeslie leaped out from behind it, grinning and whooping. The look of relief on Harry's face made me laugh too. All of us shouted and cackled the short car journey back. That evening, every time Jeslie or Harry caught my eye, we all laughed again. I was in on the joke, in with the Kaleak family in North Star Street. I was in, I was in, I was *in*.

It was back to the spot we'd fled that Billy took me, days later, to show me the two-story-high ivuniq that had formed when the sides of the lead collided. It was a solidified storm, piles and piles of shattered ice. Our beautiful camp had disappeared. I understood properly what we had been fleeing from. I climbed the ice crumble until Billy got visibly nervous. "Kiita," he said, indicating a way with a movement of his head.

I followed without a word, not something I was used to doing. Out in the ice and snow, I was at the mercy of landscapes that I had never imagined could be so beautiful or so hostile. The outside world was no longer the sanctuary it had been for me since childhood. To run when I felt like running would simply have meant death. The ice hadn't just mesmerized me, it had broken down my defenses, stormed my independence. There was nowhere to run, and the crew had something I wanted so badly with their ice, their whales, and their community. I had to give up my habit of bolting.

And against all my expectations, I found myself belonging.

PALOS VERDES TO
MONTEREY BAY

Latitude: 33° 46' 6" N to 36°46' 59" N
Longitude: 118° 20' 57" W to 121° 50' 3" W

The cliffs of Palos Verdes jut into the Pacific, south of Los Angeles. It's months since our visit to the Mexican birthing lagoons, and we are finally back in the United States, beginning the second leg of our journey. Northbound mother and baby grays come by here in droves, and as I look across the water, my heart quickens at any movement. Caro, a guide at the Point Vicente Interpretive Center, says they've been spotted in the past week. She greeted Max and me like old friends when we arrived and showed us the best place to scan the sea for whales. It's a seabird's-eye view of pure blue. Ocean and sky are in a gentle mood. The salty breeze carries whispers of wilder winds far off, as I gaze at a glistening circle through the binoculars.

"My turn, Mummy." Max reaches for the binoculars and has a quick look. "No whales. They've gone." He returns to an animated conversation between his toy van and a cactus. We arrived in LA on a flight from London yesterday. It's a relief to be taking a break from the struggle to set up a workable life for the two of us back home. We've got a month to complete the second leg of the migration journey, so there's a tight schedule of trains, buses, and ferries ahead. This is our first stop, and a renowned whale-watching spot, where a census takes place, but so far it's just rolling sea. No gray backs arching above the water, no heart-shaped blow.

A hundred and fifty years ago shore whalers also scanned these waters with hope. They used small boats powered by oars and a single sail to give chase. It was perilous. A boat could be pulled many miles out to sea by a harpooned whale, but for those men the rewards for barrels of whale oil made it worth the risks.

Max and I eat some bagels I took from the hotel breakfast buffet. I ask Caro where the census volunteers are today.

"Oh, the count finished yesterday."

I freeze, midchew. I've lost my appetite. I'd envisaged a day talking to the whale spotters, Max in my lap counting spouts and flukes. How did I manage to mess up the dates? I call Alisa Schulman-Janiger, the whale expert who coordinates the census, and try not to sound too emotional. Alisa's a marine biologist and educator. Since January 1984, she's organized teams who whale-spot daily from December to late May, sunrise until close to sunset. This year they counted 1,152 northbound whales, including 138 cow/calf pairs. That's the seventh-highest number of mother-and-baby pairs since Alisa's efforts began. The whales we kissed and patted in Baja must have been among that northbound wave. At least someone was there watching, cheering them along on their marathon.

The shrieking of schoolchildren across the cliff-top garden announces a class visit to the exhibition center behind us. I've examined every single pile of kelp to make sure it's not a whale and reluctantly put the binoculars away. We check out the exhibits. I grudgingly suppose the huge models of the grays might be better than none at all. One has hatches you can open to look at the brain, stomach, and a little curled fetus. It looks as though it's sleeping. Max is delighted. I'm slightly grossed out.

My hope is that even if he's too tiny to remember properly, the journey with the whales will somehow remain with him and give him strength. It's not been a straightforward start to our lives together, we've had to move around a lot. I've presented it as an adventure, and we are so bonded that we regularly read each other's thoughts, but I'd like to see Max find his place in the world a little. After the confines of the hostel I want it to be a world that's expansive and wild. A plastic whale wasn't what I'd envisaged. Watching him scamper through a sea cave mock-up with Caro, though, I realize he's making links between the models and the whales we sang to in the lagoons. He's exploring the world outside and also his own mind. I, meanwhile, sneak another wistful look out to sea. Where are my barnacled sea monsters?

Oh my God, maybe we've missed the whole migration.

I call Wayne Perryman, based farther north in Point Piedras Blancas, to ask if he's seeing grays. He's a marine biologist for the National Oceanic and Atmospheric Administration's Southwest Fisheries Science Center, and, yes, he spotted three cow/calf pairs the day before.

The whales are delaying the southbound migration so they get more feeding time in the Arctic, he says, and they are leaving the breeding lagoons earlier.

They are heading north earlier, that must be why we've missed them. Climate change is messing with their schedules and now ours. We'll have to race to catch up to them.

Wayne says the count is vital for assessing the health of the population, and the number of calves is linked to ice cover in the Arctic feeding grounds. If the water's warmer, there are fewer of the small bottom-dwelling crustaceans, amphipods, the whales like to eat. If females have not reached a critical weight by a certain stage of their

SOUNDINGS

pregnancy, it won't go to term. The whales are feeding all along the migration route, Wayne says, trying out other food sources. Some are wintering in the Arctic. Their choices point to fundamental changes taking place in the ocean, which is what makes them an indicator species. Often indicator species live in a specific niche, such as mosses, which absorb toxins from the atmosphere and can help with monitoring air pollution. In that sense I guess the grays, roaming up and down the globe as they do, are the mother of all indicators.

Caro and Max reappear from the other side of the undersea exhibit, talking about cars. She's finishing her shift and is offering us a lift to our hotel.

"Caro has a big blue car, Mummy," says Max, as if I needed convincing. To get here we caught the bus, but it dropped us at a gas station miles away. We hitched a lift the rest of the way with a friendly couple who were filling up. I ask what Caro's doing for the rest of the afternoon.

"I've a radiography appointment, for breast cancer."

My gratitude deepens. She's been so generous with her time and energy, playing with Max. As we wind past coastal sage scrub, she confides that she can't spot the whales unless a blue comes past, with its giant spout. I hug her goodbye when she drops us off.

All the rest of the afternoon, Max directs me in sandcastle construction: "More sand here, Mummy." Tomorrow we'll catch the train north to Monterey and meet the whales there.

But Max makes a more adventurous suggestion as he pushes some sand into place. "We need to catch up with the whales, Mummy. I will build you a boat, okay?"

The Coast Starlight speeds north. It's a romantic name for a train and a dreamy ride, dotted with surfers, swimmers, beach houses, and a bunch of Airstreams glittering like fish. Every once in a while, the sea springs out from behind a dune, then disappears behind in a shimmering streak. I get out a miniature team of Thomas the Tank Engine and friends, and some paper and pens. This is my arsenal for the long journey ahead.

"Draw me track, Mummy," says Max. "I want helicopter pad." I oblige with a big *H* in a circle and land the tiny Harold the Helicopter. "Dududududu." I remember friends' concerns about my taking a two-year-old traveling, the lack of routine, a different bed every night. But Max is so content when we're on the move. In that respect he's just like me.

As we approach our next destination on the migration route, I'm getting nervous. A complicated transfer is coming up from the train to a bus and then a taxi to our Airbnb, where we'll arrive after dark. As the whales approach Monterey Bay, they have reason to feel foreboding too.

Here, about a quarter of the way along their annual path, the continental shelf drops off into the Monterey Submarine Canyon. It's comparable in size to that geological wonder the Grand Canyon. It's also the perfect place for a deep-sea ambush by the apex predators of the seas, orcas. These distinctive black-and-white hunters are about half the size of an adult gray, but hunting in packs, or pods, they gain advantage, and they prey on the calves. Deep water allows a stealthy approach from below. Some wise gray whales stick to the shoreline here, but others cross the canyon, risking the lives of their young. Are they in a hurry, I wonder, or do they just not know any better?

The killer whales' tactic is to separate the calf from its mother and drown it. I called in advance from the UK and spoke to a renowned cetacean expert, whale-watching captain Nancy Black. She told me that tourists consider seeing this a highlight. With fresh memories of Max patting baby whales in Baja, I don't want either of us to witness it. The mere thought of dark shapes looming up toward the calves makes my palms sweat. I don't know what I'll say if we do see an attack. But this is a crucial step in the whales' journey and I can't shy away.

"Buggy, Mummy. Bag, Mummy. This one, here." At Monterey station Max directs me and our luggage onto the bus. "Clever boy, Mummy, well done," he says encouragingly, as I heave our giant rucksack onboard. We drive straight into an Ansel Adams photograph: textured sea, light streaked heavily across gray clouds. Hunched willows drip green streamers. "The trees have long hair," Max observes. It's evening when we get to our Airbnb in Seaside. Our hosts are a single mum, Teri, and her daughter, Gabby. Max is taken with their little dog, Bella. "I Rufus the traveling dog," he says. Bella looks nonplussed as he follows her around on all fours, barking. With the travel ordeal over I should sleep well, but I lie awake, watching Max breathe, for a large part of the night.

We arrive at Fisherman's Wharf on a busy Sunday morning, joining tourists and gulls on the boardwalk. There in front of us is the ominously named *Sea Wolf*, at its helm a commanding-looking woman in shades, who can only be Captain Nancy. The wind snorts and Max squeals happily as we ride the waves. Minutes later I'm throwing up over the side of the boat. I can't tell if it's seasickness or dread. A woman rubs my back. I stagger inside the cabin, shepherding Max ahead of me. I'm being told to go out again by a member of the crew, but I need to lie down somewhere or I will die and then Max will fall into the sea. I find an empty table and bench and get horizontal as quickly as possible. Pulling Max onto my chest, I wrap my arms around him with both of us wedged behind the tabletop.

"Are you tired, Mummy?" he asks, then dozes compliantly. Over the speakers Captain Nancy says we might see some late gray whales. Well, at least they're here, even if we can't see them. I am sick on the floor and fall asleep.

As we arrive back in the harbor, I wake and rouse Max. The other passengers report no orcas, nothing grisly. A couple of humpback mother-and-calf pairs appeared, to everyone's delight. No grays though. We still need to catch up with them.

I'm relieved to get off the boat, even if the land appears to be moving. Captain Nancy is standing on the jetty under a giant wind vane in the shape of an orca, and within a few seconds of speaking to her it's obvious that killer whales are her life's passion. She's been studying them here for decades, and her understanding of them is encyclopedic. They live in matriarchal groups, she says, led by an older female, often a grandmother, and are extremely intelligent. There are three ecotypes: offshores, residents, and transients. Offshore orcas eat sharks and large fish. Resident orcas eat only fish and often live peacefully alongside dolphins and seals. Transient orcas feed on sea mammals such as seals, dolphins, and whales. These are the kind that patrol the deep-sea canyon to intercept the grays. Captain Nancy thinks they find the grays by simply listening, and with echolocation.

"We'll be following some killer whales and suddenly they will be on top of a gray whale mother and calf, before we've even spotted them." Groups of up to twenty-five orcas will gather, although Captain Nancy usually sees four or five experienced females doing all the work. "They do a lot of ramming. It's pretty brutal, sad. But it's an amazing thing to see, the battle of whale against whale." Killer whales being the top predator, they usually win, Nancy says.

"Not always?"

"Not always. I'd say twenty percent of grays escape." She's seen the gray whales go at eleven knots, more than twice their usual speed. The orcas try to block them and attack in bursts, but if the grays can get into shallow waters, the aggressors will just give up. In 1998 whale-watching captain Richard Ternullo saw a pack of five killer whales surrounding a gray whale mother and calf. He watched as the mother rolled onto her back and her calf climbed on top of her in between her flippers, out of the orcas' reach.[1] That's how I held Max today on the boat, although the orcas I was worried about were only in my mind. Richard watched the mother and calf as they repeatedly rolled over, simultaneously took a breath, and returned to their positions. The calf got bitten but wasn't injured too badly. The mother also used the hull of the whale-watching boat as protection, and after a few hours the killer whales gave up.

I say I'm glad we didn't see an attack today.

"It's nature," Nancy says. "We eat cows, don't we?"

"I'm vegetarian."

I'm conveniently not mentioning all the whale meat I've eaten. I am complicit with the orcas, and they are threatened too. Being an apex predator makes you vulnerable to poisons that accumulate in the food chain, and the orcas that prowl the North Pacific, near Washington State and British Columbia, break records for the levels of toxins in their bodies.[2] Biopsies have found polychlorinated biphenyls, PCBs, which were used for making electrical equipment and were banned in the 1980s when we realized how poisonous they are, disrupting hormones, causing cancer. PCBs also affect fertility and suppress the immune system.[3]

"Yes, we keep telling those killer whales to be vegetarian." Nancy fake sighs. "They have families too, they have to feed their calves." Behind her, Max is trying to push his sunglasses down a crack in the jetty.

"Do you have any advice for the gray whales coming through Monterey?" It's a habit from my work, a left-field question to catch the subject off guard. Nancy seems as close as I might get to a spokesperson for the killer whales. Maybe she'll let slip some secret.

She laughs. "They need to stay close to the beach." It's the younger grays that try to cut across. She thinks they might not know killer whales are there. The older, more experienced grays take the long route around, make no noise, barely surface. "We call it snorkeling. The grays are trying to sneak through, stay invisible."

I know all about invisibility. It's one of my best tricks, learned as a child, and it's come in handy. At the BBC, every few years, I had to go on a hostile-environments course, run by ex-marines. It was compulsory for staff who worked in conflict zones or dangerous areas. We learned about incoming and outgoing fire and how to avoid setting off mines. We practiced first aid on actors lying in the wreckage of smoking cars or in the pitch-black, and in the final ordeal we were always ambushed and kidnapped.

It was awful, the kidnapping. I'd spend the entire week dreading it. You had to play along. Those people knew how to be scary, and you couldn't shout, "Stop!" You could, however, say you were asthmatic and have gaffer tape stuck on your back in a giant *X*, which I did in the hope that they would go easy on me, even though I'd not had a serious asthma attack since childhood. On the day, we were given a complicated route to follow, in order to conduct an interview with a fictional militia commander. As we bumped down some track surrounded by hedgerows, a gang of people in balaclavas would jump out and surround the Jeep. They blindfolded us, took us off somewhere, shoved what felt like guns in our backs, and made us all kneel on the floor for hours. During a short window, we were supposed to befriend a guard who was slightly nicer than the others, by talking about football or sharing cigarettes. Then the nastiest one came back and we had to beg individually for our lives before being pretend-shot and told how to improve our chances.

In a lecture beforehand, we had covered how to be a gray person, so you wouldn't be the one to be picked on, the first to be taken off to be executed. I'd smiled inwardly, feeling smug. I had that one down already, easy-peasy. I was so gray that when the kidnappers ambushed our vehicle, blindfolded everyone else, and pushed them along in a stumbling group, I had to cough and wave and point out that I was there too. I was standing in full view by the back of the Jeep.

As a journalist, it was useful. Something about the way I popped into being when I asked a question seemed to startle people. Interviewees sometimes laughed and found themselves answering more frankly than they meant to, or when they had not meant to answer at all.

Autumn 2006, San Francisco, the fall meeting of the American Geophysical Union. I'd been standing in a parking lot outside a conference center for close to three hours. Al Gore was inside. He'd been giving a speech on climate change, calling scientists to action. He'd asked them to be more forceful and energetic in communicating with the public. There was wild applause. My problem was, he'd refused all requests from the press to speak, even the American networks. No interviews, none. I thought he might try to sneak away out the back, through the parking lot. It was cold but I couldn't go inside to get my coat because I might miss him. The only other person in the parking lot was a security guard holding a two-way radio that occasionally barked information I couldn't make out.

"Why don't you go inside where it's warm?" said the guard after watching me for a while.

"I'm hoping Al Gore might come out this way."

We talked about the guard's children. His son was about to go to college. I'd been feeling hopeful and determined, but now, hours later, I was just feeling cold and stupid. Clearly no one else thought anything interesting was going to happen in the parking lot. I sighed, ready to go back inside. The guard coughed. I glanced up. He was looking at me, pointing to a side door, across the parking lot. I walked over and found myself standing in the path of Al Gore as he was ushered out in a half run.

I smiled at him in wide delight. "Hi! I'm from BBC World Service radio, can I ask you a few questions?" Al Gore's security detail parted and I got to stick my microphone right into his red, cross-looking face.

"No interviews. I'm leaving."

"Is anyone actually listening to you?" I asked as we strode across the parking lot, hoping he'd be unable to resist the provocation. He stopped, rolled his eyes, then started talking. It had worked! In my excitement I forgot to switch on the MiniDisc recorder and missed his first answer. I fumbled frozen fingers to slide the button. We were facing a climate crisis without any precedent in all of history, he said. I managed to catch that. Why was it such a difficult message to get across? I asked. He talked about the divide between science and popular culture, about the specialized language that scientists used, which made things incomprehensible to most people.

"The implications of what we, humankind, are doing now to the planet are so vast that it's more important than ever to translate the truth being uncovered, so we can make intelligent decisions about our future. Got to go." He folded up into his car.

"Are you going to run for president again?"

The door slammed shut.

That night Al Gore's voice traveled across the sea to London via my satellite phone, to my colleagues in the World Service newsroom. His voice carried climate change into the top three news headlines for a night. That coveted space, which reached millions of listeners across the world. For the first time in a good while I went to sleep happy.

The Niger Delta, 2003. I was holding my microphone up in front of another man who didn't want to talk to me, the managing director of Shell Nigeria, Chris Finlayson. He was trying to turn and walk away.

"I've been waiting here to speak to you for days." I moved to block his way. I'd come to the delta alone on public flights. He'd just walked off a private aircraft with a select group of male journalists. I'd battled my way through the choking traffic jam that was Port Harcourt that morning. Motorcycle taxis, cars, and buses had competed with pedestrians for every inch of space. A shiny black car, escorted by armed men on motorbikes, had come honking through the crowds. Everyone scattered.

"Oil executives' children being escorted to school," explained a man standing next to me. Oil workers were being kidnapped. Their children had to be at risk, but it still looked obscene. After a while a woman had taken pity on me, asked me where I was trying to get to, and shoved me into an overfilled bus, shouting at people to make space.

I'd spent a week traveling around the creeks and villages of the delta in a small motorboat with Daniel, a local community worker. I'd listened to people talk about the pollution from gas flaring, oil spills, and the dumping of industry waste. One activist had asked me to pray for her.

A few days later I was meeting Chris Finlayson. The stories from activists about harassment were taking their toll. I'd become nervous of the armed security that stopped the cars and guarded the buildings. Chris was impatient to go and so was I. He looked hot in his suit.

"I've been waiting to speak to you for days," I repeated.

He said okay, I could have a few minutes. He told me that the relationship with communities was long and complex, and that Shell Nigeria gave aid. Extremely substantial amounts. He sounded both irritated and bored. Could he understand the anger, I asked him, of people trapped in poverty in a place with such huge oil wealth being extracted around them? He said he could understand there was frustration, but it was not primarily Shell's responsibility to address it. The oil industry couldn't provide jobs for everyone.

"We pay our taxes, we pay our royalties, and the government has to fund the majority of development activities in the area." I mustn't forget that democracy was a new thing here, only four years old, he told me. He believed it was going to get better. I watched him leave.

I don't know that young woman anymore, the one who traveled alone, unafraid, through the Niger Delta. The one who stood in the path of powerful men and challenged them, who thought it was possible for her to make a difference, who thought she worked for good. But she had to be somewhere, I had to be able to find her. If the grays can relearn and rebound after all they've been through, surely I can too. On the surface, they are quiet, unsensational. They don't treat tourists to predictably extravagant displays of breaching and tail slaps like humpbacks. They don't have the iconic reputation or beauty of the larger great whales, or the striking uniform and fearsome reputation of the orcas. The grays are easily overlooked. But they are getting on with nothing other than one of the longest migrations we know about in the world of mammals, quietly surviving.

Max runs round and round the pole with the orca wind vane on top. He topples, dizzy. Sits, eyes tightly shut.

"Look, Mummy, I hiding behind my eyes," he shouts. I giggle, but not for long because Captain Nancy is telling me that in 1992, when she first saw a killer whale attack a gray, it was almost unheard of. Since then the phenomenon has steadily been increasing.

"Maybe they had to relearn how to do this," she says. The orcas live for up to ninety years, so some older females might have remembered how to hunt grays from long ago and could have taught the younger whales. Humans, orcas, and some other smaller whales, including belugas and narwhals, are the only species known to experience menopause. It's been an evolutionary mystery as to why, but the killer whale grannies may be illustrating the answer here, as they bring their wisdom and experience to bear. Since they are no longer reproducing, they can hunt for the benefit of the whole family.[4] Nancy thinks gray whales were so decimated by commercial whaling that the orca pods had to find a different food source. Now that grays are protected by law and their numbers have recovered, to approximately twenty thousand, the killer whales are back on the hunt.

"The orcas have got better at it," says Nancy. "When we first saw it happening, it took up to six hours for the killer whale to get the calf. Now I've seen it happen in thirty to forty minutes."

The humpbacks that were spotted today while I was seasick are also baleen whales. They've been observed many times coming to the aid of other humpbacks being attacked by orcas, and they also help other species. The previous summer, a pod of ten transient killer whales was trying to separate a gray whale calf from its mother in Monterey Bay. This wasn't unusual. What was striking was the presence of two humpback whales, who stayed close by and seemed to be making as big and as intimidating a fuss as they could. The orcas seized the exhausted calf and turned it over repeatedly to prevent it from breathing. The humpbacks moved in close, sometimes risking injury by placing themselves between the calf and the orcas, splashing and trumpeting, which is when they blow sharply, making a loud, shrill noise, a bit like a wheezy elephant. Nancy was alerted. She and Alisa Schulman-Janiger went out on a boat to observe, staying for nearly seven hours. The baby whale was killed soon after they arrived and the mother left, but the humpbacks stayed and were joined by others. The humpback adults then harassed the orcas as they fed on the carcass of the calf, "trumpeting, blowing, tail slashing, rolling, and head raising," said Nancy. "These humpback whales seemed extremely distressed," said Alisa.

It's not known why humpbacks do this, and it's tempting to see them as altruistic rescuers. In one case a humpback even carried a Weddell seal to safety on its chest. Scientists, including Nancy and Alisa, suggest that the whales could be responding to the orca vocalizations without knowing what animal is under attack, and then, once they are nearby, behaving protectively in a "spillover" of the way in which they protect their own kind.[5]

Nan Hauser, a marine biologist who works on a whale research project in the Cook Islands, experienced the whales' uncanny behavior close up. One day she was snorkeling in the bright blue waters when a humpback approached, gliding toward her. It came belly up, white against the blue, then turned gracefully to meet Nan the right way up, eye to eye. Nan stroked the knobbled chin and touched the end of its tattered flukes. It began to nudge her, lifted her out of the water, then tried to take her under its giant pectoral fin. Nan thought she was going to die. But when she saw a huge tiger shark in the vicinity, she became convinced the whale had been pushing her away from it. Yet Nan doesn't believe in anthropomorphizing animal behavior. "It's not good practice in science," she once said.[6] Most scientists insist that if you want to get better acquainted with an animal, you need to understand it on its own terms, rather than projecting human characteristics, and you should be especially careful about attributing humanlike emotions and intentions. But what happened on that day pushed Nan to the limits of what she could scientifically explain. She wouldn't have believed the story if someone had told it to her, she said, if it hadn't been captured on film. But it was.

I'm torn about anthropomorphizing. We aren't the only animals who have emotions,[7] memory, language, and societies. It isn't anthropomorphizing to recognize that. I have little difficulty in believing that a whale could feel empathy or be kind. To me, what happens between humpbacks and predators with teeth looks similar to what happens on land. Some people want a piece of you just because you come into their sights. Equally, some will help just for the sake of it, can appear out of nowhere and make all the difference.

But expecting animals to reliably comply with the place I put them into in my head, forgetting who they really are and what they need, got me into trouble as a child. Friendly or scary, large or small, nonhuman natures need freedom to be themselves, free of the caricatures we draw of them, if we are to coexist healthily. I learned that with Bramble, the hard way.

Max is standing still, concentrating hard. I know that look. Nancy is telling me that if gray whale numbers plunge because of changes in the Arctic, then orcas will also have a problem.

"Poo," announces Max. My time's up. Nancy heads out to sea with the next pod of whale watchers, and I change Max standing up. I must have done this a hundred times now, have got it down to seconds. I stow the stinking parcel in my backpack for when we find a suitable bin, and we visit a souvenir shop. Max picks up a plastic orca key ring.

"Put that back, please." I repeat myself for the toy sea turtle, otter, and stretchy octopus he grabs. The array of plastic in the shop is as diverse as the marine life in Monterey.

"Do whales poo, Mummy?" Max is examining the tail end of a rubber humpback.

Yes, I tell him, and the poo feeds the tiny sea plants, which everything else eats and which produce oxygen that we breathe.

Max looks at me aghast. "Eat poo?"

We wander down the wharf, crunching on fries from one of the food stalls. This is John Steinbeck country. Catching a trolley bus past Cannery Row, I try to imagine "the poem and the stink" of the sardine canneries Steinbeck wrote about, but they're long gone.

The next day we're due to catch the morning train, and our host Teri has offered a lift. I make toast in her kitchen for breakfast. Max is in character as Rufus the traveling dog, eating straight from the plate with his mouth and lapping water from a beaker. I squeeze in some planning, call Alaska Airlines.

"Are there daily flights to Barrow?" I ask the airline representative.

I don't hear her reply because Max barks at me, spitting his toast everywhere.

"Shhhh. You're not helping."

"Excuse me?" says the woman on the phone.

As I explain I was talking to my two-year-old, Max knocks his water all over the table. "Shit," he says loudly.

"You can say that to Mummy but no one else."

The Alaska Airlines woman laughs.

I attempt to simultaneously mop up the water with a dishcloth, hold my phone, and write down flight times. When I hang up, I realize I've booked the wrong dates and have to ring back and cancel everything before we leave for the train. Teri drives us through the Salinas Valley, where Steinbeck grew up. It's been called America's salad bowl and is one of the most important agricultural areas in California. The odor of broccoli past its sell-by date seeps into the car. To the east and west are mountains. At one time the floor of the valley was a narrow inland sea. I look up, imagine whales moving above us, and get the diving sensation like vertigo again. I ask Teri if she knows whether the whales ever swam here. She's a history teacher and points out that in *East of Eden* Steinbeck wrote about his father digging a well, fifty miles down the valley. First topsoil and gravel appeared. Then came white sea sand, full of shells and whalebone.

They were here, the ancient ones.

Our next stop following the grays' migration is Depoe Bay, Oregon. There I'll be meeting Carrie Newell, a renowned biologist and whale-watching guide who will, I hope, be Captain Nancy's equivalent in terms of grays. Max is bouncing with excitement as our train glides up to the platform. It's the double-decker overnighter to Albany. We find our sleeping compartment on the lower level. Seats at each end slide downward to form a bed. There's just enough room for the folded buggy, car seat, and rucksack to the side. A bell rings as we speed past a railway crossing, and Max rushes to the window.

"Crossing thingy. I love trains and I love crossing thingies," he shouts. This rumbling capsule will be our universe for today, tonight, and into tomorrow.

"We going to catch up with the whales, Mummy, it's going to be great!"

We sleep in the train's belly. To begin with I'm feetfirst, head to toe with Max, then turn headfirst as though ready to be born, swaying and rumbling through the dark, my son beside me.

We got past the orcas. But what about those whales we patted in Baja? I'll never know if they made it. Please, I beg the night, let them still be traveling north, all of us together.

UTQIAĠVIK: DOREEN KALEAK

Latitude: 71° 17' 26" N
Longitude: 156° 47' 19" W

"**Climate-change journalists come at** a certain time of year to try and film our people falling through holes in the ice, film our sod houses falling off a cliff. They like something picturesque and sexy about people of the north." I was in Richard Glenn's office in Utqiaġvik, and I had the feeling that I was being told off.

A geologist by training, Richard worked for the Arctic Slope Regional Corporation, ASRC, one of the land-owning associations that was created by the Alaska Native Claims Settlement Act, ANCSA, in 1971. The act was the first real settlement between the federal government and Indigenous peoples. The corporations received approximately 69,500 square miles of land and were paid $963 million. This allowed self-determination. It also denied the validity of aboriginal title, which is the inherent Native right to land or a territory.

ANCSA was a compromise that acknowledged Indigenous territorial claims but also sought to satisfy state, federal, and private oil company interests. Settling the claims meant oil extraction could go ahead. One interior Athabascan village, Stevens Village, was among several that had obtained a court injunction halting pipeline construction on their land until land claims were clarified.[1] The development of resources that made the land valuable to the US economy was brought under a capitalist system, with the federal government distributing community rights to individual shareholders through the system of corporations. Until then, the territory had been usufruct, meaning all could use the land as long as they didn't damage it. Now it was held under legal title and subject to the competing goals of development for profit and protection for subsistence.

I'd wanted to interview Richard for weeks, but he'd been busy. He'd been out hunting, as cocaptain of the whaling crew Savik, meaning "knife." He was also a politician and an ice scientist with, he said, "a bunch of degrees." His mother was Iñupiaq, his father from Nebraska. He'd grown up between Utqiaġvik and California. He looked as comfortable in the office in his crisp white shirt as he had in his parka and beanie on his snowmobile. I set up the camera nervously and double-checked I'd pressed the right button to start recording. Richard sat watching, his silence creating tension as effectively as if he had looked at his watch.

"Our people live on the edge, we've always lived on the edge." Richard told me his Iñupiat ancestors had lived on a point of land fifteen miles from the town's current site and that even in those days it was eroding. The lands along the coastal plain, including Prudhoe Bay, contained the bones of Richard's forebears, not just ancient people but also those who'd died in the early twentieth century before the Iñupiat began to bury their dead, when human remains were left aboveground, often in whatever dwelling they'd died in. The difference now was that the community had power lines, houses, large open sewage lagoons where effluent broke down, not just sod houses built into the tundra, skin tents, and ice cellars. It was harder to move around, more expensive.

Richard had a gentle voice with a forceful undercurrent. His presence and formidable intellect filled the room. He did not need to stop to think. His pitch and speed did not vary and his expression did not change. His manner suggested he'd had to explain all this plenty of times before and he was not best pleased at having to repeat himself. He'd testified in Washington at congressional hearings, in support of oil exploration onshore, in the Arctic National Wildlife Reserve.

"We try to make the best of both worlds, be the best in both worlds. It's like working two jobs, trying to be a good person in the Iñupiaq and in the modern world. Like speaking the two languages."

The local government derived its income from oil. "There is no other industry up here." The schools and health centers were financed by it. There was a whole spectrum of opinion within the community, but personally, he said, he found himself advocating for oil and gas in the region. Land could be sacred, caribou herds could thrive, and oil extraction could happen too. I nodded as he spoke, something you were taught to do. It was supposed to keep interviewees talking, reassure them that what they were saying was interesting, without interrupting the sound. Richard didn't need me to nod, I thought, as I nodded.

When he paused, I asked him what he thought of the elders' predictions that the ocean would one day be ice-free.

"I haven't heard that," he said firmly. He described the time the ice broke away from the shore-fast ice and drifted off, taking Savik crew with it. He didn't put it down to climate change.

"I floated away a few years ago and needed to be rescued by he-licopter. For me that's not a global-warming thing. It's that we didn't pay enough attention that day to what was going on. Our job is to keep a running inventory of any changes in the ice, current, wind, temperatures, cracks. Are we safe here or not?" He hoped the change they were seeing, with sea ice getting thinner, was not moving in a one-way direction but was part of a shifting pattern of oscillation.

He said he saw science as a finger pointing in the direction of truth, sometimes off a bit one way or the other. He loved the multiyear ice, *piqaluyak*. It was thick, so good for hunting and a source of unlimited pure, sweet fresh water too.

I had wanted to stay out there because it was so beautiful, I told him.

"It can lull you into thinking you're on something permanent because it can be so serene," he replied. "When you go out to make a camp, you wish it could be like this forever, but it can't. Like everything in life, it really can't, and you better be ready to move in a second."

Richard said he was sometimes more scared of what MTV was doing to the youth than of climate change. The cultural change, loss of language, loss of self-esteem, social issues, drug abuse, and suicide. "It's touched every one of us. Whether autumn starts on October tenth or October twelfth, whether the grass is going to get a little bit greener in summer, how far off the ice is, fifty miles or seventy miles. Those things are important to us, but there are other things that are important to us."

Then Richard had to get back to work and we were out of time.

Walking back to North Star Street, I thought about what Richard had said. I was surprised he hadn't heard about the previous generation's ice-free-ocean predictions, recounted so readily by Jeslie and elders I'd spoken to. Could Richard really be more worried about MTV than climate change? The devastation caused by cultural loss was undeniable. People were committing suicide, so of course that was the priority. I reminded myself that Richard was an open advocate for oil exploration. As he said, no other industry operated here, and agriculture was impossible. My first big story, as a local business journalist in the late 1990s, had been the wildcat strikes over job losses at Ford Dagenham, an iconic car plant in Essex. I'd never forgotten the faces of the people outside the factory gate. My first-ever question to an oil company boss, BP's John Browne, in April 1999, was about job cuts following the Arco acquisition. It was simple: people needed jobs. It was complex: oil companies, as a major employer in Alaska, must have enormous influence and power here. And the suicides, loss of self-esteem, and cultural loss Richard had highlighted. Wasn't it all part of the same story as climate? How one way of being had struggled against the desire of a dominant culture to define all of human meaning and existence, to own it, to break the Iñupiaq connection to land and language, to capitalize on everything, everywhere, not caring about what it destroyed.

I had many more questions for Richard, but I'd already been told so often, by Van, to stop quizzing people. An Iñupiaq word, *paaqłaktautaiññiq*, meant "avoidance of conflict." It was a deeply held value. Historically, lives depended on working well together to ensure survival. It was cooperate or die. People practiced tolerance and suppressed difficult emotions. Being demanding was not the done thing, especially as a visitor. But after speaking to Richard I couldn't shake the feeling that I'd somehow been put off the scent.

I looked out toward the frozen sea, where the light seemed to shine so much brighter. I missed the long journeys on the back of Billy's snow machine. I missed the voices of the hunters speaking Iñupiaq, missed watching them watch the weather, missed the sound of the ocean, the sigh of the whales' breathing, the roll of their backs. I missed going to get multiyear ice, I missed the taste of that fresh water. I missed turning around to always find Van or Billy there about to explain something to me or check that I was okay. The intense focus of the hunt had blocked out my thoughts, and now life was back, along with an ache in my throat that wouldn't go away. On reaching Julia's house, I made coffee and sat at the kitchen table, but I couldn't relax, kept getting up and looking out the window at the sky, as if it would tell me something. I thought about my London life. The city, the concrete, the commute, the planning meetings, the computer screens, the suits I wore to try to look the part, the managers I tried to impress. It all seemed entirely irrelevant. I just wanted to be back on the ice with Kaleak crew.

I'm good at calling ptarmigans. Those fat little grouse birds, speckled brown in summer, white in winter. You can create the growling clicks they make by opening your mouth wide and forcing the air through the back of your throat. It's a satisfying noise to make. I'd liked doing it as a child. My mother found it highly irritating. Who would ever have known that one day it would come in handy, to impress a hunter?

Billy was often the only human for miles around, he said, when he was at the family hunting grounds, Kaleak camp. "Just me and the stars. Peaceful, quiet." The tundra was where the Iñupiat went for the long, bountiful summer. *Tuttut* or caribou, *niglich* or geese, and *aqargit* or ptarmigan were all plentiful, at different times of the year. Since the weather had changed and it was doubtful we'd get back out on the ice, a few of the crew were planning a goose hunt, Julia said.

"Who's going?" I asked.

"Eli and Billy, maybe others."

"Can I go too?"

Julia shrugged. "Let's wait and see."

I was too shy to ask directly, so I hung around, increasingly anxious at the idea of being left behind, leaping up whenever I heard the sound of boots in the *qanitchaq*, the entrance hall. I tried suggesting to myself that I should now move on to northern Canada, to explore what people were saying about climate there. I searched for flights online, but after the briefest of glances at the schedules, I turned off the computer and wandered outside into the snow. Goose hunting was an unmissable opportunity to hear about climate change inland, I decided. I did more carving at the Heritage Center. Perry gave me a dense, heavy fragment of whalebone that was hard to work with. It was slow going making the whale appear, and when it did, it was more of a suggestion than a full portrait, like a word appearing in the bone. I gave it to Julia, who immediately put it in her glass cabinet of treasures.

One morning, I had my nose in a mug of coffee, drawing in the smell, when Billy came in.

"Hey, where you been?" he said. "You never here. We're off to Kaleak camp. Eli and Leo too. You coming?"

"Oh, well, maybe." I tried to sound blasé.

He turned to go. Julia stared at me, her face a question.

"You mean now? I'm coming, wait for me." I ran into my room to get my outdoor gear and camera. I could hear Julia and Billy laughing.

"Leaving in two hours," he called.

I rode pillion with him again, protected from the wind. I'd forgotten how cold it was. This time the landscape was a more recognizable white, like a snowy football field, except this was no field. It went on forever. Utqiaġvik became an irregular gray smudge on the horizon, and then there was nothing but snow. Billy had learned the way to camp from his father, he told me, as he pointed out different bits of white as landmarks. To me, it all looked the same, a totally lethal landscape.

Kaleak camp had a wooden cabin that slept ten, with bunks along the walls in the main room. Leo, Julia's eldest, was already there. We took a bunk each. In the half-light of the Arctic spring, the stars had evaporated. The tundra was just emerging, gaping soft green wounds through the snow. Eli and I played cards. Billy was busy around the camp, sorting out the honey bucket, the camp toilet. No, he didn't want help, he said. I heard the roar of his snow machine. The next morning, he said we had to leave. He'd been checking the terrain overnight and it wasn't looking good.

"If we don't go back now, we'll get stuck on this side of the river," he explained. "The water's coming out pretty fast. Forty-plus degrees. The snow is melting in hours, not days." He was calm but he was not smiling, and the three of us listened to every word. He asked Eli to call his parents on the VHF to let them know what was happening. We would try hunting geese from the other side of the river so we would be able to get back to town. It would mean we'd have to camp.

Eli called out to Rescue Base, explained the situation to the operator. "We might end up coming back tonight. It might be after midnight, when the snow hardens up. It's pretty soft out here." He repeated himself: "Leaving to Uyaġalik at midnight." Someone at Rescue Base said something back through the hiss. Julia and Jeslie weren't answering on the radio, so the operator said he'd pass on the message that Eli had called.

A few hours later I heard Jeslie's voice on the radio, calling out. "Hey, we just got home."

"Hey, Dad, we're going to come back tonight, maybe to Uyaġalik, farther north," said Eli. "It's really melting out here." It was crackly, we couldn't hear Jeslie's reply. Eli said it again. "We'll wait until it gets a little bit cooler and then take off. The snow is soft out there. We'll go to Uyaġalik tonight."

"Okay, ten-four."

No chat, no "take care" or "stay safe." No one got excited. For me, my eyes couldn't have gotten any bigger, for me it was wild. For the Kaleaks it was just how to hunt, how to live.

We waited for night before leaving. Leo decided to go straight back to Utqiaġvik. It got colder, and although it was not dark, the world had dimmed in a menacing way. When we approached the river, a thick stripe of white across the exposed green of the tundra, Billy and Eli accelerated their snow machines. The river wasn't yet impassable. A thin layer of ice still supported a topping of snow, and I wouldn't have been able to tell water was underneath. Billy led the way, with me on the back of his machine. A roar and we were over.

We circled to check on Eli. He nearly made it, but as he approached the bank of green on this side, the back of his machine got stuck.

"I'm coming," Billy shouted. I got off and watched while he drove back, took a rope out of a pack, and attached it to both snowmobiles so he could pull Eli out. Only afterward did I think about it, about how it could have been so different if Billy had not been there, how Eli and I were dependent on him, how I felt so safe.

At Uyaġalik, where the geese were gathering, there were no cabins. We set up camp, sleeping all in a row in the tent. When it was too windy for the birds to fly, we played cards again—take two, pinochle, and rummy, which I now sometimes won at. I'd got better, not only at cards but also at just being, enjoying myself and the company of others in these moments. My vocabulary grew. *Illiviñ*, your turn. *Iiqinii*, scary. *Atchu*, I don't know. *Nalaiñ*, calm down. *Atta*, be quiet. *Attai*, pretty. I wanted to learn more. I'd read that Inuktitut, a Canadian Inuit language, held a fundamentally different worldview to mine. A child would grow up learning to speak without categorizing animals. There were no generic terms, no "seal" or "bear." Each animal was addressed by name, individually. An Arctic char, a harp seal, a juvenile ringed seal, a polar bear. There were "breathers," the sea mammals, and "those that walk," the land animals. But there was no distinction between a human and animal life, no word for "it."[2] Equality of life was implied. I wanted to understand if it was the same in Iñupiaq.

Billy told Eli he was worried that the geese and caribou might stop migrating through that part of the tundra if it got too warm. This was what I'd come all the way from London for. Billy relaxed, musing about life, and at the center of his thoughts were the changes. I hadn't had anything recording him though. I'd more or less given all that up. I was no longer here for research, I was here because I wanted to be.

When the wind died down, Billy went off looking for geese, away from camp. I went with Eli to the hideout his grandfather had made. We whispered to each other while we waited.

"You hear them chattering," he said, "then you have to spot them. They can be anywhere. Try to get a direction on the sound. If they're following the wind, it brings their voices, makes it seem like you're a lot closer."

"I can't hear them."

"You're wearing your hat." He laughed.

"I know, it's cold."

Eli and Billy spent days waiting in the hides. We played more cards, slept.

"I'll record you snoring," I joked.

"You don't snore," said Billy. "We wonder if you're alive." He had a ready giggle, a deep voice, like Jeslie's.

"Want me to make noises like Ira? Your choice," I said.

"*Naumi, naumi,*" said Billy, shaking his head.

We saw an *ukpik*, a snowy owl, like a speckled chunk of snow-covered tundra cast up into the air. And far off, a single young *tuttu* on its spindly legs, stubby neck ruffed in white fluff, black face like a punctuation mark against the snow. It wasn't caribou-hunting time though, it was *niġliq* or goose, time. So we watched the calf until it sensed something was amiss, startled, and took off. The hunting code was strict, in rhythm with the animal breeding cycles. I'd read that in the 1980s Eugene Brower's late father, Harry, had reviewed the seasonal hunting limits because a whale had spoken to him in a dream.

Harry had been extremely ill, in a hospital in Anchorage. It was whaling season and the crews were out on the ice. Harry told his biographer, Karen Brewster, that while he was "dead,"[3] as he put it, a baby whale had come to him. He described how the calf took him up under the ice, all the way to where the hunt was taking place. The bowhead calf told Harry how its mother had been cornered and struck, "how they were wounded, suffered."[4] The whale pointed out the men in the hunt, including the faces of two of Harry's sons. It told Harry where its body was being stored. Harry was in the hospital for two and a half weeks. When he regained consciousness, he recounted to Eugene everything he had seen and what the whale had told him. Eugene found everything matched up, including the calf's body having been taken in its entirety to an ice cellar owned by the hunter the calf had identified. Mothers with calves were not supposed to be hunted. Harry told Eugene the deadline for hunting whales in spring would now be May 27, because most of the calves were born after May.

In Harry's world, whales had souls and their bodies carried the entire social world of a people, so he listened to the whale in his dream.

Billy checked on me continually. "Alappaa?" Was I cold, was I hungry, was I tired? When I lay on the tundra in front of a rifle, filming straight down the barrel, he appeared from nowhere and chastised me. "That thing could go off at any time." I wanted to hunt too, to contribute, and he let me borrow his gun. I took careful aim, pulled the trigger, and flew over backward.

Eli threw a snowball for me to shoot, which I missed, although I didn't fall over that time. Billy then retrieved his gun for good.

One goose he did not kill outright. It fell in a scrabble of wings and lay flapping feebly, while the gabble of its luckier companions faded into the distance. Billy ignored it, his gaze still focused on the sky.

I couldn't watch it dying slowly, walked over, looked it in the eye. "I'm sorry," I said. "Thank you," I added, thinking of the whales giving themselves. Perhaps it applied to geese too. How could I kill it? When I was little, I'd always taken injured animals—mice, rabbits, chicks—to my dad and let him do it. But he wasn't here. I took its neck but couldn't break it because it was too flexible. I bent it double. The goose was still breathing, a harsh noise. I held the bent neck tight and put my knee on the body to force out the air. It took a long time.

As a child he'd trapped lemmings, Billy said. They'd sold them to the scientists, to feed snowy owls. He explained the method, which involved string and sticks. I couldn't grasp it, but I was interested in lemmings.

"Those are the ones that commit suicide, jump off the cliffs, aren't they?"

"Jumping off cliffs, *naumi*. Lemmings don't do that."

Well, I thought, Billy must never have been to the right cliff. "They do, I've seen it on TV. They just jump off."

He shrugged, didn't argue further. He was right of course. I read later that in *White Wilderness* Disney filmmakers propagated the myth of periodic lemming mass suicide by staging the horrific event itself.[5] They clearly thought that lemmings migrating to find food after the population ballooned, sometimes swimming across rivers and sometimes drowning, wasn't compelling enough for movie-theater audiences in 1958. They bought animals from Inuit children in Manitoba, took them to Alberta, filmed them running on snow-covered turntables, then threw them off a cliff,[6] with cameras angled from below. The narrator confidently translated lemming motives and thought processes into human terms as the tiny rodents apparently hurled themselves into the sea: "They've become victims of an obsession—a one-track thought: Move on! Move on!"[7]

Eli asked me to repeat the song I'd sung to the whales, but now that I had an audience I felt self-conscious and took convincing. Billy watched me for a long time after I finished singing, so I went and hid in the tent. As I dozed, I heard a long growl from just outside. A bear! I leaped up screaming and scrambled through the tent flaps, but it was only Eli burping. He cried with laughter, imitating my face as I'd burst from the tent. He went hunting, still giggling, so Billy and I were left alone in the tent, playing cards. He lay propped up on his elbow and dealt. When he slapped the final card down with a flourish, I flinched.

"You startle easy," he said, appraising me like an animal he was hunting. I struggled to suppress this reaction, a childhood reflex to any unexpected touch or sound, and from years of second-guessing Bramble's reactions. This man kept so still that he noticed everything. I stared hard at the cards, could feel him watching me. I met his gaze. His dark eyes burned through the cold, hot as the inside guts of the earth. "I look at that whale you made me sometimes, in the night," he said slowly. "Makes me think of you." I sat beside him, thinking of him thinking of me in the night. Emboldened by his stillness, unable to resist, I leaned over and kissed him. His response was deliberate, slow. He did nothing sudden, his strength was obvious but restrained. Then came the buzz of a snow machine far off. It became a closer roar, Eli returning. Billy drew back and observed me silently. On shaky legs, I went to greet Eli. I wasn't sure this was a good idea. I was relieved Eli slept between us in the tent, but I listened to Billy's breathing become slow and regular, matching my breaths with his, as we fell asleep.

"You the first white person to ever come camping out here," he said, just before we set off on the journey back to Utqiaġvik. The luggage boxes held about thirty birds. Eli explained they were for Julia, Billy's mom, the crew, other relatives, and elders who didn't have anyone to hunt for them anymore. At first Billy let me drive the snow machine, pretending to be terrified and to fall off when we stopped. Then I rode behind him, resting my head on his back, with my arms around him.

We arrived at North Star Street about five hours later than we said we would. Julia had got worried and asked Rescue Base, always on the alert, to put out a radio call to anyone hunting on the tundra, asking if we'd been seen. I was on the Search & Rescue list as Doreen Kaleak. They had claimed me. I could not remember ever before having felt so happy.

Billy lived in a little house on Nanook Street, Polar Bear Street. It was just a large hut really and was dwarfed by his mother's sizable house next door. The walk there was a half hour from Julia's, past the Heritage Center, then alongside a main road that cut through a narrow strip of land, flanked by the frozen lagoon on the left and white expanse of ocean on the right. This part I walked slowly, enjoying the crunch of my boots on the snow, reveling in the bright, far-reaching sky. As I got closer to Billy's house, I'd walk quickly, a sensation of lightness growing inside, left past the bank on Agvik Street, then first right and on past the church and Sam and Lee's Chinese, which was snug, brown, and white-topped like a gingerbread house. There might be a jolt of urgency as an aircraft took off or landed. Billy's side of town was near the airport, which reminded me that my time was limited. Sometimes, as I approached his door, a giant helium weather balloon, released by the nearby National Weather Service station every twelve hours, would float up into a speck, then disappear, as if the sky were politely notifying me that another day had passed.

To enter Billy's house you passed through a tiny qanitchaq with just enough room to stomp the snow off your boots. The outside door was always unlocked, and if he was in and awake, the inside door would be unlocked too. If not, I had a key. It was the house of someone who existed mainly outside and held only the basics. To the right as you came in was a stove and a small fridge-freezer. An inside door led to a small toilet. There was no bathroom, so if Billy wanted a shower, he went to his mom's house. A television sat next to a radio on top of a large dresser. On top of the television was the only ornament, the tiny whale I'd carved. To the left of the entrance was a table, lit by a large window where dust motes meandered in the flood of sunlight that spilled through the dark red curtains, which Billy kept partly drawn. Behind the table was the bed and, if he wasn't in the chair or greeting me at the door, there he would be, in jeans and sweatshirt, lying back with an arm behind his head, legs crossed at the ankles, cigarette smoke curling up from his fingers to dance with the dust in the stripes of sun. It always took a moment for me to adjust to his really being there, solid and real, waiting for me.

After spending so much time with him outside, wrapped up in layers, seeing him in regular indoor clothes, especially socks, felt strangely intimate. In his house there wasn't the space to keep a distance. If we wanted to watch TV, we sat on the bed. We'd go to Sam and Lee's, and I'd feel fizzy with pride at being out with him, or we'd share a Hungry-Man frozen meal that he heated up in the oven. It was all so ordinary, such a far cry from being out hunting, yet I didn't want to be anywhere but there. I worried though. I would be leaving and didn't want to hurt him, I said.

He shrugged. "Don't worry 'bout me."

The next morning we were woken by trilling and scrabbling in the chimney. "Pesky snowbirds." He stood on a chair in his shorts, sticking a broom handle up the vent and rattling it around. The snowbirds spent winters in the southern United States, flew north each summer. They were recent arrivals like me, sounded as though they were shouting for joy at being back on Billy's rooftop, at being near him. I did worry about him.

"Guest stealer," Julia said to him, after he'd walked me back to North Star Street. I felt guilty, got to work. That afternoon she, Eli, and I were pulling feathers off geese in the kitchen. Under her instruction I was ripping and slipping off their skins. She'd forgiven me, just about, for forgetting to call from the tundra.

"My London daughter. Gizzard. Look! Some leaves in the stomach for you." She held up something that looked like grass, laughing. Since the Kaleaks had made such short work of my being vegetarian, they liked to joke about it.

"Just rinse them off," said Eli. "You don't need to buy it, it's free."

"Thanks, a nice bit of tundra," I said. He asked me how much I paid for the salad I bought at Stuaqpak. I was scared to look at the prices, I told him, just handed over however much the cashier asked for. I actually hadn't bought any recently. It had started to taste watery to me.

"Niġliq soup for me." Julia licked her lips, holding up a dead goose by its neck.

"Niġliq." Eli made the high-pitched hunting call. "Go on, Doreen."

"Nuguluguluguluk." I thought I'd got pretty good at it, sitting there in the hide with him. Once, a goose passing overhead had seemed to speak back. But Julia and Eli laughed hard. I demanded to know whose call was best.

"One sounds like from London and one sounds like from Barrow," said Julia tactfully. She named me, gave me her Iñupiaq name, Singaaġauluk. She also gave me one of the Kaleak-crew whaling jackets with her name, now my name, embroidered on the front and with a whale tail and the length of the crew's most recent catch spread across the back, fifty-one feet, five inches.

I wore the jacket proudly when Billy and I hung out playing cards at Rescue Base, where hunters milled around, played pool, and manned the radio. If anyone went missing, volunteers would launch a search. Once, I was told, Billy had to be treated for frostbite because he spent so long out looking for someone in the snow. I longed to capture Rescue Base on film but didn't dare ask. There were no other women and I was worried that, if I pushed it, I'd be kicked out.

Billy and I often just walked around the city. He showed me where he'd had an accident out at the gravel pits when he was younger. He'd been doing motorcycle stunts "like Evel Knievel." He still had a limp, a damaged leg, practically just bone left where his calf would have been. I was shocked when I first saw it but soon got used to it. With him I was calm, at peace. I'd never known me like this.

We went to his sister's house. She was Van's partner, and we all watched basketball. It was good to meet his family, but I felt uncomfortable in her spacious, beautiful house. Why did Billy live in that tiny space when she lived here? It didn't seem to bother anyone though. Billy told me he'd worked at the Prudhoe Bay oil fields for a while but found it difficult, those boss guys could be mean, it was hard work and he didn't like being away. He'd also worked as a carpenter, building houses. How exactly he existed, what he lived on, I wasn't quite sure, although I knew everyone got a regular dividend from ASRC. But then again, he was a subsistence hunter. He wasn't pretending.

Iñupiaq was Billy's first language, something that was becoming rarer, but when I asked him how to pronounce a word on a road sign and translate it for me, he went quiet. He mumbled that it had been confusing, going to school some of the time, hunting the rest. I was beginning to see that his life was not easy and had perhaps never been. When he was beginning elementary school in the 1970s, they were no longer punishing children for speaking their own language. But I thought of the boredom, coercion, humiliation, and fear I'd experienced in elementary school. I hadn't been learning in a different language, but I'd struggled with hearing difficulties and had often not understood what was going on. Confusion sounded like an understatement for a child watching and doing and learning from their family in their own tongue, which described their hunt, their land, their home. A child who then had to learn another language, to be taught another culture's ways.

His Iñupiaq name was Uvyuaq. How do you spell it? What does it mean? I pressed, but he didn't elaborate, so I stopped. Instead, I showed him the photo I'd taken of the boat he'd made, poised on the edge of the lead. He peered at the viewfinder of my camera, the tiny boat inside.

"I'm going to print it out big," I said, "frame it." With his and Julia's help, I gave it a title: *Uvyuam Umialiaŋŋa*, which translates as "the boat that Uvyuaq made."

When Billy worked on the boat in the first weeks I'd known him, he told me he'd learned the skills from his father. He didn't need to read to make the umiaq. His father had been his book. I'd seen Billy read the ice, clouds, currents, temperature, wind, terrain, the whales. I had watched everyone, and he was always the one getting on the radio to communicate any change, sharing information, so that all the crews combined were effectively a superbrain, keeping safe and increasing the chances of a successful hunt.

During the days we hunted for whales and geese in that frozen, white universe, my feelings for the landscape and for him became intertwined. He was inseparable from the ice and those vast expanses of tundra. This was his home, part of him, and he was part of it.

Billy didn't need to read words. He could read the world.

As for me, there was nowhere else to go, nothing else for it, other than to fall in love with him.

DEPOE BAY TO THE SAN JUAN ISLANDS

Latitude: 44° 48' 30" N to 48° 32' 6" N
Longitude: 124° 3' 47" W to 123° 1' 51" W

I'm woken by the phone. Rain roars against the motel window. I fumble for the receiver.

"No boats are going out today," says a voice. I haven't even said hello. Who is it? No one knows I'm here. It's by order of the coast guard, continues the voice, because the swell is too extreme. There will be no whale watching. The voice, which eventually says it is calling from reception, informs me that Morris will be available at the museum.

"Morris? Museum?"

I notice through half-open eyes that Max is taking off a poo-filled diaper. Then the voice is gone. Leaving me to wake up, deal with the poo, and let the information sink in. I feel gray. We eat gray porridge for breakfast. Outside there's gray rain, gray sky, gray buildings. No sodding gray whales, apart from a big plastic one in the flower bed outside the motel. I walk on, head down against the rain, being misdirected by several people to a seemingly nonexistent bus stop.

"Does that say 'bus,' Mummy?" says Max from under the plastic buggy cover. He looks like a goldfish in a bowl and is pointing at some large letters on the asphalt ahead. It does say BUS, and maybe it's pure guesswork on his part, but if he's learning to read on this journey, that's something else I can use against any critics. Just then, the bus to Depoe Bay growls past the stop and past us, soaking me with spray from the road puddles. There's another one in three hours.

This part of the journey was the most difficult to plan. By the time I'd worked out the travel logistics by phone from Jersey, Kitty at the Depoe Bay Chamber of Commerce recognized my voice at "hello." The bay is about a third of the way along the migration route. On a fine day it would be one of the best places to see grays in Oregon, but with no whale watching I'm wondering how I will entertain Max. To top it all off, the biologist we'd planned to meet has emailed her apologies that she's had an emergency and is away.

I'm weary. We arrived last night as the light was beginning to fade and ran to Nye Beach to play in the surf. At a café, I ordered veggie burgers and chips for our dinner and marionberry cobbler for Max. The place was full of people laughing around the tables. I felt conspicuously lonely, without another grown-up to speak to. While Max explored his dessert, I watched the faces around me as though observing another species.

"Anything else I can get for you?" The waitress had appeared. The warmth in her voice left me momentarily unable to answer.

Max looked up at her, nodded seriously, and paused for a long second before speaking. "A whale, please."

"Well, someone's hungry." She took our plates.

I giggled, and Max's face cracked wide open with an ice-cream-smeared grin as he realized he'd made a joke. Those moments, the best ones, sometimes hurt more than the difficult times, with no one familiar to share them with. But the gray whale cow-and-calf pairs did it all by themselves, I told myself sternly. So could we.

We've not seen the whales in such a long time they might as well be figments of my imagination. But sitting at yet another bus stop as the rain bounces off the pavement, it's safe to say this journey feels in no way dreamlike. Whales, as I'm learning from following them, are not mystical but intensely practical. There are different theories as to how they navigate through the treacherous currents and storms along the coastal route. One is that their spectacular hearing allows them to follow the sounds of waves on the shore, or noises of creatures hanging out in the kelp beds. Some scientists suggest they use the stars, or landmarks, spy-hopping with heads above water to see cliffs and beaches. An alternative theory is that they are guided by the earth's magnetic field or that the possible presence of small particles of magnetite or iron oxide in their brains might allow them to detect magnetic contours. Others suggest they are guided by bathymetry or contours on the sea bottom. They also appear to help one another during the migration, have been observed stopping and waiting for individuals or pods to catch up before moving on together.[1] It's been hypothesized that they might leave a chemical trail, some kind of scent, for others to follow. None of these methods help me. I'm relying on Amtrak and bus timetables.

Depoe Bay, when we finally catch the bus, is pretty, even in the rain. A giant sign says WHALE, SEALIFE AND SHARK MUSEUM. We duck into the building and are greeted by a man who introduces himself as Morris. So this is what the voice on the phone was talking about. I tell Morris we're unsuccessfully chasing grays up the West Coast.

"Well, Captain Ahab herself," he says.

"Didn't he want to kill the whales?" I've a hazy memory of attempting *Moby-Dick* as a teenager, but I didn't have the stamina to finish it.

Max sticks his head through portholes to look at the displays of underwater life. Model starfish lounge on pretend rocks with clams and spiral shells of all sizes. It's like being at the beach but with labels.

Max and I move on to an exhibit of toy whales suspended, grays and orcas, side by side, as though they were friends.

Morris says the gray whale mothers have to be crafty to get their calves safely through this leg of the migration. "Every year we get calls from people worried about baby whales getting stranded on the beach." He explains that adults put their young in the swash to hide them from the killer whales, who can't sense them in the crashing surf. "It's an acoustic screen. The little baby whales become invisible. The mothers outwit the predators."

I'd been discharged quickly, twelve hours after the birth. I'd planned to have the baby in Ireland, where I had an aunt and uncle who treated me as their own. Pavel wanted me to stay in London, so he could meet the child, but I couldn't remain in my rented room and hadn't been able to afford the mortgage on my flat for years. In Jersey, as a recent returnee, I would have to pay for health care, including during the birth. In the end it was academic because the baby came early, in London. Pavel made a brief appearance at the hospital after the birth and returned the following day with a huge bouquet of flowers, which I carried awkwardly behind him as he took the car seat containing Max. We went to his home. But, he said, the next day, I was to find somewhere else to stay for a night, for reasons he did not specify. But when morning came, Max's skin was a strange color and he had hardly fed. I called a midwife help line for advice, trying to explain my concerns, while Pavel stalked the room, his tawny hair leonine about this head. I was making excuses, trying to force him to let me stay, he said.

"It won't work," he growled.

"You sound very flat," said the woman on the other end of the line. A midwife would visit the next day, she said. I gave her the address where I would be, the home of a friend who was on holiday and whom I'd contacted by text. Of course I could stay at her flat for a night, she'd messaged. Pavel drove us there. I realized I'd not eaten and asked him to stop for a pizza. He pulled up wordlessly at a take-out. I did not dare speak again. That evening, while I tried unsuccessfully to breastfeed Max in my friend's flat, my brother called from Canada, where he lived, to congratulate me on the birth. I told him I couldn't confidently describe the baby's color. My red-green color blindness meant I had difficulty with some tones.

"It just looks wrong," I said.

"Go to A and E. Now."

We were admitted to the emergency room immediately and stayed in the special care unit for a week. Severe jaundice, blood tests every hour. A kind Nigerian nurse kept me buoyant in the small hours of the night, through the pain of learning to breastfeed. Pavel visited. I said I thought we needed to behave differently, now that we were parents. He said it was my fault, that I'd agreed to leave and go to the empty flat. He turned to walk out, pushed open the double doors of the hospital room. I begged him not to go, said sorry, agreed it was all my fault. A week later Max and I were discharged. We returned to Pavel's house. A few days later he went on holiday.

Cradling the baby in my arms in Pavel's empty home, I leaned back against the wall opposite a framed picture of Billy's umiaq. I'd given Pavel a copy, which he had hung on the small landing at the top of the stairs by his bedroom door. I gazed at the boat in the blue night, at that moment before we fled the incoming ice pack. Behind me, a panel clicked. To my surprise, it opened like a door, onto a staircase leading to what looked like an attic room. Pavel had never told me about it. A secret room. I shivered, as if I were about to discover some awful truth about him. Something that would explain everything, including why he'd forced us out when Max was just one day old. His very own Bluebeard's secret chamber. I looked back at Billy's boat, waiting there. You need to leave, the picture was warning, get the fuck away, like you did when the ice was coming in. But I needed to know.

Breathing shallow breaths, cradling Max, I took one careful step after another up the stairs. The attic was cold and empty, a cluster of boxes at the far end. I felt stupid already. I peered at the contents from a few steps away. The boxes contained neatly filed artworks, probably Pavel's. I exhaled, left the attic, and pushed the hidden door firmly shut. I really must control my imagination, stop making things up about Pavel, or I will ruin everything, I scolded myself. It was just a cleverly designed, space-saving door. Becoming a father must have triggered difficult emotions for Pavel that I hadn't properly appreciated. I cleaned the house, scrubbed the bathrooms. He'd like that, would be pleased with me when he came back.

I was deluded. Pavel returned from holiday and told me to leave by the end of the week. Max had not been given the all clear by the doctors, I pointed out, and I didn't think it was wise for us to travel. There were hospitals in Ireland, Pavel said. I called my dad and asked if he could come over and accompany me on the ferry. He booked a flight immediately. When he knocked on the front door of Pavel's house, I was that child again, carried on his shoulders.

I did not see that I was executing an escape. It was as though it had been perfectly planned, by someone else.

"This," says Morris, his voice ominous, "is the real star of the film *Jaws*." He holds up the mounted head of a shark, its jawbone full of razor-sharp teeth. It's a bull shark, he explains, more fearsome than the great white but not as big or photogenic. Morris's enthusiasm has infected Max—who is biting my leg, pretending to be a shark— and to my surprise, me. The museum is carefully curated. Nestled in a nearby display case are fossilized dinosaur eggs, sixty-five million years old, says the label. What were the ancestors of the grays doing when those were waiting to hatch?

Geneticists have compared genomes from ancient gray whale skeletons with those of modern whales. The genetic diversity in the older bones suggests the oceans once held approximately ninety-six thousand gray whales.[2] The eastern population of grays is thought to have been at least three times larger than it is now. Low diversity in some genetic markers shows inbreeding, telling us the population built itself back up from a small pool of survivors. Researchers can tell when it shrank too by looking at the genes. I don't suppose Charles Scammon ever imagined that he would leave such a fundamental mark on the species. But along with food shortages and an increase in predators, the whalers of his time are a possible cause of the collapse in gray whale numbers. Today's shrunken genetic pool could reduce their ability to adapt to change.

A family tree of gray whales has been drawn up, showing genetic similarities that point to migrations between the Atlantic and the Pacific, through the Arctic Ocean, during warmer periods of the late Pleistocene and Holocene ages, when sea ice was light. The ghost population of the Atlantic Ocean, extinct for centuries, still speaks to us through fossils that are from a few hundred to fifty thousand years old. Bones have been found in Sweden and England. Current models predict the range and distribution patterns of grays will shift toward the poles and that they may repopulate the Atlantic.[3] Individuals have been spotted in recent years off the coasts of Israel, Spain, and Namibia. In 2021, a young whale was seen off Morocco, then swam past Naples, Rome, and Genoa to the southern French coast, possibly passing through ancient calving grounds. The Atlantic is utterly changed from the last time it was home to grays, busy with shipping lanes, invaded by noise, oil exploration, drilling, and industrial fishing operations. Sea-level rise might provide increased shallow habitat for feeding, but that's only if ocean acidification and warming do not decimate the whales' prey.

I wish the grays all the resilience, endurance, and adaptability that their fossils sing of, and more. As for Max, what about him in a future where change is building momentum like an avalanche? What can I wish for Max? I wish him whales, in all his dark moments, their songs filling the ocean all around him.

It was pitch-black when I got up. Max was tiny, four months old. He slept as I lifted him from bed to car seat. Pavel had threatened court, had ordered me back to the house he'd demanded I leave with a sick one-day-old. He wanted my immediate return to London and 50 percent custody. He had no say in what Max ate or wore, he had complained on the phone.

"But he's breastfed." He wore baby clothes that I'd mostly been given, I told him.

Did I have to go back? I asked three different lawyers. One was in Ireland, where I was staying with my aunt and uncle. Another was in the north of England, where I had friends from my university days, and the third was the best family law advocate that Jersey had to offer. In the first days after Max's birth, when Pavel had told me to leave his house, I'd spoken to a lawyer in London.

"If you take the baby to Jersey," she'd said, "he might try and accuse you of abduction." I didn't call the London lawyer again. I'd pushed her words to the back of my mind. They were still there, though, tiny and silvery, like pins dropping in the dark.

The three new lawyers ummed-and-aahed a little. Then suddenly their advice converged. Go home, to where you grew up, they said. You will be stronger here, said the Jersey one. You might want to go soon, said the one in Durham. He put you and Max out on the street, said the Irish one, think about that. After another phone message from Pavel demanding my return, fear took over. I booked an early-morning flight and sent an email the evening before, to inform him of my movements. I fled at dawn. I chose my moment and ran. I did not look back. The time I'd spent as a child observing Bramble's reactions, when to startle, when to bolt, came into its own. The day I arrived in Jersey, I went to the lawyer's office and filed for a residence order.

When a bright spot appears through the clouds, Max and I rush out from Morris's museum to look at the sea. The air is warm, water-heavy. Then another downpour sends us running into a café. Inside is Clyde Ramdwar, serving *nearly famous homemade chowder*, fries, and brownies. Clyde says he's retired, this is his daughter's café. He grew up in Trinidad and left, as a teenager, on a ship bound for Chile, washing dishes. Ten years later he was a marine engineer on oil tankers sailing from Saudi Arabia to Brazil.

"Wanted to see the world for free," he says. "And you? What are you doing here?"

"We following migration of thurr gray whales," says Max. Clyde and I both do a double take. "I'm a whale!" shouts Max, puffing out his cheeks and blowing out a long sigh.

"Very good," says Clyde. "Now, what would this whale like to eat?"

"Whales love chowder," I say, seizing the chance to feed Max something other than chips, porridge, and peanut butter. "Sometimes, when they've eaten their chowder," I tell Clyde emphatically, "they get a brownie."

Max looks suspicious. Clyde insists that, yes, the whales that frequent his café always have chowder first and a brownie second.

A couple comes in. They're celebrating their sixtieth wedding anniversary, they tell me as they sit. I congratulate them and the man asks me how long I've been married. They blink as though they've discovered an alien when I divulge I'm a single parent. "Don't worry," he says, "the next one will be a keeper."

Max is my keeper, thank you, I think.

The woman looks at us long and hard. "He's a change maker."

"Pardon?"

"Your boy, he's a pattern breaker." What's she talking about? "Watch what happens, you'll see."

That's strange, I've heard this somewhere before but I can't think where.

Outside, the ocean is all shades of gray. The sky is still falling. We get the bus back to our motel. A silver streak lies across the sea as we leave, and Max falls asleep on my lap. I carry him to bed and pack our stuff, ready for the next day's early start, watching his mouth move as he talks in his dreams.

I was sitting on a plastic chair, in a room with institutional-green carpet tiles, opposite Lola, the family liaison officer from the Royal Court of Jersey. Lola had shining black hair, beach-tanned skin.

"What gender was your pony?" Lola's job was to scrutinize me and find out if I was capable of being a good mother because Pavel said I wasn't. He'd written a statement to the court, listing reasons why I was not to be trusted with bringing up a child.

For the first hearing, I'd called on the ancestors for help. I'd raided my aunt's closet and borrowed my Jersey granny's swirling black cape. I'd asked my dad for something personal of hers, and he lent me a jeweled brooch. I walked, carrying Max, around the tiny fishing village where my great-grandfather had built a house. With the cape wrapped around us, I prayed for protection. In return the island delivered a gray, sodden porridge fog for the morning of the hearing. Planes were not able to land. Pavel was stuck at Gatwick.

For the second hearing, he'd arranged to provide testimony on video link. He'd accused me of abduction because I'd come to Jersey, which is a separate legal jurisdiction from the UK, and he'd submitted the statement that Lola was holding in her hands. Pavel wasn't under scrutiny, just me. I'd written fifteen pages about him, but because I was a journalist, they said I'd written "a story." That's what Lola's colleague said, while I was waiting at reception. Sitting opposite Lola, I felt peeled and split open, like a tangerine. Max, five months old, was sitting beside me on the floor, preparing to attempt a crawl. I'd forgotten to bring any toys, I realized. I must not look like a very good mother. I couldn't see Max because I'd frozen as I heard Lola's question and stared at her mouth, as if I could read her next words as they emerged from her lips, to lessen the shock of hearing them when the sound waves caught up with the light. The soles of my feet were hurting. I always feel fear or shock in my feet. I planted them firmly on the floor, kept an eye on them, to make sure they didn't start to move toward the door. No more words were coming from Lola. What gender was my pony? I was going to have to answer.

"Female."

Lola shifted in her chair. Max shuffle-crawled behind her. He was heading slowly, with determination, toward an empty bin.

"Female," she repeated. "Do you know why he might have written this?"

I didn't answer. Max had reached the bin now. He picked it up and put it over his head. Lola continued to read from Pavel's statement, in which I stood accused of developing a bizarre relationship with the family horse. As well as looking after it, I'd apparently disciplined it and used it for sexual gratification. The animal's inability to defend itself and being in my control had, Pavel claimed, excited me.

I imagined Pavel typing at his computer late at night, angry, possibly drunk. I wondered what Lola would be asking, had Bramble been male. She was looking at me, waiting. I had to say something. I had to explain. I didn't know how.

"I had a pony," I said quietly. "She was called Bramble. She was a very big part of my childhood." Then, more quietly, "She died."

Lola coughed. I looked at Max, remembered what was at stake. "I had orgasms when I was riding her, a couple of times in about . . . We had her for about ten years. I didn't know what they were at the time, I was young. I told Pavel that in a moment of intimacy." There. It was out. She could go ahead and judge me, all of me, the bewildered child, the so-called adult, the total fuckup.

"So he has taken that information and changed it into something socially unacceptable?"

"He's changed it into something totally different," I said quickly. Had she not understood?

"Do you know why?" Lola explained that research showed people who were cruel to animals were more likely to be abusive to children. "He is questioning your suitability to look after a child."

I remembered Pavel telling me about the cat that he and his friends had tortured. "We pretended it was . . . What do you call that instrument?" He'd pulled his hands apart and pushed them together.

"An accordion?"

"Yes."

I had imagined him in his youth, gripping the cat as it writhed, bending its body as it screeched.

"It ran away eventually," he'd said.

I had watched his full lips move, thinking this man is damaged but love will heal him. I thought about the sex, the gradual introduction of force. Swept along by his charisma and attrition from accusations of prudishness, inexperience, and frigidity, I'd learned to acquiesce, lost sight of me. I felt sick, wondered if I would ever be able to trust myself again. Max took the bin off his head and chortled, rolling it around the floor. In my head I put up a barbed-wire fence around both of us to keep everyone out.

Lola said she would do a home visit before the third court hearing. We were staying at my parents' house. At home, I got little sleep. There was Max, there was trying to fit in some work, and there was my mom, who woke us every time we tried to nap. She couldn't remember not to, and we upset her routine. She found me cooking pasta in the kitchen one afternoon and stared at me from the doorway, her face displeased. She could sometimes be calmed by chatter, by Max, or by touch, an arm around her shoulders. But today Max was hungry, tetchy, and I was sullen with exhaustion.

"Hi" was all I managed. I could not care for them both. She said nothing, crashed the dishes around. I made a mental list of foods Max could eat that didn't require cooking, gave him his pasta as quickly as possible.

"I need to disappear." She walked purposefully out the door. Dad followed, cajoled her back, his hands shaking.

I got out of the kitchen. This was the mother I'd known as a child. Except now that she was losing her memory, it was worse, and as I had a baby, it was harder to stay out of her way.

I was worried about Lola's visit. My parents sat on the sofa. Lola took a chair to start the interview.

"I'm Granny," my mom said repeatedly. Her eyes shone as she held Max on her knee. The illness granted her just enough time to fall in love with her grandson. "Now you," she cooed at him, "are the one who will change everything, aren't you?" He regarded her seriously, reached for her face.

I went for a walk so Lola could speak to my parents in private. The old farm buildings looked beautiful, the granite illuminated by the sun and the trees in full bloom. When they'd finished talking, I put Max on my hip and led Lola up the steps to the playroom I'd made in the conservatory above the kitchen. Through the glass you could see a giant chestnut tree, towering over the house, and the track that led up through the fields.

Lola looked around. Sun streamed in over the cot and the toys strewn around the floor. A friend had sent them, a plastic bottle full of dried beans, scraps of glittery material. Lola examined the home-made rattle. "You've made some sensory toys."

I looked down at her car parked in the gravel yard. It had a surf-board on top. I imagined Lola riding the waves. She walked out of the conservatory, clanged down the metal steps. I followed. "You might find that you stop looking for a father figure for Max," she said, "and get on with your life." Her tone was professional, brisk, but the words were different. I was confused. She said goodbye and got into her car. I lifted a hand to wave. What did she just say? Did she think I might be enough on my own? Was she on my side? Then she was driving away down the lane. I'd thought I was calm, but when I went back into the conservatory to sit down with Max, my legs buckled before I reached the chair.

My alarm goes off at four o'clock the next morning. The bus back to Albany station leaves at half past. I look around our room in New-port, and the excitement of an early-morning start fades. The hope-lessness of our journey sinks in and I feel bone-tired. The whales will be up and swimming already, though. I just need to follow them. If I keep moving, nothing can get us.

The bus driver who brought us here from Albany told me he'd be on shift this morning and could pick us up outside the motel. He's true to his word, saving us a walk to the bus stop in the dark, and I'm so grateful I tip him more than the fare. Only one other passenger is on the bus, a single silhouette. We're lucky there's any public trans-port here at all.

"This is a lovely bus, Mummy," says Max as he settles into his car seat. It's still dark when we arrive back at Albany station, and we've a three-hour wait before our train to Seattle. We watch freight trains materialize in yellow out of black that slowly turns gunmetal gray. A man appears and unlocks the main door to the waiting room. We follow him in, but it's just as cold inside. I sit on the curved wooden bench, Max on my knee. At least I have someone to cuddle, am not hunched on a bench on my own looking weird. Or does it make me weirder, being here with a child? I'm not sure what Lola would say if she could see me now. I wonder if the stationmaster is at this moment reporting a hobo with a child in his station. I sit up straight, whisper at Max to shhhh his chatter so as not to attract attention from my imaginary observers. I should have brushed my hair, wiped the sand off our shoes. Max is oblivious, engrossed in watching for trains as I collapse internally. Perhaps I'm not sensible enough, strong enough, to look after a child. Perhaps this journey is just running away from the responsibility and drudgery. Most people make do with the living room, some toys, and the local park. I wish I were easier to please, took fewer risks, felt less lost. As I flounder, I make a pact with the strengthening daylight: I will let go of everything, everything, if I can only be a good enough mother to my son.

The northern waters of Puget Sound, the area where we are heading next, are frequented by a female gray, nicknamed Earhart by researchers. While I'm sitting in the station, she is nearby, probably nosing somewhere in the muck. Earhart is the founder of a group of whales called the Sounders, who have discovered a new food source, the ghost shrimp near the shore. Marine biologist John Calambokidis first spotted her in 1990 and has observed other whales following her. Earhart and the others spend approximately three months of the spring sucking up mud soup and filtering out shrimp in the intertidal zone before continuing their journey to the Bering and Chukchi Seas. It's a risky maneuver as the whales are sometimes as much as a mile and a quarter from deeper waters and could easily become stranded on an outgoing tide if they misjudged their direction or timing. Inland waters are busier and the mud may also have higher levels of toxins. But the area might be a sort of emergency food bank, which helps those who know about it when other sources are scarce. Not all pioneers look the same, that's what makes them pioneers.

Sometimes they might just look lost. If I want to change my story, perhaps, like Earhart, I have to take risks.

"Cuddle," Max demands, wriggling around on my lap. "My mummy." He leans his cheek into mine. The earth rotates a little, into the morning's first sunbeam. He's unfazed by what I perceive as my failure, trusts me more than I do myself, and I'm growing in line with his expectations. What's failure anyway? It's only me judging. The whales are out there, traveling on through the storm. Following them is a lesson in second chances, third, fourth, fifth chances, as many chances as you can believe in.

Holding the talisman sperm whale carving up to my face, Max sings, cheering the early-morning sun. He's on message: "Whales, we're coming to find you."

"There's a café over there, Sidekick, if y'all need some breakfast." The stationmaster is pointing through the window. "Does good coffee." Sidekick delivers croissants and a revolving cake stand taller than me.

"Can I have lemon cake, Mummy?" Max is eyeing up a giant bright yellow creation that is rotating slowly and majestically into view.

"Finish your croissant first please, Maxim."

"I finished, Mummy." Max repeats this three times, getting progressively louder and more tearful.

I am in no mood for a battle. "Are you lovely?"

"Yes."

"Are you clever?"

"Yes."

"Are you a marshmallow?"

"No."

I enjoy his smile, this long moment of happiness. If this is enough for him, then it's more than enough for me. We are far from the four walls of the hostel, far from Pavel, and we are having cake for breakfast.

I'm aiming to get to Anacortes, on the coast, tonight. It will be our springboard into the ocean, the gateway to the San Juan Islands. From there the plan is to ferry-hop to Canada, while scouring the sea for migrating grays. On the train to Seattle I realize we are cutting it fine and we'll need a taxi to the bus terminal. We get there seconds before the Anacortes bus pulls away from the curb. Max is tired and wriggly. It's a relief for both of us when he's in his car seat and asleep.

The farther north we travel up the Pacific coast, the thinner the soils become, the more dependent on the sea people are. The vast, diffuse clouds of summer plankton that support life have no terrestrial equivalent. This is the home of Indigenous whale hunters, where whales have shaped human culture, carried it on their backs. Reading about the Makah whalers of this area, I learn they used to imitate the grays before the hunt. They would dive deep and stay down as long as possible. On surfacing, they'd spout mouthfuls of water and try to sound like a whale. An account from the 1920s said that the most determined divers would push themselves so far that blood would trickle from their ears.[4] It's a reminder to me of how little I can hope to understand of what it is to be whale, to face Earhart's challenges, how the human body starts to break when we attempt to enter the whales' world just for the length of a single dive. We will never fathom their depths.

"Get up, Mummy, it wake-up time." Max's face is pushed into mine. The light from the marina has crawled around the curtains like a cat and patted our faces, waking us. On the way out, I ask the hotel receptionist about grays. There aren't any around at the moment, she tells me nonchalantly, but people are seeing the Sounders on the boats that leave from Everett, about fifty miles south.

I can't believe we've missed the whales again.

We find a pancake café for breakfast and elbow our way through a teeming ferry terminal. Today we're heading for Friday Harbor on San Juan Island, the biggest of the archipelago. There's no particular reason to stop there, but it's Friday, so that'll do. Max is impatient, gets close to a meltdown, even though he's not usually given to tantrums. We wave off the US mainland as the ferry moves gently out onto the water. The trip through Rosario Strait and Lopez Sound is a vision, the islands a scattering of luscious forests floating past on flat-calm blue. Max runs unsteadily around the deck. I circle him, ready to catch him, knees bent, arms wide, as if I were about to do a rugby tackle. I'm looking forward to a rest and have booked an eco-guesthouse as a treat. It's a bus ride away from the Friday Harbor waterside, and as we arrive, every cell in me lightens. The house is set in a mossy garden, was built by craftsmen. Floorboards creak a welcome. In our room, orange silk curtains frame a view of spread-eagled green, lapped by a tide of purple lavender. A dark, knotted forest exhales silently in the distance. While Max sleeps, I sit on the floor next to the window, feeling purple-and-green peace.

The ferry to Vancouver Island, our next stop, leaves first thing in the morning. We go down to the kitchen early to heat up brioche rolls for breakfast. There's loud birdsong and a woman in luminous Lycra washing dishes. She smiles curiously as Max toddles in. She's getting ready to go kayaking with her boyfriend, she says, as she splashes mugs in the sink.

"Is it just the two of you?" she asks.

"Yes."

"Nice. I'm a single parent too, of four."

Four?! How on earth does she feed them? "What do you do?"

She's a psychiatrist, she says. "Three are mine, one's adopted." The birth mother of the adopted child was a drug addict and asked her to take in the boy.

I feel as if she's guessing at my story in her head, so I tell her. "I went through family court with him." I nod toward Max, who is sitting on a stool, looking out the window, eating his roll.

"That's tough."

I change the subject. "We're following the gray whale migration, but we can't find them." I try to laugh but it comes out harsh. "Isn't it wonderful here? I want to move in after just one night."

"Why not start again here?"

"Oh, I'm too old. I'm forty."

She came to the islands at forty, she says, when she split from her husband. He was bipolar. Her friends sided with him after the divorce.

"Was he a narcissist?"

"Oh, yes. And big control issues. Yours?"

"Same. I mean, I think so, probably." I don't like to think in detail about Pavel's issues anymore. It all feels like a swamp I nearly got stuck in.

"Kind people look for the kind people. I'm looking for the kind people"—she pauses—"and I'm sleeping with them."

I see a handsome man through the window. He adjusts a strap on a van with kayaks on top, then looks around. She waves at him through the glass. He walks in and high-fives Max. She puts her head back around the door as they leave, winks, and hands me her card. "Big house, spare room. Come and stay if you are in between or starting off."

I try not to stare at the two of them as they fool around outside. They are laughing as they get in the van. Kind people, kind people, I repeat over and over in my head as I get Max ready to leave. I wonder if I could ever pull off her Lycra look, her laugh.

There's no bus this early, so we get a taxi back to the harbor and board the boat to Sidney, on Vancouver Island, where we'll go through border control into Canada. Whales obviously glide through political boundaries without noticing, but I feel nervous. I put my hand in my bag to feel the plastic wallet that holds my legal paper-work. A moment later I delve again to check it's still there, and this time I keep hold of it. As a single parent I'm eyed with suspicion by border officials and usually asked to show proof that I'm allowed to travel with my child. We join the passport queue at Sidney. When it's our turn, the immigration official takes my paperwork and examines it. *Royal Court of Jersey*, it says at the top. I sometimes worry people will think I've made Jersey up. It's a small island, not English, not French, and lots of people have never heard of it. The man takes his time. Acid rises in the back of my throat.

During court sessions, I stayed at a women's refuge. I didn't want to be at my parents' house while Pavel might be on the island, and the staff provided someone to look after Max during the hearings. The large house was painted in subtle colors. It had high ceilings, spacious bathrooms with vintage fittings, and a luxurious kitchen. It must have been a rich person's home once, before it was donated to the charity.

There was always someone you could talk to there, even in the small hours, and that night Jolanta was on shift. Jolanta had a light Polish accent and was unsmiling, straightforward, almost busi-nesslike. She made me think of a surgeon. Usually I went to sleep with Max after he'd nodded off breastfeeding. That night, though, I needed to talk, and I trusted Jolanta. I got out of bed, walked slowly down the wide, carpeted stairs in the dark, and knocked on the door of the office. With shame hanging like heavy curtains around me, I began to talk to Jolanta about sex.

We didn't speak about sex in our family. When I was seventeen, my mother returned from holiday to find me on the living-room floor asleep, fully clothed, in the arms of a boy. She saw him off by giving him a pile of Samuel Beckett books to read. She then told me all men were bad and, with disgust, that they could get erections just from the vibrations of a bus.

"Your father is different from all the rest, Doreen," she clarified some time later. I took her at face value, not fully understanding what she carried with her. Even when I ended up having sex, I never got any better at talking about it. So I was talking about it for the first time really, to Jolanta. I talked about the sex I'd had with Pavel, how I'd wanted to be close to him, to feel protected, to belong to him. He was born in the cold north, he'd told me, and that in itself reduced me to jelly.

"These are the hands that held the reindeer's reins," he said, laughing, after seeing the effect on me when he talked about driving a sleigh as a child. He was a political dissident, he said. After all those interviews with the brave and politically persecuted, there I was, in the arms of one. Here was a man who understood what it meant to suffer for freedom and truth. He had been through the worst, he knew best. I didn't even need my own opinions anymore, his were better. "So desperate to be touched," he'd whispered, "and so scared." He'd scented my vulnerability. I was like an iron filing stuck to a magnet. His pillow talk was soft, hypnotic speech. "You are my little girl, my tight pussy, you are not allowed to run away." As I opened up to Jolanta, shame at my compliance billowed up in poisonous clouds. It choked me so I could hardly speak. I'd allowed him to take me apart, had made excuses for him, aided him, had been so willing to abandon myself. He could be so gentle, though. I thought he would change.

"I feel so stupid."

Jolanta nodded as though she'd already known it all. "These people rarely change. But, Doreen, it doesn't matter what anyone else does, you can change. You already have. You're the winner here."

I told her about the accusations involving Bramble that Pavel had made in his statement to the court.

"Well, sex with horses is a very common theme in porn in the

Eastern Bloc, where he and I come from"—she sounded bored—"because of Catherine the Great."

Heat rose in my cheeks. I thought I was embarrassed but then felt burning anger in my throat. *Get your hands off Bramble,* I said to Pavel in my mind. *Get your stupid, stupid porn the fuck out of my head.* As soon as I'd thought it, I felt a weight lift.

Something about the quiet, about there being no one else, made the time with Jolanta feel like a gift, just for me, a little extra slipped into my life. Time for me to rearrange things, to let some darkness go.

"It feels like people want Max around but not me," I whispered. "Like they want me to disappear." I could not have said this in daylight. In daylight I smiled and got on with things.

"You carried him for nine months, Doreen. He is yours."

I went upstairs. The conversation was lost to the night. The shame and contortion dissipated into the dark. I went to my room, to Max. We shared a single bed. He didn't want to sleep in the cot, and I didn't want him to either. It was snug, soft, safe. I kissed him all over his face. I'd worried about kissing him too much until then, had held my affection in check, as if there were something wrong with it. I made a quiet leap into the unknown, trusting myself again. I claimed him and claimed my space beside him.

At the third hearing, Lola's report was not mentioned. Pavel hadn't come. He'd sent another statement to the court, agreeing to my having a residence order for Max. It had taken six months and all my savings. I had no job, no money, and no home, but my baby would live with me.

The Canadian border official greets Max by name, presumably to test his reaction.

Max skips the hello. "We going to catch a boat to find the gray whales."

The man raises his eyebrows. I take up the baton and describe the whale migration, fast, blow by blow, to prevent any questions.

He looks from me to Max as a small voice chimes in, "Whales eat chowder and brownies. And then they poo."

The official wishes us a nice stay and waves us through. It's another sprint for the next ferry over to Tsawwassen. About halfway across the Strait of Georgia, a humpback whale surfaces close by, waves its tail around. There's wild enthusiasm on board as several hundred people rush to the window. I give the humpback a casual nod. I'm holding out for my grays.

On the SkyTrain into central Vancouver, Max insists on sitting at the front, and we fly into the city. We dump bags and car seat at the youth hostel. The traveling is getting easier, we have let go of all routine, found our rhythm, and it feels as if the world is getting friendlier the farther north we get. I'm no longer the armor-plated woman who eyed her surroundings with suspicion at the start of the journey. We play on the beach, collecting sticks to use as boats. Then we stroll along the pontoon toward the Aquabus, which is buzzing closer on the darkening ripples. Paddleboarders pass. I feel luminous, weightless. Max takes my hand as we step aboard the Aquabus, and all the misery and difficulty, all my fear and fury, dance away across the water.

UTQIAĠVIK: SOUNDING

Latitude: 71° 17' 26" N
Longitude: 156° 47' 19" W

Sedna is the mother of the sea. She protects the sea animals and provides food for all the Inuit. Her story is told from Greenland to the central region of North America and varies in each place. In northwest Alaska, she is the woman at the bottom of the ocean, who holds the souls of the sea animals in the bowl of her lamp.[1] I was first told of her by Aleqa Hammond, who was foreign minister of Greenland at the time. She explained Sedna was the original Inuit goddess and was also called Sassuma Arnaa, "mother of the deep."[2] In some stories she is Nerrivik,[3] "the food fish." In others she's Uinigumasuittuq,[4] "she never wants a husband." Or Takanaluk arnaluk,[5] "the woman down there."

Sedna was a beauty and refused all the men who tried to woo her. In the story told by Piita Irniq,[6] who as a child lived in Nattiligaarjuk, or Committee Bay, in Nunavut, she was called Nuliajuk. Nuliajuk fell in love with a dog and gave birth to many children. Some became Inuit, some Qablunaat or white people, some Qarnuktut or black people, some Itqilik, Chipewyan, Chinese, Japanese, all the world's peoples. In some stories, including one told on Baffin Island in the 1880s, Sedna was seduced by a seabird that flew from over the ice and took the shape of a man.[7] The birdman, a fulmar, enticed her with promises of a life of ease.[8] But life on bird island, living on fish, in a tent of fish skins, was hard. Sedna sang a song of woe to her father, who came and killed the bird husband. They fled by boat and the other birds gave chase, beating up a huge storm with their wings. To try to save his own life, the father threw Sedna overboard. She clung to the boat, so he took a knife and cut off her fingertips to make her let go. They fell into the sea and became whales, the nails turning into baleen, but she held on tighter. The father cut off the second finger joints and finally the stumps, creating seals, walrus, and all the other sea creatures. Sedna lives at the bottom of the ocean now, and when animals are killed by hunters, their souls return to her. She can give them new bodies, but if anyone breaks a hunting taboo, killing an animal without the proper ceremony and respect, Sedna will become angry and keep the souls below, causing scarcity above. Then, a shaman must visit her.[9]

The drumbeat was straight to the heart, such a clamor it seemed to echo off the sky. The dancers were finned. Their skeletons morphed, upper arms fused to their bodies, forearms swaying, fingers together, wrists loose. Knees slightly bent, their bodies swept this way, that way, synchronized, following the flow of an invisible current. Long lines of song were cut by high animal cries.

In the gym at the Ipalook Roller Rink, members of the Nuvuk-miut dance group, meaning "people of Nuvuk"—the point—were meeting. The group was led by Jeffrey and he'd said I could film. I sat at the back for a while, not wanting to intrude. The echoing hall reminded me of dance classes at primary school, the discomfort and embarrassment of having to wear a scratchy red leotard while I clumsily leaped about.

But when the drumming started, it wiped the building out.

The dancers moved through the air as if it were water, heads held at a stiff angle. Their limbs were those of a different creature, the curve of the back just so, as they dived and flowed through the music. Movement and voice merged. Wide white drums waved in a line like surf. I felt a change in me after watching. Whereas before something inside had felt dense, predetermined, I felt a formless, shifting space.

JJ, Julia's youngest son, got up to dance on his own. He looked both bashful and proud. His son, tiny J3, ran across to join him, fingers of one hand in his mouth as his dad stomped, crouched, flailed. JJ was a hunter in a boat, looking for whales, hand shielding his eyes from the sun as he scanned the horizon. He was paddling. His arms showed the sweep of whales, surfacing all around. One whale came up close, right by the boat. The dancer briefly became the whale, rising. Then he was the hunter, driving the harpoon home.

"Arigaa"—good—the women cheered at the end of the song. They murmured in Iñupiaq, pointed, and laughed at me crouching with my camera. There were all ages, a tiny baby, elders. Some were wearing hoodies, some their Kaleak-crew whaling jackets.

Ay yah yah yah yah—the men in the front row were beating their skin drums. A slow, light beat. The stick was held underneath the drum, batted the rim loosely upward. Then the drums began to boom as the sticks struck the skins. It was a heartbeat getting faster, more urgent. It was a chase. The drums were held up and the sticks beat hard. The taut skins filled the air. Voices were scattered over the top. The room was now full of men turning and stamping in rhythm. J3 stood still, in the middle, staring.

Was this the voice of their ancestors? What would those who lived long ago have thought about the changes we were seeing? I wanted their wisdom. The present was such a mess and the future so ominous. It was comforting to think of the faces of the past, from a time so mysterious they said people here had been able to change into animals and then return to human form. I wanted that time back, a time when Western culture had not named everything else as other, colonized, categorized, and dominated everything. I couldn't understand the words being sung in the hall, but I understood that they were in unison. And I understood the easy giggles and chatter. The song was about community, a conversation with the nonhuman world, a give and a take.

The dancers wiped sweat off their faces. It was a fierce workout too, loads of squats. I wondered if it was partly to keep in shape for the hunting season. There was a loud *niġliqiġliqiġliq* in the middle of the next one, and the room was suddenly full of geese pecking at the floor. At the end, the dancers were earthbound, wings spread back.

Billy came into the hall, looking for me. They called to him to join in.

"Billy! Come on, Billy, *come on*," shouted his aunt Rhoda. He went out again. I don't know what stopped him. I'd have loved to see him dance.

Pickled maktak, the whale skin and glistening pink blubber, was now my favorite snack. I couldn't get enough of it, greedily accepted it whenever it was offered. I didn't recognize myself. I was learning patience, getting rounder, heavier. Bound more tightly by gravity's pull, I felt the earth holding me in place, this place.

"What would you do if I came back?" I asked Billy.

"Probably marry you."

I supposed I was being stupid even thinking about it. But I was thinking about it, a lot. Though I didn't like that it was only "probably."

"What would you think if I stayed here and, you know, learned how to hunt and, well, maybe got married?" I asked my mother on the phone.

"I think it would be very interesting for you," she said without hesitation, taking the idea of seeing me rarely, if ever again, in her stride. I never did hear her express surprise. Not even when I arrived home with a shaved head when I was fourteen. She had me all worked out, she said once. I did not tell her that the hunter with whom I was discussing marriage lived in a one-room hut. He had few possessions, but he was rich in other, unquantifiable ways.

Billy and I talked as though we had a future. He told me about driving the ice roads and said he'd take me to see the caribou migrate across the tundra. You had to be careful where you camped, and it was really something, seeing all the running bodies. Once in summer, he said, he'd climbed down into the ice cellar when he got too hot, to cool off. The ice cellars were deep holes dug into the permafrost, with ladders going down to the bottom, large enough to store enough meat to last a family the winter. It was an image that stayed with me, Billy sitting down there, being recalibrated by the earth.

When I got serious about anything, or the conversation turned to work or climate or that I was going to have to leave, he'd tell me to stop thinking. "You'll have an aneurysm if you carry on like that." He turned on the radio. Stevie Nicks sang about the room being on fire. Billy took my hand.

We would sit entangled, breathing each other in. He'd repeat my name, and each time I'd feel a little more deeply called into being. We'd intertwine fingers for long enough that I could no longer feel whose hands were whose.

"You got my baby in there?" he said one morning, looking at my belly. "It would be smart. Like mommy, like baby." He'd produced some school photos of his nephews and nieces from a drawer and displayed them for me with pride. That made me ache. I wondered what our children would look like. Billy was a beautiful man.

He introduced me to his mother, a poised woman. His father, who'd served in the military, had died several years earlier. Billy was deferential, nervous around her, so I was too. They shared the most elegant of noses, but apart from that there was little resemblance. She had waves of curly dark hair and an oblong face, whereas Billy had straight jet-black hair and a rounder face. Just being next to her made him look like a little boy.

She eventually seemed to warm to me a little, told me that she used to have a snowy owl. "They make good pets. Quiet." She suggested we drive a little way off through the snow to the edge of town and spot wild owls. Billy pointed one out, perched austerely on a post. It glared piercingly at us, a little like the way in which his mother was keenly observing me.

Each crew that had landed a whale hosted Apuġauti, a communal feast, when they brought the boat back to shore. I helped one successful family prepare and washed dishes for several hundred people afterward. The women laughed at my hands, spindly and useless compared to theirs, which were muscular and capable: "Those haven't seen much work."

"What's going on with you and Billy?" A woman I'd barely met, a girlfriend of one of the crew, had appeared out of the crowd.

I told her we weren't sure.

"That's not the Barrow way. It's not how we do things here."

I asked her what she meant. She was dual heritage, one parent white, one Iñupiaq. Perhaps she'd know if I'd unwittingly broken some taboo, but she didn't elaborate. I finished the dishes, wondering what was being said around town. People were enjoying themselves, having a few drinks. The party was mellow. I wished Billy would come and we could have a drink together. The whaling captain's wife gave me a beer, which came in a small can, and a piece of whale heart to eat. The meat was chewy, did not easily shred or disintegrate into fibers. It was clearly part of a whole, carried a message about entirety. After I swallowed it, I sat still and quiet. It took me down into the ocean, sounding, down below the light, where benign goliaths swam by.

Billy didn't show up. I didn't see him for several days. When he reappeared at Julia's, he said he'd been partying. Just how much time did he spend drinking and with whom? What was his deal? Was that the reason he lived in that tiny place, at the bottom of the pile?

"They took my shoes once when I was drunk," he told me, sounding injured. It struck me as particularly cruel, stealing someone's shoes when he was inebriated, in subzero temperatures. Protected as I was by living with Julia, I didn't fully understand the dangers Billy lived with until later, but a man staggered into his hut a few days after, shabbily dressed.

"I want to see Billy," he said, slurring. "Okay?" It wasn't really a question. I left. I couldn't ignore the issue anymore.

"Would you stop drinking if I stayed?" I asked Billy. "I'd need you to."

"That would be hard for me."

It wasn't the answer I'd wanted. I'd needed a yes. Out hunting, Billy knew the way. In town, he got lost, and I struggled to find him.

The whales had gone. The hunt was over. I'd been there months and my grant money had run out, but Julia said I could stay on without paying rent. I extended my ticket for as long as I could, used up all my annual leave. Julia had a party to mark the end of whaling season. The house was full. Billy was supposed to come, but after several hours he still wasn't there. I felt strung out, thin somewhere in my throat. Where was he? My need for him weighed on my lungs, my heart. I slipped out of the house and walked to Nanook Street, let myself into his hut with the key he'd given me, and fell asleep in his bed.

"I might hide your passport, so you can't go," he said, a week before my flight. "Why do you want to go back out there anyway?" He suggested I could find a job around here. "Something secretarial." He didn't know me and I realized I knew little about him, other than that I loved him. He'd been kind, he'd known not to startle me. In that blinding, deathly environment, my life had depended on others, a situation I'd not experienced since childhood. I'd felt safe with him. Billy's compassion had shone out of him, he had healed some old, old wounds.

My flight was in three days. I pictured myself staying. Billy, working as a carpenter, he'd built the umiaq so beautifully. We'd have a baby. In the school-district books gender roles seemed clearly defined, so if it was a boy, he'd grow up learning all about weather and the different stages of sea-ice formation, the parts of a boat, the harpoon, whale physiology for butchering. If it was a girl, she'd be learning food preparation, how to work the skins, and to stitch mukluks, clothes, and the boat. Or, if she wanted, she'd learn to be a hunter too, from her father, at Kaleak camp. I could see Billy, the best father, patient and gentle, schooling her on the land and on the ice. Our daughter, learning to put her full weight and intention behind the heft of the gun, the butchering knife, the harpoon. I couldn't see myself quite so clearly. But I could see Billy, drinking. The sea ice disappearing. The dangers out hunting increasing. The land eroding as the ice buffer against the storms disappeared. All of it unfolding slowly like a horror film.

Billy helped me pack. Sitting quietly on the bed, rearranging things for me as I tried to get all the equipment back into the cases.

"They won't let you through customs with that." He pointed to a piece of baleen Julia had given me. "Draw on it, then it'll be handicraft." He found me a nail. I roughly sketched a whale tail. "You're good. You could sell it, make a living." I wasn't sure about a white woman selling whale art in an Iñupiaq city, I said with a wry smile.

We clung to each other all night. When morning came, we refused to let go of each other, ignored the birds scrabbling on the roof, kept the curtains shut against the light, did not allow the day to come in.

A car horn in the street outside marked the moment time finally defeated us. Julia had offered to drive me to my flight, since Billy had lost his license for driving drunk. At the check-in desk in Utqiaġvik's tiny airport, a man was loading rifle-shaped cases onto the conveyor belt. Julia pulled me into a long hug as I dabbed at my eyes with my sleeve.

"I'm your Iñupiaq mom now. You better stay in touch."

Billy stood there awkwardly, his hands by his sides, our intimacy unable to cope with a public goodbye. "Come back, even if it's in fifteen years, even if it's just for a visit."

I wasn't sure if this was him imploring or just pretending this was all totally fine. He was silent after, watching me carefully, as though he were hunting. His eyes so dark, his body so still, getting smaller and smaller in the swell of people as I went through security. Walking toward the gate, I could still feel him watching. Turning back, I saw his eyes were full of distance, as though I were already flying away, far above. I closed my eyes briefly. The next thing I saw, when I opened them, was the tarmac and the plane. Billy's smell lingered comfortingly on my clothes.

After I'd left, they kept on seeing me, Julia told me on the phone. Once she saw me walking along by the side of the frozen lagoon, the path I used to walk to Nanook Street.

"That's Doreen! What's she still doing here?" Julia pulled over, but on closer inspection, she said, it was "just another tanik," not me.

It happened to me too. In the airport, on my way back through Canada. A man in glasses approached me. He was taller than Billy, he had a thin, brown face, and his baseball cap was on forward instead of backward. He was staggering drunk.

He came up close and stared at me with Billy's eyes. "I love you."

I looked at the drunk man, who was not Billy. My lips formed the words *I love you too* but made no sound. I turned and fled across the departures hall. I knew it was crazy, but I could not shake the feeling that I had been visited, was being called back.

I stopped off with my relatives in Edmonton. Aunt Kathy is an older sister of my mother. She is tall and slim and stately. She gave me the small, peaceful room that had belonged to her eldest daughter. In the photos of that weekend I am smiling and fat, sitting with my cousins, their children, and a puppy. Aunt Kathy told me about her work as a nurse with First Nation children, many of whom had fetal alcohol syndrome, resulting in learning difficulties. I saw so many homeless First Nation people. Injustice was right in my face every time I walked down the street. *Eskimo* or *Native* sounded different here because the words weren't spoken with pride from the mouth of one of my Utqiaġvik friends. I felt self-conscious of my whiteness, ashamed to be on this side of the cultural divide. This was a reality I hadn't yet encountered. I'd gone looking for ice and whales and had traveled in a stratum of health, with hunters who were still connected to the land. I'd lived with a family that had refused alcohol and all its pathological connections. I'd barely even seen anyone drinking. It had happened indoors because it was so cold. And Billy, he had kept me away from it.

I listened to some Iñupiaq language tapes I'd bought and thought about the names given to things, people, and places. I felt honored Julia had given me her own name and loved the sound of Billy's Iñupiaq name, Uvyuaq. He hadn't wanted to use it, though, and he'd lived in a place called *Barrow*. That was the name of an explorer, Sir John Barrow of the British Admiralty, who'd never even visited. All sorts of Western misconceptions, ambitions, and romantic notions had been projected onto this place, the home of the Iñupiat. What had been done to Barrow, which had been called Utqiaġvik in the past and would later have its name changed back? At times I felt I'd been a fraud myself, unable to speak Iñupiaq and walking around seeing everything in English. I couldn't work it out.

Back in London, I'd grown bigger than all my clothes and was living on peanut butter and cheese. I avoided salad and vegetables and hated the noise of the city. My old life didn't fit me. I agonized with friends. Some of them listened, some of them laughed. A Japanese colleague married to an Englishman advised me to be pragmatic about the difficulties of cross-cultural relationships and to let it go. What if it went wrong after you'd had children, asked another, and you then wanted to come back? Far too complicated, she said.

Billy was doing good, he said. He'd ring during his lunch break. He'd got a job, skilled labor, and was waiting for a carpentry vacancy. The guys all looked out for each other, like a crew.

"You missed out on lots of fun at the Fourth of July games." He would be paid on Friday and would have money to go boating. "About time I finally got off my butt." His birthday was coming up. I telephoned the authorities in Utqiaġvik and asked if I could pay off his driving fine, so he could get his license back and drive for work. They said no, the money had to come from him, so I transferred him enough for a barrel of fuel for the boat. He called to tell me about the day he'd spent out on the water with a group of relatives. I got an email from his niece. Billy had dictated a message, "I sure do miss you Doreen."

"I might just go and buy a ticket and come over. What's good for hunting in London?" he asked during one phone call. I wondered for a second about squirrels and pigeons before telling him there wasn't anything. He laughed loudly. Even when I realized he was joking about the hunting, I wasn't sure what London would offer him, what I could offer him.

"Would you like to live in a city?"

When he'd visited Seattle with Jeslie and Julia, he'd been glad to get back home, he admitted.

Once he called drunk, distorted and unguarded. "I love you," he said. It was the first time he'd said it.

I didn't want him to hear me crying, ended the phone call straight-away. Why did he have to be drunk to tell me that? And so far away.

Then Julia emailed to tell me he'd been flown to Anchorage with pneumonia. I saw the message first thing in the morning and spent the day waiting for enough time to pass so I could call the hospital.

"Hold on," said a nurse.

There was a long wait.

I heard the handset being picked up again. "Doreen?"

"What happened?" I was suddenly furious. "You need to look after yourself."

"One thing makes me want to get well again, hearing your voice."

I felt pain in the back of my head. The room began to swim. The handset felt eely, I gripped it tightly so it didn't slip away. I told Billy to get better, that everyone would be missing him at home.

I felt like a pollutant that had gone to Utqiaġvik and left a harmful trace. Was I stringing him along? A man already wounded by the slow attempted annihilation of his culture. I waited until he was back from hospital. Then I called him.

"It's not going to work, Billy. I can't come back."

"Sure. I miss you."

I stopped calling him, stopped answering the phone. I'd watch it ring, put my head in my hands when it stopped. Then he stopped calling too.

At work, I pushed through a previously impermeable confidence barrier and got a presenting job.

"You've been hiding your light under a bushel," a manager said. I went to Greenland to report on the scramble for Arctic resources and interviewed Aleqa Hammond, who told me the story of Sedna. I filed a story on climate once a day, skeptic-free, for a week. I was on a roll.

Back in London, I set up an interview with a whaling family, but when I went into work the next day, I saw it had not aired, had been dropped.

"They're eyewitnesses to climate change," I protested. "We never hear from them, it's important." Was something happening here that I didn't understand? Some viewpoint that was dominating?

I remembered my early days working in the World Service Newsroom, when I'd learned that BBC practice was to refer to the military in Northern Ireland as simply "the army," rather than "the British army." I'd thought about my Irish grandfather, who died long before I was born. He'd been decorated for fighting with the IRA against the British forces in the 1919 Irish War of Independence. What, I'd wondered, would he have made of his granddaughter broadcasting from the perspective of those he'd have seen at that time as the oppressors, the colonizers?

If a political viewpoint might be seen as emerging in the output from just one word, in this case the word "British," or from the absence of it, then what other paradigm might I be broadcasting from, without even realizing?

"You're not one of those Eskimo soul-walkers are you?" said a copresenter one night. We were preparing to go on air and I'd been telling him about hunting on the ice.

"We say *Iñupiat* or *Inuit* now, not *Esk—*"

He'd already turned back to the brief he was reading.

I stopped talking about Utqiaġvik. It was becoming unbearable to think about it, the multiyear ice that was being lost, the Kaleak family whom I so missed, and Billy, the fact that I was not with him.

Julia had given me a black-and-white print by a relative of hers who lived in Point Hope. I hung it in my room. It was a picture of a bowhead whale swimming, with an Iñupiaq man sailing in a boat above it. In the belly of the whale was another man. This Iñupiaq Jonah was different from the despairing Jonah of my childhood. He was banging his skin drum and dancing.

I had the photo I'd taken of Billy's umiaq poised at the lead edge printed out as a poster, which I framed and hung alongside. In the blue light, the umiaq looked for all the world as though it were waiting to take people on that final journey, across the water, away from the land of the living. As well as the Iñupiaq title, *Uvyuam Umialiaŋŋa*, I added a title in English: *I Will Carry You.*

GLACIER BAY

Latitude: 58° 27' 3" N
Longitude: 135° 49' 21" W

Our ship blasts its departure on the horn. At last, the open sea. After weeks of glimpses of the sea between train and bus rides we're joining the grays on their patch, for the last stages of the migration. Max and I wave, and people lining the quay wave back. Vancouver opens up along the skyline and then shrinks into the distance.

We are Alaska-bound. As we stand on the balcony of our luxury cruise ship, the *Norwegian Sun*, I feel a tinge of shame. This is not my idea of roughing it on the high seas. It's way above our budget. There's even a swimming pool sloshing around on the top deck. But the Alaska Marine Highway ferries weren't running when we needed them, so I negotiated a cheap ticket, saying I'd write about the trip for a glossy Jersey magazine that's read by bankers. In our cabin, I study the map of our route. It winds through a jigsaw of islands, making stops at Ketchikan, Juneau, Skagway, and Glacier Bay. Every so often a whale tail emblem has been drawn emerging from the sea, which must be a good omen. Our ship will stay in the calm, protected inner channels, away from the rugged and wild outer coast. We will arrive in Whittier in seven days. I start counting the fragments of land, but there are too many and Max's head is blocking my view. He's clambered onto me, smacks his open palm onto a photo of a seaplane on the opposite page.

"Airplane, I love airplanes. What those feet?" He points to the floats.

"Those are so it can land on the water."

Max stares at this previously unknown vehicle with wonder.

We wake to a view of dark ocean through our balcony door. Upstairs, pancakes dripping in maple syrup are brought to our table by Ayu, a waitress from Bali. Other staff I meet are from Nepal, the Philippines, and India. Nine months of every year, Ayu leaves her child to work on the ship. She can't get enough of Max. They do moony eyes at each other over the tall glasses of orange juice she brings. She uses Skype, she says, to stay in touch with her family. Her voice is light. How must it be to have your love stretched that thin, like elastic, so far over time and place? I don't feel like eating, look out the window and see small dark gray dorsal fins breaking the waters around us. They appear and disappear so quickly I think I'm imagining them. I leave a large tip for Ayu and rush Max down to our room. From the balcony, we can see white-striped bodies surfacing.

"Whale, Mummy, whale!" Max shouts. I search online until I identify the pod playing around the boat as Dall's porpoises, the fastest of all dolphins and porpoises. TV screens dotted around the decks have our coordinates displayed at all times. That is as exciting as it gets, though. We wander the carpets, go up and down in the glass lifts. I check the pool rules and find children are only allowed to swim if they're toilet-trained. When I tell Max, he starts to take off his diaper immediately. I hustle him to the nearest loo and explain that he needs to go three days with no accidents. A rumor spreads of a whale being spotted, and I rush to gather intelligence, debrief the spotter. It was black, she says, showed off its white-splattered tail, breached several times. She demonstrates a leaping whale with a swoop of her arm. My heart sinks in disappointment. A humpback, not a gray.

The next day we arrive at our first port of call, Ketchikan. The city began as a fishing camp and is known as the salmon capital of the world. I don't want to spend money on a tour that isn't whales, so we just walk around. In Parnassus Books I find an illustrated book, *The Oceanic Society Field Guide to the Gray Whale*. It feels like I'm getting closer to them just touching it. We continue down the road and onto a bridge that overlooks a jostling crowd of yacht masts, then stumble on a Salvation Army thrift store and have a good rummage. Max uncovers a raucous Elmo laptop, which I try to negotiate back onto the shelf. That is not coming back to our cabin. I barter, offering a plastic train with a single joyful toot, then add an Etch A Sketch, and finally a wooden log cabin set. Max isn't sure, still clutches the laptop. I do a hard sell, explaining to him that people here can make houses out of trees. He goes for it, swayed by the ax-wielding frontiersman and his faithful plastic hound. He swaggers out of the shop, piled high with his new acquisitions. I'm not sure I struck a very good deal. Someone stops me and asks for directions. When she hears my accent, she says she thought I was Ketchikanian. Now Max and I are both strutting with pleasure.

I have kept the gray whales at bay all day, but that night I pore over my new book, searching for clues. That gentle curve of the mouth. The wise eye. It feels as if I were looking for unicorns. There is absolutely no mention of grays anywhere in the cruise ship handbook. It seemed straightforward, the whales go up and down the west coast every year, so surely if we went up at roughly the same time as them, we'd meet them along the way. I have scanned the sea and horizon for spouts and blotched bodies thousands of times now. I have found only their absence. The disappointment has accumulated into something that feels solid and heavy inside. They must be farther out, away from all the people and our enormous ships. Where else? How foolish of me to think that such intelligent animals would voluntarily cross paths with those who hurt them most.

Nirvana's "Come as You Are" was playing, and the Hautlians, a smoke-filled club in St Helier, was dancing. I was seventeen and off my face on three green monsters. I'd watched the barman mix the half of cider and half of lager, the final shots of blue Bols liqueur magically transforming the whole lot to swamp green. As I cycled back home, the world gently turned upside down. I was on the road on my back, pedaling into the air with the bike on top of me. When I finally reached Bramble's shelter in the old pigsty, she hardly looked up. She was slight now, still fairy-tale beautiful. I curled up next to her on the sawdust, was so drunk I wet myself, felt the warmth slowly soaking through my jeans, then turning cold. I slept fitfully, an arm touching her all night. Close enough that her hooves struck me when her legs jolted in the dark.

I'd found her lying in the field weeks ago, nickering at me, unable to get up. I'd cared for Bramble for nearly a decade. When I reached my A-level years, though, I became unable to care about anything— school, exams, getting out of bed. I got drunk a lot. Most days all I managed for Bramble was to trudge buckets of water down the path to the field. I'd enlisted a classmate to come and ride her instead of me. Bramble threw her onto the road and her arm was in a sling for a month. I even put an ad in the local paper: "Pony for loan." No takers for my betrayal.

The vet carved a hole in her sole with a knife. "This will help," he said. Neglected once more, Bramble had been gorging on the spring grass. The laminitis, the foot disease she'd had when I had first found her, was back. Her front hooves were hot. "That's the pressure released," said the vet. Beige stuff oozed out of her hoof. The smell was like a noise, deafening. It entered my nostrils at the pitch of something pleasant, was almost sweet, but resonated on a register deep down, carrying something base, putrid, up into the air. Bramble's foot tissues, enclosed in horn, couldn't swell to accommodate the excess nutrients and water in the blood vessels. The structures had collapsed like a bruised fruit. She was in agony.

From then on, I did everything the vet told me. I tried to make her walk and asked the blacksmith to come and fit special shoes. After the burning-hot iron was fitted to her hooves, Bramble swayed and staggered and leaned so far back on her haunches that she was almost sitting. I mixed sachet after sachet of painkiller into her favorite foods, but she wouldn't eat anything at all now.

It took a long time for me to accept that I couldn't make it right, couldn't get a job and pay for Bramble to be sent to England for treatment. At night in bed, I conjured up imaginary articles in *Horse and Pony* magazine about her miraculous recovery. But it was already too late. This was one thing Bramble could not run from.

"This needs to be put an end to," said my mother. I wanted her to be wrong, but I couldn't watch anymore. I called the vet. My parents went on holiday, took the boat to France. I watched the dawn come, my arms around her neck.

The vet arrived early in the morning. He wanted to restrain her because he was worried she would smash her way out of the pigsty. I refused to let him touch her.

"How long have you had her?"

"Dunno, nine years," I mumbled.

"Oh God."

I held her head in my hands. Two injections. One was a sedative, he said, one a lethal muscle relaxant. He had to stab hard, to get through the thick muscle of her neck. She jumped up, and a thin line of blood spurted onto the sawdust. She was standing for the first time in days, trembling. Our eyes locked. Her legs crumpled slowly. She fell and I went down with her, cradling her head.

The vet jabbed a finger into the blue pool in the middle of her eye, to check for a muscle response. I curled around her face, blocked him with my back. I stroked her, trying to remove that final awful touch. I stroked her upper eyelid, her eyebrow, her shining cheek. Her velvet lips and nose. I stroked the bristly hairs on her chin, around her nostrils. I stroked her body, her bedsores, her legs, her perfect round feet.

A van was waiting in the yard.

"You should go inside now," said the vet.

They must have dragged Bramble with ropes into the back of the van. I came out and studied the marks in the gravel and I ran. I reached St Helier, five miles away, and sat crying on a bench in the main shopping street, needing to be in the constant wash of people. As it got dark, I walked in the opposite direction from home, around the coast to St Catherine's Bay, through the wind along the breakwater, toward the end where waves crashed gray and horrifying on the black rocks where the conger eels lived. I wanted to be water.

Was it music? Wind on the railings? In one of the granite fishermen's alcoves, where Josie and I had sometimes searched for discarded bits of glittering fishing tackle to treasure, a group of young men sat around a fire with a guitar. In broad Scottish accents they invited me to join them, asked what was wrong. I mumbled that my pony had died. They shared their Marlboros, asked nothing else. Bramble was free now, free from pain. And her death had cut me adrift and set me free too.

"Get out," I heard her say. "Get help, or you will be next." I knew then that I would be leaving. One of the men passed me his phone number on a piece of cigarette packet. I sat there silently, hugging my knees, until dawn. Until I had lived past the day she died.

"She was my responsibility too," my mother said some months after. She was trying hard. She cleared her throat. "You were just a child." It did not take away any of the pain or guilt because I knew it was my fault. Bramble's love had been mine and I had been wholly hers. Whether my eyes were open or closed, she was always there, looking into me, reminding me that never, ever should I take responsibility for another life, not ever. I must keep my distance from every living thing.

I gently close the book about gray whales, put it down beside the bed, and look at Max, sleeping next to me. He is practically part of me. Such fear of inadequacy comes with this love. I could never have fitted him into my old life, I realize. To cope with the fear of getting it wrong, I've had to devote everything to him. But I've reached a balance now. I am suddenly content with not seeing the whales. The scientist in me knows the careful observation and work that went into writing that field guide. Thanks to that, I can understand the whales and appreciate them for what they are. It's enough that they exist. I'm glad we can't see them, that they are somewhere else, away from human interference, just being whales, being free.

We reach Juneau, Alaska's state capital. About twenty of us get into a small boat. Our guide, Emily, is of Tlingit heritage. *Tlingit* translates as "people of the tides." They've cohabited with the whales since time immemorial and have always had a strict taboo against eating them.[1]

"In our creation stories people turned from animal to human and then back to animal," says Emily. Every sentence she speaks is lit with a persistent ecstasy. Her hair is long and she has the grace of something undersea.

Max is also captivated. "Is she talking about the humpback whale, Mummy?"

My little scientist is taking so much in. We are close to land, and the water is so flat it looks solid. The bay is teeming with humpback and killer whales. These "resident" orcas eat fish and live peacefully alongside other whales, Emily says, very different from the "transients" that attack gray whale calves back in the deep waters of Monterey. Humpbacks the size of buses frolic close by.

"Look, a baby orca, Mummy!"

Max's observation is met with an approving smile from Emily. She comes over and he reaches for her hand. "And there's the mom," she says to him.

The mother and baby killer whales leap clear of the water together, splashing silver from their black-and-white suits. Their bodies rhyme, their beauty is distilled sharp above the surface for just one intake of breath.

Then, an adult orca comes straight for the boat.

The dorsal fin cuts silently through the water toward us. The dense black sucks in all color. It is a messenger from the void, ready to devour. The tip is at chest height, even though I'm well above the surface up on deck. Gripping the rail, I can see the body, long, moving with intent. I imagine the helplessness of a gray whale calf. The precision of the orca's path makes me feel like a marked woman. I have a sensation of being above the boat, looking down on myself as the predator approaches, and freeze in primeval horror as the head breaks the surface a few boat lengths away. Is it going to ram us?

The seconds stretch and twirl. There's a collision of memories. Shuttered moments. Me, as a girl, as a woman, frozen in fear.

From above, I see three figures, Emily, Max, and me. Gray whale mothers don't freeze when those toothed torpedoes bear down on their calves. They hold them close, they *move*. I reach for Max's hand, become mobile, and at the last second the orca dives under the boat. I remember Captain Nancy telling me how intelligent they are. Was it playing? Perhaps the orcas enjoy frightening tourists. The alien intelligence glides away, hardly disturbing the surface. I swing my arms, box the air, jump up and down, wave off the orca. Max laughs and copies me.

———

A year or so before her mind started to fail her, my mother came to visit me in London. She said she wanted to talk about us. We went out to a Turkish restaurant. She wore a pink silk taffeta top, and I'd dressed up nice for her too, in my favorite striped cashmere jumper, from an Orla Kiely sample sale. She beamed at the waiter, who asked if we were sisters. My mom threw back her head and laughed, but with her hair still jet-black, her perfect skin, and her energy, talking to everyone in the vicinity, she did always seem twenty years younger. She started on her mackerel.

"Delicious!" she exclaimed at a passing waiter, then looked at me expectantly. "Well now." She smiled.

I was nervous, ordered red wine.

"I'll have the same." My mother rarely drank.

We were very different, I said to open, and that was no one's fault. That was okay. "I can't talk about books and theater like you. Those conversations make me feel stupid, disappointing."

She put her fork down and considered what I'd said, ripped up some flatbread, and moved it around on her plate. I concentrated on shoveling forkful after forkful of moussaka into my mouth.

"When you moved into science, it took you out of my ken." She looked into the distance.

A waiter materialized next to her immediately. "Can I get you something?"

She shook her head, then inquired where he was from. They had a conversation about Turkey and Ireland that took me to the end of my moussaka.

My mother looked back at me. "I've often been afraid for you, Doreen."

Here we go. I struggled not to narrow my eyes at her and sulk, my teenage defense. "But you don't actually see me, you just project your fears. Shit!" I'd missed my mouth, spilled wine down my jumper.

"Swearing shows poverty of language, Doreen."

"It's how I fucking speak," I snapped as I dabbed the stain with my napkin. "You called *me* a shit, don't you remember?" My impersonation of a reasonable adult had lasted all of three seconds. I went to wash my jumper in the bathroom, splashed my face, held on to the basin, took some deep breaths. When I sat down, my mother and I ate neatly, silently.

"Sorry." *Sorry I'm me*, I wanted to say. Perhaps if we got dessert that would help, desserts here were good. I lifted my hand and smiled at the waiters, who didn't notice.

"Everyone does their best, Doreen," she said as though from a great height. She delicately swabbed the last of the mackerel juice from her plate with the bread.

"Shall we get the bill?" Dessert wasn't worth the sermon.

We walked toward the bus stop, my mom's face joyful as she gazed at the evening crowd milling about. I loved watching her when she looked happy, though I never knew whether she really was.

"You know, Doreen, I was looking around the house before I came, and all the beautiful things are from you." I'd brought gifts from every work trip: rainbow glass beads from Ghana, a minty-striped plastic teapot from Burkina Faso, Arabic Scrabble from Jordan, glass seascapes from Prague. I'd wanted to give her the world. I reached to take her hand as we walked through the night.

Back at my flat, I gave her my bed and arranged cushions for me on the floor alongside. I was woken by the god-awful scream of a child in terror. My mom's face was a grimace but she was still asleep. She always slept like a rock, she used to say.

I climbed in beside her and stroked her forehead. "You're safe," I whispered. "I'm here." I kept my arm around her all night. Whatever ghosts from her past came near, they would not get past me. My mom wrote to me later that, for her, our conversation "had put to flight many of the monsters that were between us." But by then I had finally understood that the woman who'd screamed in the night was haunted by other, older monsters.

On subsequent visits to London, she asked repeatedly which tube stop we were getting off at, forgot what we'd been talking about the day before, forgot what she'd been saying in the previous sentence, then in the current one. Her expensive head furniture, her reference points, were being stolen, piece by piece.

"I feel like you are leaving me," I told her.

She laughed. "I want to forget," she said repeatedly, determinedly, over the years of her decline. She got her wish. She was always unreachable, is forever unreachable now.

Max and I say goodbye to Emily and walk off the boat. I hold his hand as he jumps from the deck to the jetty. He pulls me running along the boards.

"I winned!" he shouts as we reach land. I have my son. I make him happy, he makes me happy. This is already so much more than my mother and I had. We are lucky, Max and I.

The next stop on our cruise is Skagway, which means "beautiful woman" in Tlingit.

"That one, Mummy," says Max, pointing at a corner store with an onion dome as we walk into the city. Inside the shop is a selection of matryoshka dolls with an Alaskan influence. I am drawn by one doll, exquisitely painted. The outside is an Inuit woman in furs, paddling her kayak, smiling, with a baby girl in the front, who holds a large pink salmon. Seals and fish play in the sea around. When I look at the woman, I feel proud that I'm paddling my own canoe too and smile back. Inside the woman is a man riding a caribou across the tundra, inside him is a boy with a bow and arrow among musk oxen, then a second little girl carrying another big fish, and finally, in the middle, a tiny husky. The doll is pricey but has a little crack down the front of the woman's jade-green parka, so the cashier allows me to haggle. As she wraps it carefully in tissue paper, I make a wish that my family will grow to match this doll. A few doors down we find a woolly-Siberian-husky hat. Max watches anxiously as I hand it to the saleswoman and puts it on his head immediately when she passes it to him.

"You look wonderful, Max, just like a real husky!" I hold out my hand to take his.

He bites it. "I not Max, Mummy, I Rufus," he growls.

Ghosts of the gold rush start to appear. A sign for Keelar the Money King, advertising, "Barrels of money to loan, liberal advances made. Grips, trunks, gold-pans and picks." We walk past long log cabins. A picture in a church shows a trail of tiny people struggling up through the snow. A memorial to those who died attempting the journey over the mountains at White Pass.

Looking through a pile of leaflets and papers at the local library, a copy of the *Skagway News* dated December 31, 1897, grabs my attention. There's a stern practical guide for women taking the perilous journey north. It catapults me into the past.

"Women have made up their minds to go to the Klondike, so there is no use trying to discourage them," the writer, Annie Hall Strong, warns. "For when a woman will, she will, and you may depend on it."

She continues, "Delicate women have no right attempting the trip; it means utter collapse." For the hardy, she gives a list of essentials to take.

1   good dress.
1   suit heavy mackinaw, waist and bloomers.
1   summer suit, waist and bloomers.
3   short skirts of heavy duck or denim to wear over
       bloomers.
3   suits winter underwear.
2   pair Arctic mittens.

1   pair house slippers.
1   pair heavy soled walking shoes.
1   pair felt boots.
1   pair German socks.
1   pair heavy gum boots.
1   pair ice creepers . . .

The list goes on. I'm gratified to see that she includes chocolate among the essential foodstuffs. More than a thousand women crossed over the Chilkoot or White Pass trails between 1896 and 1900. Annie Hall Strong herself contracted what she termed "acute Klondicitis."

I allow myself to imagine for a moment that I too am an intrepid, pioneering woman at the gateway to the Klondike. Then I remember my Gore-Tex and the cruise ship, and those people struggling up the mountain path. I swear I'll never complain, about anything, ever again. Not even that we haven't seen a gray whale since Baja.

"Mummy, let's go." Rufus is crawling toward the door. I'd wanted to stay longer and read about the Native women. How did the pioneers look to them? Some Native people found jobs hauling supplies or as guides, but the gold rush caused long-term damage to their rivers and forests. The hunter-gatherer Han people, dependent on the salmon run before the arrival of whites, saw their hunting and fishing grounds ruined and were relocated to a reservation. It must have felt like the end of the world.

The children's playground has a view of the peaks and a bust of Mollie Walsh, who traveled the pass alone and set up a grub tent, feeding home-cooked meals to the gold-crazed freighters passing through. Her story doesn't end well. She married but left her husband, taking her baby son to live with another man. Her ex pursued her. She had him arrested for drunkenness and threatening to kill her, but withdrew the accusations, a fatal mistake. He chased, shot, and killed her. I wish Mollie had not looked back, had continued on her way, escaped. It's a strange story to be learning about in a playground, but then Skagway was born out of extreme times. It's also a reminder of how often men have written women's stories for them, decided their fates. I wonder how the women who'd fled domestic abuse that I met in the Jersey Women's Refuge are doing and whether they're back in charge of their lives. I look at Max, who's climbing the ladder to a forest-themed slide. I am mother to a boy who will be a different kind of man.

The following morning we wake up surrounded by glaciers. As we go out on deck, they are laid out around us like a panoramic postcard. The water is green and oily looking, with a scum of ice floating on the surface. It's flat calm, but the presence of our boat is shaking the reflections of the ice and the mountains behind into crisscross pulsating images. Seagulls sail past on the air, screeching. *Choc, choc, choc,* says the water against the boat. Chop, chop, chop, the postcard below us is reordered.

Max runs around the deck, laughing, pretending to be Thomas the Tank Engine. "You're Clarabel, Mummy," he yells. It's an order to follow behind.

As I jog after him, I realize he's been diaper- and accident-free for five days now. That was easy. Promise him a swim and he toilet trains himself. He's definitely a water baby. People are emerging from below for a talk by an ocean ranger. She looks like an ad for a hiking holiday, so healthy, outdoorsy perfect. I sidle up alongside, hoping to catch some of what she's got.

"The Tlingit people were the first observers of glacial change," she tells us. There have been two or three pulses of advance and retreat in the past fifteen million years. The periodic freezing and melting of recent ice ages, only a few million years ago, which is the final moment in whales' fifty-million-year evolutionary history, have created conditions that powered the abundance of the seas. The summer swarms of zooplankton set the scene for the giant whales we know today. Hearing about things that happen in geological time is comforting to me. We don't matter, shrink pinprick small. The glacier fields lining the mountains are like benevolent older relations, watching our toddler-like human activities. We will go and they will continue, shaping the earth as they breathe out and in. But looking at Max, I wonder. The Arctic's changing beyond recognition. These glaciers, how long will they be here? Worldwide, most glaciers are retreating, with the melt contributing to sea-level rise. What's Max going to see in his lifetime? I don't want to think of him being older, just want to stay on this journey with him, in this moment, where he's safe.

"The most dramatic movement has been within the past five hundred years," the ranger says. The Huna Tlingit observed it from the entrance to Glacier Bay, which had young Sitka spruce and mature rivers, with salmon to catch and berries to pick. She describes how, during the Little Ice Age, the Tlingit saw the glacier moving toward them as fast as a running dog, watching the movement from their canoes. I reassess the glaciers, the power they hold. The weight of ice that surrounds us. "The Tlingit have been very important partners here. It's a special place for them because of their ancestral connections." As she speaks, a piece of glacier calves off at the end of the bay and plops into the water. The passengers move toward the rail as one, cameras at the ready.

"After the forward rush, the fastest retreat we know of then began," the ranger continues. Another piece of ice starts to tumble in front of us. I run with the others, to try to film the fall. The ice crashes into the sea.

We hear how Captains Cook and Vancouver sailed up here. Many then came to know about Glacier Bay because of John Muir, the Scottish-born naturalist who came up in 1879 and "coerced," as the ranger puts it, some Tlingit people to guide him. Muir believed that his beloved Yosemite Valley had been carved by ice long ago. His visit paved the way for a succession of scientists and tourists. The ocean ranger sounds like a narrator in a play, introducing the characters, who are mainly white men, as though the story is predictable, planned, with a happy ending. I realize that what I'm listening to isn't really about the glaciers. It's a human history of exploration, scientific discovery, empire building, and colonization. It's not seeing the earth as home, not treating it with love and respect as the Tlingit did. It's categorizing it, owning it, abusing it, wrecking it. The glaciers don't seem quite so friendly to me now. It's as if they're pissed off, throwing things.

The ranger tells us how when snow sticks around, the snow underneath is compacted into ice. The glacier thins and retreats or thickens and advances depending on how much snow there is higher up. As ice bulldozes down the valley, it picks up rock. Max is playing with his toy train on the deck, quietly crawling around people's legs. I get the odd disapproving look, but most people ignore him. It's a constant weighing up of the situation, traveling with a child, checking his safety, watching his mood. I pick him up as we all stampede to the other side of the boat toward another calving, caught up in the sliding, cracking metamorphic-rock-crumbling-as-spectator-sport.

The greasy-looking water in the bay is fresh and salt water mixing, I learn. The ranger doesn't mention climate change or how vulnerable the Arctic and its human and nonhuman residents are to ocean warming. I guess she doesn't want to ruin our day. The humpback whales to whom Glacier Bay is home need the cold waters. It's high stakes, being big and specialized in what you eat. A marine heat wave known as the Blob emerged in 2013, stretching from Alaska to Mexico. It lasted six years and killed off krill, and whales. Fish whose activity is reduced in cold waters were fully awake and competed for less food. Humpback and other whales fed closer to shore, and record numbers became entangled in lines from crab traps and fishing gear. Calves didn't survive and bodies washed up on beaches in Alaska and British Columbia. For a number of reasons related to warm water, they had basically nothing to eat.[2]

It's like I'm in an isolation suit on this boat. We're so contained in our little consumerist bubble that we would probably film the end of the world with mild interest. The pace of human behavioral change in response to what the scientists have been telling us for decades is so glacial, it had also better be as powerful as one. I feel heavy, tired. I've got my period, the first since getting pregnant with Max more than three years ago. It's not the glaciers that are angry, it's me.

The boat is moving, powering north again. I don't like my ice from far away anyway, I like it close up. Moving northward, following the migration route, we are drawing closer to Utqiaġvik. That's where I got close to the ice, in all its emptiness and deadliness, where I got reduced down to my bones by the white. I lived it, breathed it, drank it. In Utqiaġvik, the ice got inside me.

RETURN TO UTQIAGVIK

Latitude: 71° 17' 26" N
Longitude: 156° 47' 19" W

Max launches himself toward me, arms thrashing, teeth bared.

"Sweetie, look, everybody on the plane is wearing their seat belt. Just let me do up the clip."

Earsplitting screams followed by snarling as he tries to bite me. "No, Mummy, Mummy. Nee-nee, Mummy. Pleease, I don't want to take off. I want to *get off*."

We're heading for Utqiaġvik, the penultimate and most northerly stop on our journey. Our plane is full. It's cool in the cabin, but sweat is trickling down my back. Glancing up, as I both fend off attacks from, and try to reassure, my small assailant, I see only men, of varying degrees of toughness. Heavy work boots, jeans, shaven heads, bulging, tattooed muscles. All absolutely still. A guy in a checked shirt mumbles something, but he's several rows off and I can't hear it above Max's roars.

The plane taxis and takes off. Seconds later Max is sound asleep and my heart rate normalizes. It's a short flight to Utqiaġvik. We make a quick stop at the Prudhoe Bay oil field. So that's why the plane is full of men. As the oil workers file past me, I apologize for the screaming during takeoff. Most of them nod or ignore me and carry on past. But the checked-shirt man stops. I press myself into my seat, brace myself for the complaint.

"That's exactly how every guy on the plane felt." He smiles. Suddenly, instead of strangers, I am surrounded by boys who want to go home, and Max's reaction to the tension makes sense.

As soon as I'm through security in Utqiaġvik, I see Jeslie, smiling luxuriously. I can't stop grinning either. It's been seven years. Julia's away for work until tomorrow, so he's come alone to pick us up.

"Only four days?" she'd said indignantly when I called from half-way up the west coast. "Could you have timed it any worse?" I did my best to explain that it was the maximum possible, given the gray whale migration and the monthlong travel limit. Jeslie folds me up into his arms.

"Hello, you must be Max. You coming home with me?" Jeslie bends double to shake Max's hand. Strictly speaking, I should have gone to a different village nearby, Point Hope, where Julia's from, for this leg of the migration. There's a gray whale count in Point Hope. But I couldn't afford to visit both, and I couldn't not come to Utqiaġvik. I walk out of the airport, trying to breathe in the whole place. Why didn't I come back sooner? I was trying not to fly for holidays, worrying about my carbon footprint. Worrying about Billy too. The sadness about our relationship never went away.

Jeslie drives us home to North Star Street. I'm light-headed, slightly hysterical. I notice everything as though it were for the first time. Roads are unpaved because putting anything on the permafrost makes it heat up, melt, and swallow whatever's on top. I take in the prefab houses on stilts, the yards scattered with motorboats, snow machines, umiaqs, trucks, whalebone, and walrus tusks. No picket fences, no pretense of control.

In the house on North Star Street Jeslie makes hazelnut coffee, gives Max a Sailor Boy cracker, and updates me on reported sightings of Sasquatch, a bigfoot, in a neighboring village. He retells a story from my first visit, of the little people, the Iñuqułłigaurat, who rescued someone lost in the snow. The hunter was caught in a whiteout, saw a light, and went toward it. He found a small person who told him to follow in their footprints and led him back home. There is a baby to meet, Jeslie says. JJ and his wife, Lillian, live next door and their new addition is a little girl, Jessa. There is also an absence. Eli, who was such a friend to me, died two years ago in a road accident in Arizona. Jeslie talks about going to identify his son's body. Jeslie is a tall, strong man. It is not an easy picture to carry in my head, Jeslie looking down at the body that had held Eli and his soft voice, the body that had laughed and dreamed as Eli. Max and I sleep in what was his room.

Julia is there when we get up the next morning. This time I am not a paying guest, I am a long-lost London daughter. We talk fast. Julia turns regularly to raise her eyebrows, to laugh or to update me on something as she potters in her kitchen. She makes Max oatmeal and promises him a ride in her truck. We drive to the store. Max runs along the giant aisles. Then we look for Billy, go to the Search & Rescue Base, where I used to play cards with him. I thought about calling to tell him I was coming, but in the end I didn't. I was too scared of creating expectations and didn't know what to say after all the years. This time around the door of Rescue Base is not open to me. Women don't usually go in, and I definitely can't go in with Max. Julia pulls up outside and slides down her window.

"Billy Kaleak?" she yells at a man by the entrance. He goes in, then comes out again, shaking his head. Julia has to go to work, so I take Max to the library and watch as he plays with the other children and the cast of Arctic-animal figurines. Owls, foxes, bears, whales. At home it would be domesticated-farm-animal toys, here it is creatures of the wild. There's even a fiberglass walrus in the playground, where we go with Lillian and her four children. Jessa, the baby, is snug in the hood of Lillian's parka. Katelyn is the eldest and there are two boys, in between. Katelyn and I used to play together with toy cars in the snow outside Julia's house. When I was leaving, I remember she asked Julia how Billy and I were going to see each other, how long it would take him to walk to where I lived. She was seven then. She's grown up into a breathtaking teenager and a basketball ace.

"Can we stay here for years, Mummy?" asks Max, clambering down a ladder from a truck-climbing frame. He sits on one of the boys' knees going down the walrus slide. I want to say yes. I'm not sure why I thought I could be happy anywhere else. Lillian and I talk about everything. Motherhood, juggling work, about my last visit, about Billy. He is best friends with her husband.

"I guess he got it wrong," she says, "thought you guys were more serious than you were."

"He didn't get it wrong." I think about how I left, taking his heart with me, and leaving mine behind.

From the playground the sea ice is visible, still right up against the shore. That's bad news for us. No boating. No whale watching. Deep breaths. We scud rocks across the ice. When we get back, Julia says Billy came by to see me. I feel sick—nervous or excited, I don't know which. I focus on the gray whales, my ostensible reason for being here, and call the local wildlife department. One of their experts, Billy Adams, answers the phone. He's so kind and offers to pick us up the day before we leave, to talk to me about grays. I'm slightly cheered when he tells me they are coming more and more into the bowhead feeding grounds. They are out there now, he says, we just can't see them because of the ice. I ask if it's possible to charter a plane. It is, but not on what remains of my bank loan. I check emails on my phone. I've no reception here so can't make calls, but at least I can connect to Julia's Wi-Fi. I've been firing off inquiries to every whale-watching captain I can find in Kodiak Island, our next and final stop. I've missed the season and will have to hire a boat especially, they say. I reply to their messages, asking how much that would cost. I email a woman who seems heavily involved in a whale festival on Kodiak, then post on an internet community page, explaining our journey. *Can anyone help us find the whales?* I write.

Julia and I talk late into the night about what's been happening in our lives since we last saw each other.

"You're one strong woman," she says. The next day she's working and flies off on another overnight trip to a nearby village. Max and I spend the day with Lillian, and our dinner is pizza at Anne Jensen and Glenn Sheehan's place at NARL, the former naval research base outside town. It was Glenn who first opened the door to Utqiaġvik for me, lent me the scientist's hut for the first night and then pushed me out so I found my way into the community.

"I figured that's what you wanted," says Glenn, as Max explores the living room and sizes up the huge gray fluff ball that is their cat. Anne and Glenn met when they were both young archeologists. Anne's been featured all over for her work at a coastal site, just south of Utqiaġvik, called Walakpa Bay. The work of the team she leads is important to locals. The bones of Iñupiat ancestors are found, often in unmarked graves, everywhere in the region. Anne was at a dig once when a Search & Rescue helicopter landed on the beach. A family had thought there might be the grave of a child in an area where people wanted to drill holes for pilings and needed Anne to check the terrain. Walakpa has an unbroken history of use for camping, fishing, and hunting from four thousand years ago until the present day, but it's vanishing, melting and eroding. Anne is excavating in a race against time as the Arctic Ocean laps at the beach.

With their knowledge of local and international politics, of history, of evolution and deep time, I can't help hoping Anne and Glenn will have some perspective on climate change that will make some sense of it all. Recently they've written of the onslaught of Western-style consultations on offshore development, shipping, and climate, which demand participation from the Iñupiat.[1] To keep their seat in crucial discussions, North Slope residents have had to make huge, ongoing efforts. The processes interfere with culturally and economically important pursuits as they've had to sacrifice time they would have used to go subsistence hunting. After all that, agencies have proceeded as though locals had never spoken. Glenn talks about a demonstration that was held against what was then the US Minerals Management Service, which was in charge of offshore activities. "MMS has no ears" was one slogan. Iñupiat representatives testified on the effects of various activities for years, but their comments were always put in quotes in sidebars. "Agencies and organizations have used public meetings to baffle any effort to do anything," says Glenn.

We get to talking about my journey.

"The grays are coming farther north, into the bowhead feeding grounds," I say importantly, pleased to be able to share an interesting fact.

"Or they might be coming back," says Glenn. "Back to what used to be gray whale feeding grounds before." The Jensen-Sheehans don't do oversimplification. Two reputable information sources, my journalistic maxim learned in the World Service newsroom, don't cut it in this NARL hut. Their knowledge is based on material remains and data, nothing other than primary evidence.

They tell me stories about the Diomedes, two islands in the middle of the Bering Strait. One is American, one Russian. Before the collapse of the Soviet Union, American Iñupiat were able to deliver much-needed supplies from the Diomedes to Russian Yup'ik on the Chukchi Peninsula. Silently, in darkness, they would paddle across the sea in their umiaqs, following historical trading routes. The seal-skin craft didn't show up on Soviet radar, and the officials couldn't tell people apart in their traditional dress. Hearing about the invisible support that came by night, I am set alight. The bravery and simple ingenuity of this mission, the disregard for centralized authority, are rare magic to me. The bonds between Inuit whalers seem to make short work of political and geographical divides.

Once the Soviet Union fell, Glenn tells me, the Russian Yup'ik's economic safety net disappeared. The North Slope Borough mayor arranged for a generator to be airlifted to one of the Yup'ik communities. Hunting was now vital to survival, and the borough authorities also flew a Yup'ik elder who had hunted gray whales in his youth from Chukotka to the United States for an operation to remove his cataracts. Once his sight was restored, he was able to teach a new generation how to catch grays.

Craig George had told me how gray whales forged an unlikely international alliance in Utqiaġvik during the Cold War, in October 1988. Operation Breakthrough was an effort to rescue three grays that were starving to death. A hunter, Roy Ahmaogak, found them stranded in a hole in the ice and called the biologists. It touched off a global media frenzy. Craig's office got hundreds of calls a day. Nightly TV footage was broadcast from the ice, showing the captive whales. The US Department of State asked for Soviet help, and Moscow sent two icebreakers. Iñupiat hunters cut a trail of breathing holes to a channel forged through the ice by the Soviet ships. Two of the three whales made it at least part of the way to freedom. The operation cost well over a million dollars and was both widely applauded and criticized. It wasn't possible to establish for sure whether the emaciated animals survived, but it showed how strongly people all over the world feel about whales, and how these beloved sea creatures can bring even enemies together.

Glenn drives Max and me back down the road to town. I don't know how on earth I'd be useful here, but I ask if he can think of any jobs I might be able to do. Glenn says it's unlikely, but he'll give it some thought. We get an early night. Tomorrow morning we've our meeting with Billy Adams from the wildlife department.

"Nee-nee, Mummy." Max falls asleep within seconds. I wriggle away to check my email. The Kodiak Whale Fest organizer, Cheryl, has replied, saying she can lend me binoculars to whale watch from land, and there's a response to the message I posted on the Kodiak community page. A mom has given her email. *I can't promise we'll find whales but we can take the kids to the beach and try.* I message both of them. *Fingers crossed for some gray whales*, I type, trying to sound hopeful rather than desperate. I put my phone on the bedside table and arrange myself around Max. As I drift away from the day into sleep, my mind wanders not to whales but to Billy, my Billy. His dark eyes, his fingers entwined with mine.

Billy, I'm here. I've come all this way to see you. I haven't got much time. When are you coming? Billy, what will we do?

Max and I are up early the next day, ready and waiting for Billy Adams. A truck rolls up outside JJ and Lillian's house. I go to check it out. The motor's running but there's no sign of the driver. It's chilly, so after a few minutes I go back inside. I don't want to seem pushy, so I wait forty-five minutes before calling the department office. I get the secretary. Billy Adams chartered a plane to Point Hope for the day, she says. He was going to take us, came to pick us up, but didn't see any sign of us. For a moment I can't fathom it. The truck. The driver that wasn't in it. It must have been him. I must have missed him by seconds. I say thank you to the secretary in a small voice.

I imagine us soaring over the sea ice, over my grays. We were so close. I fold in two, onto the sofa, try to muffle my sobs with my sleeve. What am I doing chasing whales? Who do I think I am, Doctor bloody Doolittle? I wanted to show Max our connection to the grays, but there's no connection, just a badly planned trip. I give up. I just want to go home now. Either that or stay here forever.

"What wrong, Mummy?" Max has left his dolphin jigsaw to investigate. He lays a hand on my shoulder. "Don't worry, Mummy, you will feel better soon, everything will be okay," he says firmly. Shocked at his assurance and ashamed that a two-year-old is taking care of me, I pull myself together, more or less.

Julia comes in, just off the plane. She sees my face. "You okay?"

"Fine." I wipe my eyes. "How was your trip?"

She gives an exasperated sigh. "Fine? That's why your eyes are all red?"

"It's just . . . The whales." I gesture toward Max. "We've come so far." Julia's face says nothing. I look away, draw in a long, shuddering breath. "I just thought we'd see him," I say plaintively to the floor.

"Him?"

"Them, I mean. Them—the whales."

We have Julia for one whole day. I push the grays to the back of my mind. The Kaleaks hold a barbecue in our honor out on the deck, cook us the best salmon. Lillian's children show Max their toy snowmobiles. We admire Katelyn's purple sneakers.

"We have to get basketball shoes, Mummy," says Max.

"That's so adorable," says Lillian. "You like Katelyn's basketball shoes?" And to me, "Maybe you found something he likes." I think we've found everything both of us like, all in one place. Julia gives Max an Iñupiaq name, as she gave me on my first visit. I got her name, he gets Jeslie's, Akootchook. Max has an Iñupiaq granny now, I saw my Iñupiaq mom. That's wonderful, that's enough, it has to be.

We clear up slowly. Billy still hasn't come. I consider my options. I can't ask Julia to run me around looking for him and can't wait in his hut for him the way I used to.

Inside the living room that is still like a big soft hug, with its sofas and pink carpet, Julia opens the glass cabinet where the whale I carved for her sits on a shelf. I was proud of that one, the piece of bone was hard to work with, but the whale came out for me. She takes something from inside, presents me with the eardrum of a bowhead. "This is for you."

It is an unbelievable thing to hold, rests heavy across both my palms like a giant cowrie shell, bone curving protectively around the middle ear, with heavy frills on the internal lips. It's a structure inherited from the whales' deerlike ancestors. The way it thickens and separates in different areas helps maximize resonance underwater. I hold it to my ear, seeking a message in the whispers. The deepest sea envelops me. I cannot think of anything to say, except thank you, over and over. I don't think I can take the eardrum through customs. I'd probably need a permit, so I reluctantly ask Julia to keep it for me.

"Was good to see you," she says. "Make it longer next time, okay?"

Julia, Max, and I are already in bed in our respective rooms when the phone rings. I know instantly who it is and why she is calling.

I hear Jeslie pick up. "Slow down, I can't understand what you're saying. . . . She's already in bed." Katelyn is calling me over from next door. Billy is visiting her parents, I just know it. She remembered us together, always thought of us as together. I close my eyes tight. How could he leave it so late? Should I go? Take Max with me? Might Billy be drunk though? I can't take Max, can't leave him here. I have to see Billy. I can't go. There's a loud pulsing in my head, sounds like the sea on shingle, making Jeslie's conversation difficult to hear.

"Yup, your *aaka*'s in bed too. Okay, good night." By *aaka* Jeslie means "granny," Julia. It's definitely Katelyn. Jeslie doesn't knock on my door to wake me. The room is suddenly so cold. I'm shaking. I'll get up. Am I getting up? It's as if I'm not even in my body. I smell rather than feel that I'm sweating. I can't move. I can hear my heart thudding like hooves.

I cannot say goodbye.

We oversleep. I must have set my alarm wrong. We've got one hour to get to the airport for the flight to Anchorage. Julia dresses Max while I shove clothes into our rucksack.

"Katelyn called for you last night," says Jeslie. "Billy was visiting next door. I told her it was too late to call." Sometime in the night, Billy left Lillian and JJ's and walked back to Nanook Street, away from me.

Julia holds Max in departures. He laughs and chants his Iñupiat name: "Akootchook, Akootchook." Their smiles nearly meet in the middle of the photo I take. For a moment I remember Billy's face, watching me seriously as I walked through the same airport security seven years ago.

I leave Utqiaġvik for a second time. This family, the Kaleaks, have held me gently, once again, in all my confusion and despair. I have been remade by this place, by what has happened here. I follow the line of people out to the plane, holding on to Max's hand. I think of the grays moving breath by breath through the ocean.

Billy and I weren't meant to meet this time. Max is too young. We can't go out hunting yet. It was only seven years. I'll come back in fifteen years, as he said. I'll see him then. Whenever I look up at the sky and see white, he is there anyway, like the white sky that blanketed our journeys when we traveled together. Whenever I see sun, shining through the blue sky, he is there, on one of those bright Arctic days out on the ice. Whenever I see stars, he is there, watching them on his own from Kaleak camp. He is always there when I look up because I know the sky can see us both. I still love him and I'm sure he knows. Billy and his boat will be there when it's time for me to die. I'd like to slip into the sea at the end, with the whales. Perhaps we'll be together then. I always imagined that we'll know each other when we are old.

KODIAK ISLAND

Latitude: 57° 47' 24" N
Longitude: 152° 24' 26" W

By the time we get to Kodiak Island, our final stop, we have chased the gray whales by bus, boat, train, and plane, up the west coast of Mexico, the United States, and Canada, to the northernmost tip of the Alaskan Arctic. In Los Angeles, they'd already left, just days before. In Monterey, there were humpbacks only. Depoe Bay, too stormy to go out. At sea between Seattle and Vancouver, one humpback. On the boat from Vancouver to Whittier, humpbacks and orcas. Utqiaġvik, too icy to whale watch, and I missed the Department of Wildlife Management's chartered plane by seconds.

Our last chance is this remote island in the Gulf of Alaska, where we'll spend the final two days of our journey. As our tightly packed flight buzzes lower, Kodiak reveals itself, an untamed sprawl of green in an austere blue ocean. There are plenty of coastal nooks and crannies where whales might be feeding. We are not the first, nor the only ones, to come here looking for them. Locals and ecotourists from all over the world gather every April to celebrate the return of the migrating grays. We are two months late, but the festival organizer,

Cheryl, has assured me by email that whales are still about. That is, if I had a boat to go and look for them. I've got just about enough money left for two days' food. Hiring a boat would cost a thousand dollars. It's not going to happen.

The airport is small and crammed with a surprisingly large number of people. A procession of long cases slides onto the baggage carousel, full of hunting and fishing gear, I guess. Or maybe full of parts meant for secret and deadly weapons. My imagination has been fed by reading a guidebook on the plane. Kodiak is home to a major US military base. It's been a strategic outpost for both Russia and America during its history. There's mystery here and I have my own small mystery to solve. I received instructions by email: *Look for two small girls chasing each other around and a mom chasing them around, that'll be me.* Alex, a math teacher, has offered to take us whale-spotting from the beaches and cliffs. I know her as soon as I see her. She's unruffled amid the chaos of the arrivals hall, while her children play on a bench. We barely have time to speak. Max, five-year-old Tatiana, and three-year-old Alicyn, plus the buggy, car seat, and our collection of bags and toys need to be organized through the crowd into Alex's minivan. We synchronize immediately, directing children and grappling luggage through the parking lot. I feel relief. This must be a sign that the journey is finally going right.

Alex drops us at our B&B, which is on a hill a little outside the city center. Through the window, the sea is just visible, shining under the setting sun. I'm not venturing out, though. I'm worried about the island's celebrity resident, the Kodiak bear. It's an unusually large subspecies of brown bear that sometimes attacks people and likes human food and garbage. Max and I tell each other stories about baby whales coming up to the boat when they hear him singing, until we fall asleep.

I'm up early the next morning, looking forward to meeting a local biologist, Bree Witteveen. I'm hoping she'll give me insider information on where to find the grays. Max and I go to the harborside café where we've arranged to meet. When Bree appears, she brings sea air in through the door with her. She's wearing ripped jeans and her hair is short and tousled. I want her life.

"I'm a humpback girl," she fires off almost immediately, pointing out that gray whales are less charismatic, don't breach as much, and generally stay away from boats in the open sea. I loyally defend them, their iconic endurance and the astonishing playfulness of the mothers and babies we met in the Mexican lagoons. How exciting to be talking whales again. They feel near. Before we part, Bree gives me a precious tip. I fancy I've earned her respect in our clash over the titans of the ocean. A drive through the mountains, she says, would take me to Pasagshak Beach. That's where the grays hide from the predatory orcas, or "jerks," as Bree describes them. She saw a killer whale attacking a calf right here in the harbor once as the mother made indescribable noises.

"I recently saw a juvenile gray rolling in the surf over at Pasagshak," she tells me.

A baby whale rolling by the beach! I can't wait for Max to see that, and to tell Alex, who, within minutes, has arrived to sweep us up in her van. We set off, loaded up with children, toys, and clothes, only stopping briefly at the Java Flats café for provisions. Max chooses enormous cookies labeled *Electric Banana Monkey Love*. We are all set.

Following Bree's instructions, we head toward Pasagshak, a wide, sheltered bay cradled by cliffs on either side. As we come out of the mountains, we take a sharp turn toward the coast. I can't believe what I'm seeing. The view is entirely fog. This isn't happening. The binoculars borrowed from Cheryl feel like a joke. It had all seemed so promising.

We walk down the pebbles onto the sand, to check visibility closer to the water. We can't even see the sea, never mind any grays. The children make whale-song noises to try to call them in. I turn toward the sound of the surf. The fog engulfs my last hope. It hurts to breathe.

"Let's go," Alex says softly. We trudge back to the van and wind up the hill away from the coast. As we surface above the ghostly fog, an ominous sign appears: WELCOME TO KODIAK LAUNCH COMPLEX. Gray buildings squat on the horizon with huge satellite dishes near the road. We are being treated to a close-up view of one of the island's most classified sites. From there, Alex tells me, the US government fires rockets and launches satellites into space. Polaris, Aries, Athena, and Minotaur have blasted into polar orbit from Kodiak. As we drive past the base, I wonder how much we really know about what's being tested there and whether the operations affect the whales. I learn later that a hypersonic test missile launch after our visit ended badly. The rockets propelling it exploded seconds after liftoff, and several beaches had to be closed for a while because of whatever had landed there. That caused consternation among some locals. If it was too dangerous for people even to go on the beach, what went into the sea?

As we drive, the children drop off to sleep one by one and Alex probes gently, "Why gray whales, what made you come?"

I'm monosyllabic. I can't justify the expense and effort that I've put into this stupid quest. Then I tell her. I might as well, I can't look any more idiotic. I describe Max's birth and how I summoned the whales, how I thought they'd helped me, how I wanted to thank them. Then the words are all over the place as I finally admit to myself and to Alex that the whales were meant to take me back to Billy. They couldn't, though, because I was too scared of losing him again.

"It's our last chance to see them. For Max to see that we've followed them all this way, to show him their strength."

Alex listens to it all, drives in silence for a while.

"I really want this journey to be successful for you," she says eventually. We drive in the direction of the town. "Would you like to come to my nephew's birthday party?"

I'm taken aback. I have been demanding and then miserable company. Evening draws in with Max dancing like a crazy thing in the sunset among Alex's relatives. She tells them about our journey, and I start to see the funny side of my expectations. *I will go to the sea and press the on button. The waters will calm. Whales will appear for me to wonder at.*

"Dance, Mummy!"

It's hard to refuse an invitation to dance with Max. We sample a tower of key lime cupcakes and dance some more. Alex introduces me to her husband, Chris, who used to spend weeks at sea, fishing for the world-famous Alaskan king crab. It's an incredibly arduous and dangerous profession. Faced with a person of such vast experience, I feel embarrassed to admit I'd expected whales to play ball with my schedule.

"You came all the way here to see gray whales and you haven't seen any? That's bullshit!" exclaims Chris. This man of the sea surely knows what he is talking about. Alex told me that once, out fishing, Chris stitched up his own wound after an injury. He wanders off, chatting on the phone. I resolve to stop thinking about whales, look around at the community that's welcomed me, a total stranger. We are introduced to the family chickens.

Then Chris reappears. "We have a plan." The plan comes in the shape of a boat, about twenty-five-feet long, owned by Brian, Chris's old friend. They've arranged an impromptu trip out halibut fishing tomorrow, to treat themselves for Father's Day. Alex and the girls, Max and I, are all going too, Chris says. "On the way, we'll make a small detour to the gray whale feeding grounds." The feeding grounds, the holy grail, in search of which the whales and their calves, and Max and me, have traveled thousands and thousands of miles. This man might as well have a direct line to the god of the sea, Sedna herself. And he is on my side.

———

It's an early, cold start among the fishing vessels the next morning. At the back of the boat, *Raven II*, I obsessively examine every inch of sea as we cruise out of the harbor. Max stays up front, out of the wind, sitting on Chris's knee as he powers the motor up fully. We round Cape Chiniak, on the easternmost tip of Kodiak, in a freezing blast. I grip the side of the boat. My knuckles are bright white. I remember the story of Sedna, clinging to the boat by her fingertips as she fled her bird husband. I imagine her sinking, wounded and hopeless, down through the water, whales streaming from her hands. Thousands of whales, sweeping the seafloor, stirring up a muck, restoring the balance of the ocean. Sedna falling upward, caught in the whales' slipstream as they rise, ripping through the surface and bursting into the air. Great masses of displaced water meeting behind them as they breach, with a thunderclap that echoes off the contours of the earth.

The boat slaps down over a wave and I open my eyes to a dark, crumpled quilt of sea. No whales, of course. Then, far off, close to the cliffs that roar openmouthed out of the water, I see two gargantuan black backs rise among the waves.

"There's your whale!" Chris shouts triumphantly. It feels churlish, but I can't hide my disappointment that they are humpbacks, not grays. The boat moves southwest between Kodiak and the tiny island of Ugak, toward the mouth of the bay of the same name. A gasping blow to starboard. Humpbacks again. They submerge, then the air seems to still as I see the humpbacks aren't alone. Not far off, a pair of slate-gray knuckled backs gently break water. My mouth drops open and I hold my breath, trying to imprint indelibly on my mind what I've just seen. I examine the world again, find nothing but waves. Were my eyes lying? Perhaps it was wishful thinking, a mirage. A few seconds, another blow. I scramble for binoculars. Unmistakable. My barnacled grays are here. It's them, really them, a mother and a juvenile, feeding alongside the humpbacks. Signature heart-shaped blows, mottled gray-and-white humps are suddenly everywhere. They have made it. They are here. They have come all the way from Mexico, like us.

"Whale tail," shouts Max.

A chorus erupts.

"There!"

"Look, whale!"

"There, Mummy, there!" Max tallies five, then Tatiana takes over and reaches thirty-nine before losing count. Grays escort us on either side as the boat dances slowly eastward. I'm leaning so far overboard I have to catch myself to avoid toppling in. My eyes sting with salt but I try not to blink, I don't want to miss a moment. I can't believe they've done it, we've done it. This is a wonder of the world, a migration like no other. I can't feel my body, can't speak. Every surge of water, every pair of rolling backs splitting the waves, every breath fracturing the air with spray, sings of life and survival through unimaginable distances and challenges. This is what the ocean should be like everywhere, what it once was. Populated, a home to wild and teeming communities, to the most incredible of lives, journeys, and ecologies. I try to summon a sign that the mother and baby we first sang to in Mexico are here. Through the binoculars, I see an adult rotate ninety degrees onto her side, into a position where she can observe us fully. I see her eye. She's watching us.

After an hour or so, Chris steers us slowly away. I am smiling so widely my cheeks ache. Throughout this journey the whales have brought me so many friends. They've shown me a world where there is help, if only I can keep reaching out. It was worth having no hope so I could experience being given it back.

That evening Max and I stand at the top of a cliff among purple fireweed blossoms, looking out at the sea with Chris, Alex, and their girls, soaking up the shimmer of blue.

"Bye-bye, migration of the gray whales," says Max, repeating the mantra he's heard over and over as I explained our journey to everyone we met. "Bye-bye, whales," he says softly, "thank you for coming." He waves at the sea. Then he remembers I'm there, turns. "Mummy, do you want to say bye-bye to the whales?"

We leave Kodiak at four in the morning. As dawn breaks on the deck of the *Kennicott* ferry, Max and I take a walk in the cold, salty air. We look out to sea with bleary eyes. Shapes appear among the waves to port. The shapes seem to be coming straight for us. By now I can spot them a mile off. It's a pair of grays. I have no doubt that these are the mother and baby we met at the beginning of our journey.

"Look, Max!" I point. We jump together on the deck, waving. "The whales you sang to, they followed us, to say goodbye."

Who could convince us otherwise?

As they approach the side of the boat, they blow glittering hearts of spray up into the air in unison. I have time to gasp. Then they dip under the ferry and are gone.

HOME

One morning, six years after our journey with the gray whales, I find an email from Julia. We haven't called each other for nearly a year. *Doreen, I really need to speak to you as soon as possible. Please call.* It's too late in Alaska now. I'll have to wait until evening. All day I speak in a slightly higher pitch than normal. I must have a cold coming on. I skype Julia as soon as the children are asleep.

"We buried Billy a week ago, Doreen."

For the briefest instant, I am nothing. No movement, sound, or thought. Too soon I am back, trapped in the moment of knowing. I keep very still.

"Oh God," I whisper.

"The strangest thing. He texted Lillian your photo just two days before. It was as though he knew, it was really like he knew he was going to die."

My right eye releases one fat tear after another. My left eye is completely dry. There's a delay on the line. I have to say something, but I'm not here. I'm in Billy's hut, finding it empty.

"Did they find the whale?" I ask finally. "The little iŋutuq I made for him out of whalebone, was it still there?"

"I don't know who's been there. No one had seen him for days so his family called the officials and they broke in." He was working at the Heritage Center as a security guard. It was early January, the darkest part of the year. They found him in bed, clutching his chest, a week after he'd died. Those same days I had been writing about him.

He'd gone to the doctor with chest pains. They sent him home.

"Oh God," I repeat. I should have been there. I should have stopped it happening. I think about him living and breathing, all that time, without me. "I thought I would see him again. I thought he would always be there."

"He was always talking about you, Doreen. He was talking about you until the end."

Under the sea ice, where the light filters down as though through heavy clouds, aġviġit are massing. A group moves toward the open water. They burst the surface. At their center, one whale is flowing, rather than swimming. The aġviq moves as if alive, supported and steered by the others. I read about this bowhead funeral in an Alaskan magazine. Now Billy is gone, I call on the whales again, to help me say goodbye.

Following the lead, toward the open ocean, aġviġit carry the body of their beloved kin. The procession gasps, heaves, through the meeting of air and water. The party stays close, gently nudging the central animal on a path away from land. The body, heavily scarred from the battles of life, is borne far, far out before it is let go. The whales dance and dive, down past where the light fades, where the color gives way to black. In the deep sound layer, they remember him. Voices call in from far around the ocean basin, singing goodbye. Returning to the surface, the bowheads trace the body for the last time. Then they leave him, surrounded by music, wheel away from him in the dark water. He moves slowly, glides, his body taken by the waves, as if he were flying home. Billy did not die alone.

My children sit around the kitchen table, eating pancakes, hooting and screeching. They have ganged up on me, rejected the porridge I'd been about to make for breakfast.

"Not again," said the middle one, sighing and rolling their eyes.

Max leaped into action. "I'll make pancakes."

"This one," my uncle Patrick said to me, the last time we were in Ireland, with the youngest having claimed his lap, "is just like your mother at that age."

"I can well believe it," my cousin Sally said. "She's such a wee boss." I marvel at how loving and articulate, how riotous, my children are, how unafraid of me. Perhaps Max really is a change maker, as my mother and the woman in Depoe Bay foretold. Perhaps all children are. Perhaps it was the whales. Who knows. On a shelf next to the talisman sperm whale sits the Inuit matryoshka doll family, inexactly fulfilled. For one thing, instead of the husky in the middle, we have two cats.

Max and I go swimming. He's ten years old, tall and excitable. I watch as he folds, bunches, flows, like an animal made in the water. I've kept him off school for the morning so we get some time, just us, without his siblings, who are too little to swim properly.

"Watch me. Watch me swim underwater, watch me dive!"

I watch. I can't take my eyes off him. I'm so happy watching his joy.

After I've dropped him at school, I sit at the kitchen table, going through videos of my first Arctic trip, looking for dialogue and images that will help me remember. I thought at first the tapes were lost. They'd been hidden away in a box for more than a decade. I was sitting on the ice next to the lead when I filmed this shot. The screen is white, cut diagonally by a dark streak of water. Looking down along the lead, the water sky looks like a plume of smoke coming from a far-off fire, dispersing into a soft gray caress as it widens above me in the blinding white. It's early in the hunt. There are no whales yet, not even belugas. I am playing with different angles, putting the camera on the path to film boots passing as crew members walk between the camp and the blind, the ice barrier that blocks the whales' view. The path is shining, lightly dusted with snow. Leif throws crumbs for a disheveled small sparrow that hops along it.

"Maybe a whale bird," he says. What on earth is it doing out there? I wonder. What an opportunist. Such a lot of effort to put in for a few crumbs, flying miles from land over the desert of ice. Recently I've been thinking about food security.

"The weather is angry," the elder told Warren Matumeak eighty years ago. Looking at the bird and the crumbs, I realize I am biting my thumb. I've left indents. The bird hops out of view. I am still looking at the ice, thinking about the bird, when I hear Billy.

"You wanna go up?" he asks. He is standing behind me, out of the shot, as though he were just over my shoulder, in my kitchen, speaking to me. As though he has come to visit, from where the white and ice and whales are.

"I can't go, in case I miss a whale."

He must be going back to town to pick something up. "You should go rest, in the tent," he says.

I'm mesmerized, swallowed by the landscape, haven't thought of resting. He's been watching, has understood all this about me. I haven't really noticed him yet, but he's already taking care of me.

"I will," I say. "I'll just finish filming first."

He gently leaves. Thirteen years later, I am suddenly crying. I want to tell him I'm coming.

———

I long to see Julia and the family. She, Lillian, and I share our news on the phone. I send pictures of my children. Katelyn got a basketball scholarship, Jessa is getting big. I listen to Julia's soft melodic voice, the slow rhythm of her speech. I let it all calm me.

"It's December and there's still no ice," she tells me. There isn't much to say. It's 2019 and not as if we didn't know this was coming. "It was, like, sixteen above yesterday." Hardly any bowheads were seen in the fall. The community caught only one on November 16, later in the season than any bowhead in anyone's memory. The whales are changing their migration patterns. The ice as the Iñupiat elders knew it, as the ocean knew it, as our global weather systems knew it, as the whales knew it, is gone. Billy is gone. Jeslie is gone now too. Eli, Van, Warren, and Jeffrey are gone. As Julia and I talk, I see Billy standing there smiling at me, see his face turn serious, see him shrug.

"Looking back," my dad said once, "I find it's not that relationships ended that's important, it's that they happened at all." Grief is woven through all of life after all, it means we are connected. I can't stop death. I can only face it and my life with as much openness and generosity as possible.

For some people, the end of the world came a long time ago. The Han, forcibly relocated to a Klondike reservation. The Iñupiat in the epidemics of the nineteenth century. I remember the gray whale mothers, fighting to the end for their calves. I think of the bowhead calf speaking to Harry Brower in his dream. I think of Aaŋa, the hunter trapped and pulled down by the ice floe, how he smiled when it was time to go.

Billy and I had such a short time together. We didn't even have a night as I'd known them. It was just one long day in the light. We actively kept in touch for only a year. But his gentleness and kindness toward me remain unparalleled in anyone I have met before or since.

I wonder if there is a memory of us together out there, on the tundra, or somewhere in the ocean, where aġviġluat and aġviġit, grays and bowheads, meet.[1] I wonder if a whale mind somewhere might remember our voices mingled above.

I can still see Billy's wide brown hardworking hands as clearly as if they were holding mine.

"Things are always changing," he says tenderly. "Watch out for cracks, be ready to move. And don't think so much, you'll have an aneurysm." That still makes me smile. "You did good out there, Doreen." I hold on to my memories of him and to those fleeting months that I was Doreen Kaleak, when the world cracked open and the love poured in.

With the recognition of false balance, media coverage of climate has changed, gradually. In 2018, the UK's broadcasting regulator Ofcom ruled that the presenter of the domestic BBC radio program *Today* had not sufficiently challenged false claims made by Lord Nigel Lawson, a climate skeptic and former British conservative finance minister, who appeared on the program following an interview with Al Gore. Lawson claimed global temperatures had declined over the previous decade, dismissing Gore's statements as "the same old claptrap." The BBC apologized for breaching editorial guidelines and, shortly after Ofcom's ruling, managers issued guidance on covering climate that admitted "we get it wrong too often."[2]

In autumn 2020, I'm back at work. A coworker asks me if we need a skeptic to balance a piece about how hurricanes can be intensified by climate change. I reassure them, categorically, no. When the conversation ends, I feel heavy. It should be simple, but even with the organization's stance now so clear, sometimes the most well-intentioned of people still get it wrong.

A few weeks later I'm having lunch with a group of old journalism school classmates. We are talking shop, and someone brings up the increase in extreme weather events, and climate change. Rob, my former coursemate, says that the debate isn't whether climate change is happening anymore, it's what's causing it. Always a good story-teller, Rob has drawn the attention of the whole table, but no one contradicts him. I stare at the menu. It's tapas. I had practically the same conversation at work recently. I don't want to go through it again. I get up to go to the restroom. But then something makes me sit back down. I think of the oil company executives meeting in their boardrooms three decades ago, and that whole ocean, all the life there that has no voice. I say that in fact there's no need to debate the cause of climate change, as the science was settled years ago. At first Rob disagrees. As I'm explaining how the IPCC works he concedes.

"Perhaps you've more up-to-date information than me."

There are nods from across the table.

Change is always a process, I suppose. It takes work, careful dia-log, and sometimes it feels like nothing is happening. I remember the glaciers, their movement sometimes imperceptibly slow, sometimes as fast as a running dog.

There is no longer any shortage of eyewitnesses to the impacts of climate change. There are wildfires, floods, heatwaves, catastrophic storms. Leading medical journals across the world, more than two hundred of them, jointly call for emergency action, saying the failure of world leaders to cut emissions and keep the global temperature rise below 1.5 degrees centigrade and to restore nature is "the great-est threat to global public health."[3] There are scientists crying on TV.

"I'm a father," says one, as his voice cracks. In the Amazon, an-other Indigenous forest protector is found shot dead near his village.[4]

Now, climate is an easy pitch. Sometimes, in the office, that makes me feel useful, pleased. Sometimes, at home, when the rush of the day has faded, and my children are in bed, the science makes me cry too.

It would be easy to spot the gray whales along the migration route the year I've been finishing this book, 2021, because they've been washing up dead on the beaches. A die-off began in 2019. Emaciated juveniles and adults have been found. Food scarcity in the Bering Sea is the suspected cause, possibly along with growth of the gray whale population.[5] The Sounders are still going. Earhart, the ghost-shrimp pioneer, was hit by a boat off Whidbey Island in 2017. She's scarred but seems to have recovered.

Lockdown during the coronavirus pandemic led to what has been called an anthropause,[6] a reduction in human activity.[7] A temporary and partial decolonization of the ocean. It gave scientists a chance to listen in on a less disturbed undersea world, and to hear it recover. Marine mammals started to behave differently, were seen in parts of the ocean they'd not frequented for decades. A generation of whales have never known the sea so quiet, researchers said.

"The moment we turn the volume down, the response of marine life is instantaneous and amazing," said Carlos Duarte, who led the study. A significant drop in underwater noise was registered in seabed observatories. Scientists scanned the sound signals for new conversations, aware that there may never be another chance to hear some of them. We are getting noisier and the voices are getting quieter. For some species they are silenced.

Here comes the gray whale, from the beginning of time, say the fossils. They pose a question too. *All this you know. Now what?* Human thought and intention are part of the global ecosystem, the most powerful driver of change, the most powerful obstacle that both we and the whales have encountered through millennia. We are writing the next chapter of the story of all life on earth.

I'm taking the children to school and nursery on a hot summer's day. Above the road is a heat shimmer, and the exhaust fumes hang heavy. My hands are sweating on the handlebars of my bike, and I'm thinking about the Met Office confirmation that the UK climate is changing.[8] The man quoted in the paper mentioned warmer and wetter winters, heavier summer rain, more heat waves. Farmers predicted wheat yields would be down by a third. The UK could become a net importer of grain rather than an exporter.

What is going to happen to us all?

Cycling through the heat, I remember the whales' endurance, the resilience and adaptability they have inspired in people. I think of the relationships they helped communities forge across the Bering Strait, between Iñupiat and Yup'ik, and the cooperation between the US and Soviet governments in Operation Breakthrough. The color of the dappled deep murk rising to the surface comes to mind. I keep my eyes on the surface, just ahead, looking for light. Whales do not deal in hope or hopelessness, or even in getting stressed-out, I remember. They deal in living, taking each breath as it comes. They keep moving. They travel to the end of the earth for themselves and their young. I remember their eyes, their breathing, and how one year Max and I shared their journey. I remember that they saw us, heard us, and that when I was desperate, they helped me rewrite our story.

"Do you still remember our whale journey?" I ask Max later, at home. "How far we traveled with them?"

He lifts the pencil drawing he's working on so I can see. It's a humpback, shaded and barnacled, with an inquisitorial eye. His pictures of grays are stuck all over the fridge, all over the walls. In Max's room there's the photo of Julia holding him in the airport and one of him patting a calf in Mexico.

"I think of them swimming along sometimes," he says. "I like to imagine swimming with them."

Throughout the history of the Iñupiat and of Western industrialization, whales have carried these human cultures, and throughout my life, in some sense, they have carried me. They carried my son and me to a new beginning. I am woman, human, animal. I bore my child in water. We sang to the whales. We listened to them breathing. We listened to the sea. This book is what I heard.

AUTHOR'S NOTE

The relationships and events depicted in this book are as honest as I can make them, based on my experiences and memories. Some characters have been disguised, with changed names, physical descriptions, and other distinguishing details.

I'm giving a share of my proceeds from this book to the Barrow Volunteer Search & Rescue and the Iñupiaq Studies Department at Iḷisaġvik College, Utqiaġvik.

Barrow Volunteer Search & Rescue is an organization of volunteers who often risk their own lives looking for missing people in extreme Arctic weather conditions on the tundra and sea ice. Donation checks made payable to Barrow Search & Rescue, Inc., can be sent to: PO Box 565, Barrow, AK 99723-0565.

Iḷisaġvik College is Alaska's first federally recognized tribal college and is unapologetically Iñupiat: https://www.ilisagvik.edu /about-us/unapologetically-inupiaq/. The Iñupiaq Studies Department develops and delivers full- and part-time programs aimed at indigenizing the curriculum, incorporating the history, values, traditions, and knowledge of the Iñupiat. You can learn more about the work of the college and can also donate on their website, at https:// www.ilisagvik.edu/we-are-ilisagvik/.

ACKNOWLEDGMENTS

I would like to thank the women who made this book happen. Jessica Woollard, whose belief in it after reading the first few pages helped me believe in it too. Rose Tomaszewska, for her commitment and heart. Valerie Steiker, for her warmth and the careful listening that gave me so much courage. Sally Howe, for her precision of thought on the final draft, and Zoe Gullen and Steve Boldt, for their eagle eyes on the details.

Quyanaqpak to the Kaleak family and Kaleak crew, especially Billy Uvyuaq Kaleak, Julia Singaaġauluk Kaleak, Jeslie Akootchook Kaleak, and Lillian Tuigan Kaleak, for everything.

Thank you to Damian Le Bas, Ramita Navai, and the other judges for the Royal Society of Literature's Giles St Aubyn Award 2021, which gave me an unimaginable moral and financial boost. Thank you to the Society of Authors for the generous Foundation Grant and to the Eccles Centre & Hay Festival Writer's Award for the encouragement and financial help that came with being placed on the short list. Thank you to Pierre Vicary for his steadfast support on many occasions, and to Leyla Yusuf and all at NUJ Extra, which kept me afloat during the most difficult of times.

Thank you to the experts, scientists, and academics who were so patient and generous with their time in helping me with clarifications and explanations. Dr. J. Craig George for all the reading and for the "swimming head," Dr. Barbara Bodenhorn, Professor Hugh Brody, Dr. Glenn Sheehan, Dr. Anne Jensen, Debby Dahl Edwardson and George Saġġan Edwardson, Etta Patak Fournier, Professor Jason Hall-Spencer, Dr. Kate Stafford, Alisa Schulman-Janiger, Dr. Sue Moore, Dr. Linda Weilgart, John Calambokidis, Dr. Frank Fish, Professor Hal Whitehead, Professor Patrick Hof, Dick Russell, and Dr. Sven Uthicke. Any inaccuracies or oversights in the book are mine, and I welcome clarifications and updates on the science as it evolves.

To the writers and readers who have given transformational feedback, advice, and encouragement throughout: Elena Cosentino, John W, Sarah Austin, Stef Pixner, Carrie Gracie, Judith Keany, Elena Seymenliyska, Penny Wincer, Kate Burls, Anna Vickery, Sarah Davis, Dr. Andrea Mason, Dyan Sheldon, Maria Y, Emma B, and Mavis Gulliver. At Goldsmiths, Professor Blake Morrison, Dr. Erica Wagner, Dr. Tom Lee, and Ardu Vakil. Plus all the members of the Goldsmiths Isolatin' Workshop, especially Christine Marshall and Nikkitha Bakshani.

To Maureen Bebb, formerly of the BBC Alexander Onassis Bursary Trust, who set me off on my journey in 2006. And Frances Marsh and Eleanor Peers from the Scott Polar Research Institute, for their help during lockdown.

To the professionals and volunteers everywhere who make women's shelters and food banks possible.

Thank you to my dad for giving me the sea, for having my back, and for granting me freedom on the page by telling me it was important I write what I wanted. Thank you to my mother and my siblings, and to my extended family in Jersey, Ireland, and Canada for the love and support. Thank you, over and over, to the friends and neighbors whose kindness and generosity helped keep me and my family going as I wrote, including Carolina S-B, Ann T in Cornwall, Kathy C, Barbara B, Jacqui, and Rebekah.

NOTES

Prologue

1. S. E. Moore and K. M. Wynne, "Gray Whale Occurrence and Forage Southeast of Kodiak Island, Alaska," *Marine Mammal Science* 23, no. 2 (February 2007): 419–28, https://www.researchgate.net/publication/229786781_Gray_whale_occurrence_and_forage_southeast_of_Kodiak_Island_Alaska.

Los Angeles

1. Neela Banerjee, Lisa Song, and David Hasemyer, "Exxon Believed Deep Dive into Climate Research Would Protect Its Business," *Inside Climate News*, September 17, 2015, https://insideclimatenews.org/news/17092015/exxon -believed-deep-dive-into-climate-research-would-protect-its-business/.

2. Neela Banerjee, Lisa Song, and David Hasemyer, "Exxon's Own Research Confirmed Fossil Fuels' Role in Global Warming Decades Ago," *Inside Climate News*, September 16, 2015, https://insideclimatenews.org/news/16092015 /exxons-own-research-confirmed-fossil-fuels-role-in-global-warming/.

3. M. S. Glaser, "CO2 'Greenhouse' Effect, internal briefing material. Exxon Research and Engineering Company," November 12, 1982, http://www .climatefiles.com/exxonmobil/1982-memo-to-exxon-management-about -co2-greenhouse-effect/, pp. 1, 4–5.

4. Joseph M Carlson, "Internal Memo on the Greenhouse Effect," Exxon spokesperson, March 8, 1988, http://www.climatefiles.com/exxonmobil /566/, pp. 2, 7.

5. G. Supran and N. Oreskes, "Assessing ExxonMobil's Climate Change Communications (1977–2014)," *Environmental Research Letters* 12, no. 8 (2017): 084019.

6. Sharon Y. Eubanks, "Testimony Before the Subcommittee on Civil Rights and Civil Liberties. Section E. Denial Campaigns in the Media and False Solution," June 26, 2019, https://congress.gov/116/meeting/house/110126 /witnesses/HHRG-116-GO02-Wstate-EubanksS-20191023.pdf, p. 8.

7. Joe Walker, "Draft Global Climate Science Communications Action Plan," American Petroleum Institute, April 3, 1988, http://www.climatefiles.com /trade-group/american-petroleum-institute/1998-global-climate-science -communications-team-action-plan/, pp. 4–5.

8. "Understanding the #ExxonKnew Controversy," ExxonMobil, February 10, 2021, https://corporate.exxonmobil.com/Sustainability/Environmental -protection/Climate-change/Understanding-the-ExxonKnew -controversy#WhatisExxonKnew, introduction, paras. 1 and 2.

9. Martin Hoffert, "Written Testimony to Civil Rights and Civil Liberties Subcommittee Hearing on: 'Examining the Oil Industry's Efforts to Suppress the Truth about Climate Change,'" October 23, 2019, https:// docs.house.gov/meetings/GO/GO02/20191023/110126/HHRG-116 -GO02-Wstate-HoffertM-20191023.pdf, p. 4, para. 8.

Utqiaġvik: Aġviq

1. Bowhead whale: singular: *aġviq*; plural: *aġviġit*.

2. K. M. Stafford, C. Lydersen, Ø. Wiig, and K. M. Kovacs, "Extreme Diversity in the Songs of Spitsbergen's Bowhead Whales," *Biology Letters* 14, no. 4 (April 2018), https://royalsocietypublishing.org/doi/full/10.1098 /rsbl.2018.0056.

3. National Snow and Ice Data Center press release, "Sea Ice Decline Intensifies," September 28, 2005, https://nsidc.org/news/newsroom /20050928_trendscontinue.html, para. 1.

4. Melanie Phillips, "Global Warming or Global Fraud?," *Daily Mail*, April 28, 2004, https://www.dailymail.co.uk/columnists/article-229940/Global -warming-global-fraud.html.

5. David McKnight, "A Change in the Climate? The Journalism of Opinion at News Corporation," *Journalism* 11, no. 6 (December 2010): 693–706, https://doi.org/10.1177/1464884910379704, abstract para. 1.

6. https://www.bbc.co.uk/news/stories-53640382, para. 40; "Deep Pockets, Useful Allies," presenter Peter Pomerantsev, producer Phoebe Keane, episode 9 of *How They Made Us Doubt Everything*, BBC Radio 4, 3:57, https://www.bbc.co.uk/programmes/m000lf9n; Ted Koppel, "Is Science for Sale?," ABC's *Nightline*, February 24, 1994, 14:50, 12:20, 13:30, 5:30, http://www.climate files.com/denial-groups/1994-nightline-special-science-for-sale/.

7. "Ripe for Change," *Guardian*, June 30, 2005, para. 3, https://www.the guardian.com/environment/2005/jun/30/climatechange.climatechange environment6.

8. Naomi Oreskes and Erik M. Conway, *Merchants of Doubt: How a Handful of Scientists Obscured the Truth on Issues from Tobacco Smoke to Global Warming* (London: Bloomsbury Press, 2010), p. 6.

9. Centre for Climate and Energy Solutions, "Climate Basics. Climate Science. IPCC Fifth Assessment Report. Growing Certainty on the Human Role in Climate Change," https://www.c2es.org/content/ipcc-fifth -assessment-report/, bottom table: 2001.

10. Ewen MacAskill, Patrick Wintour, and Larry Elliott, "G8: Hope for Africa but Gloom over Climate," *Guardian*, July 9, 2005, para. 13, https://www.theguardian.com/politics/2005/jul/09/uk.society.

11. H. Brower and K. Brewster, *The Whales, They Give Themselves* (Fairbanks: University of Alaska Press, 2004), p. 41.

12. Ibid.

13. K. Bergsland, R. Senungetuk, E. Kakinya, and S. Paneak, *Nunamiut Unipkaaŋich Nunamiut Stories* (Barrow, AK: North Slope Borough Commission on Iñupiat History, Language and Culture, 1987).

14. R. Fortuine, "The Health of the Eskimos, as Portrayed in the Earliest Written Accounts," *Bulletin of the History of Medicine* 45, no. 2 (March–April 1971): 97–114, 113 para. 4, https://pubmed.ncbi.nlm.nih .gov/4932202/.

15. National Library of Medicine, "Native Peoples' Concepts of Health and

Illness, Native Voices, Timeline/Defining Right and Responsibilities/1900: Measles, the 'Great Sickness,' Strikes Alaska Natives," https://www.nlm.nih .gov/nativevoices/timeline/392.html.

16. Robert J. Wolfe, "Alaska's Great Sickness, 1900: An Epidemic of Measles and Influenza in a Virgin Soil Population," *Proceedings of the American Philosophical Society* 126, no. 2 (1982): 98, para. 1.

17. Richard Gray, "The Places That Escaped the Spanish Flu," BBC, October 24, 2018, https://www.bbc.com/future/article/20181023-the-places-that -escaped-the-spanish-flu.

18. A. Keenleyside, "Euro-American Whaling in the Canadian Arctic: Its Effects on Eskimo Health," *Arctic Anthropology* 27, no. 1 (1990): 11, para. 2.

19. Barbara Bodenhorn, personal communication, June 2021.

20. H. Napolean, *Yuuyaraq: The Way of the Human Being* (Fairbanks: University of Alaska Fairbanks, 1996), p. 11 para. 2, https://epub.sub.uni -hamburg.de/epub/volltexte/2011/4559/pdf/Yuuyaraq.pdf.

21. Ibid., p. 11, para. 4.

22. Ibid., p. 2, para. 1; p. 11, para. 2; p. 14, para. 1; 15 para. 1.

23. S. Z. Klausner and E. F. Faulks, *Eskimo Capitalists: Oil, Politics and Alcohol* (New Jersey: Allanheld, Osmun & Co., 1982), p. 115.

24. B. Bodenhorn, *Documenting Family Relationships in Changing Times*, vol. 1, *Family Portraits: Oral Histories; Sharing Networks*, vol. 2, *Sources of Stress: Loss of Autonomy in Relation to Land and Animal Resources, the Court System, Education, Alcohol*, chap. 21: "Alcohol: Culture & Politics," p. 329 (Barrow, AK: North Slope Borough Commission on Iñupiat History, Language and Culture Commission, 1988).

25. E. Burch, "Property Rights Among the Eskimos of Northwest Alaska," paper delivered at the 4th International Conference on Hunter/Gatherers, London School of Economics, 1986, pp. 7–10.

26. J. Hamer and J. Steinberg, *Alcohol and Native Peoples of the North* (Washington, DC: University of Press of America, 1980), introduction.

27. Bodenhorn, *Sources of Stress*, chap. 20: "Alcohol on the North Slope: Household Summary," p. 316.

28. W. Hunt, *Arctic Passage* (New York: Charles Scribner's Sons, 1975).

29. W. H. Oswalt, *Eskimos and Explorers* (Novato, CA: Chandler and Sharp, 1979), p. 293.

30. B. Bodenhorn, *Documenting Family Relationships in Changing Times*, vol. 1, *Family Portraits: Oral Histories; Sharing Networks*, and vol. 2, *Sources of Stress; Loss of Autonomy in Relation to Land and Animal Resources, the Court System, Education, Alcohol*, chap. 21, "Alcohol: Culture & Politics" (North Slope Borough Iñupiat History Language and Culture Commission, 1988), p. 330.

31. Ibid., chap. 21, p. 331; H. Brody, "Indians on Skid Row: Alcohol in the Life of Urban Migrants," in Hamer and Steinberg, eds., *Alcohol and Native Peoples of the North*, pp. 210–66.

32. Barbara Bodenhorn, personal communication, March 2021.

33. Bodenhorn, *Sources of Stress*, chap. 20 ("Alcohol on the North Slope: Household Summary"), p. 317.

34. Capt. C. L. Hooper, *U.S.R.M. Report on the Cruise of the U.S. Revenue-Steamer* Corwin *in the Arctic Ocean, November 1, 1880* (Washington, DC: Government Printing Office, 1881).

35. R. Fortuine, *Chills and Fever: Health and Disease in the Early History of Alaska* (Fairbanks: University of Alaska Press, 1989), pp. 296–97.

36. Bodenhorn, *Sources of Stress*, chap. 20, p. 318.

37. Ibid.

38. Ibid., chap. 20, p. 319.

39. Ibid., chap. 20, p. 299.

40. Bodenhorn, *Sources of Stress*, chap. 20, p. 303.

41. Ibid., chap. 20, p. 301.

42. Ibid., chap. 20, p. 300.

Laguna Ojo de Liebre

1. Dick Russell, *Eye of the Whale: Epic Passage from Baja to Siberia* (New York: Simon & Schuster, 2001), p. 46.

2. Erle Stanley Gardner, *Hunting the Desert Whale: Personal Adventures in Baja California* (New York: William Morrow, 1960).

3. "The Surprisingly Social Gray Whale," Dr. Toni Frohoff interviewed by Terry Gross, *Fresh Air*, NPR, July 13, 2009, https://www.npr.org/transcripts /106541921?t=1610631193989, paras. 10, 13.

4. Charles Siebert, "Watching Whales Watching Us," *New York Times Magazine*, July 8, 2009, para. 33, https://www.nytimes.com/2009/07/12 /magazine/12whales-t.html?_r=2&scp=2&sq=toni%20frohoff&st=cse.

5. D. Toren et al., "Gray Whale Transcriptome Reveals Longevity Adaptations Associated with DNA Repair, Autophagy and Ubiquitination," bioRxiv, September 1, 2019, https://doi.org/10.1101/754218. Now published in *Aging Cell*, https://doi.org/10.1111/acel.13158, abstract, para. 1.

6. Nick Pyenson in Robert Sanders, "Gray Whales Likely Survived the Ice Ages by Changing Their Diets," *Berkeley News*, July 6, 2011, para. 13, https://news.berkeley.edu/2011/07/06/gray-whales-likely-survived-the -ice-ages-by-changing-their-diets/.

Utqiaġvik: How to Wait

1. T. Lowenstein, *Ancient Land: Sacred Whale* (London: Bloomsbury, 1993), 148, para. 1.

2. Whaling captains: singular: *umialik*; plural: *umialiit*.

3. G. W. Sheehan, *In the Belly of the Whale*, Aurora: Alaska Monograph Series VI (Anchorage: Alaska Anthropological Association, 1997), p. 20, paras. 1–3.

4. A. Jensen, "The Archaeology of North Alaska: Point Hope in Context," in *The Foragers of Point Hope: The Biology and Archaeology of Humans on*

the Edge of the Alaskan Arctic, ed. C. Hilton, B. Auerbach, and L. Cowgill, Cambridge Studies in Biological and Evolutionary Anthropology (Cambridge: Cambridge University Press, 2014), pp. 11–34, https//:doi .org/10.1017/CBO9781139136785.00.

5. Charles D. Brower, *Fifty Years Below Zero* (London: Robert Hale, 1948), photo no. 14.

6. H. Brody, *The Other Side of Eden* (London: Faber and Faber, 2001), p. 242, para. 3.

7. Ibid., p. 246, para. 2; p. 248, para. 3.

8. F. Darnell and A. Hoem, *Taken to Extremes: Education in the Far North* (Oslo, Norway: Scandinavian University Press, 1996), and O. A. Kawagley, *A Yupiaq Worldview: A Pathway to Ecology and Spirit* (Prospect Heights, IL: Waveland Press, 1995).

9. Bodenhorn, *Sources of Stress*, chap. 12, p. 121, para. 12.

10. Ibid., chap. 12, p. 122.

11. Ibid., chap. 12, p. 129.

12. Eben Hopson, "Inupiaq Education," in *Cross-Cultural Issues in Alaskan Education*, ed. Ray Barnhardt (Fairbanks: Center for Cross-Cultural Studies, CHRD, University of Alaska Fairbanks, 1977), para. 3, http://www .alaskool.org/native_ed/historicdocs/PEOPLE/INUP_EDU.html.

13. Brody, *Other Side of Eden*, p. 189, para. 3.

14. Diane Hirshberg and Suzanne Sharp, *Thirty Years Later: The Long-Term Effect of Boarding Schools on Alaska Natives and Their Communities* (Anchorage: Institute of Social and Economic Research, University of Alaska Anchorage, 2005), p. 11, para. 5; p. 12, para. 5; p. 14, para. 4, https:// iseralaska.org/static/legacy_publication_links/boardingschoolfinal.pdf.

15. Harold Napoleon interviewed by Rachel Naninaaq Edwardson in *History of the Iñupiat: Nipaa I!itqusipta / The Voice of Our Spirit*, 2008, DVD, at 13:45, https://vimeo.com/126341194.

16. Jasmine Clark and Randy Hobson, "PC (USA) Leaders Issue Apology to Native Americans, Alaska Natives, and Native Hawaiians," Presbyterian Church US website, February 9, 2017, https://www.pcusa.org/news /2017/2/9/pcusa-leaders-issue-apology-native-americans-alask/.

17. Stephen E. Cotton, "Alaska's 'Molly Hootch Case': High Schools and the Village Voice," *Educational Research Quarterly* 8, no. 4 (1984): 30–43, http://www.alaskool.org/native_ed/law/mhootch_erq.html.

18. Bodenhorn, *Sources of Stress*, chap. 12: "Schooling on the North Slope," p. 132.

19. The situation with schooling in Utqiaġvik, and across Alaska more generally, is complicated. Many different schools were attended with very different memories and views of what happened at them.

20. Hirshberg and Sharp, *Thirty Years Later*, p. 7, para. 5; p. 8, para. 4.

21. Pat Aamodt, *Impact of ANCSA in the Arctic Slope. Taking Control: Fact or Fiction? A Curriculum Unit Plan*, 1993 message to students of the North Slope Borough from Mayor Jeslie Kaleak, http://www.alaskool.org/native_ed/curriculum/aamodt/tc.html.

22. *Healthy Alaskans*, vol. II, *Strategies for Improved Health. Creating Healthy Communities: An Alaskan Talking Circle. Difficult Decisions: Barrow Local Options Stories*, Alaska Department of Health & Social Services, Division of Public Health, November 2002, p. 51, para. 7; p. 49, para. 5, http://dhss.alaska.gov/dph/Documents/HA2010/Volume%202/06_Barrow.pdf.

23. Bodenhorn, *Sources of Stress*, chap. 19, p. 287.

24. Jana McAninch, "Baseline Community Health Analysis Report," North Slope Borough Department of Health and Social Services, July 2012, p. 24, para. 4, http://www.north-slope.org/assets/images/uploads/Baseline CommunityHealthAnalysisReport.pdf.

25. Pronounced "Aanga," *ŋ* makes an *ng* sound.

26. Charles Wohlforth, *The Whale and the Supercomputer: On the Northern Front of Climate Change* (New York: North Point Press, 2004), p. 9, para. 3.

27. "Alaska Operations: Alpine," ConocoPhillips Alaska, https://alaska.conocophillips.com/who-we-are/alaska-operations/alpine/, para. 5.

28. Martha Itta in "Nuiqsuit Subsistence Users Speak Out against Court Decision," press release, America's Arctic, May 26, 2015, https://trustees.org/court-upholds-u-s-army-corps-of-engineers-decision-on-colville-delta-development/.

29. "Sustainable Development: Environment: Air Quality," ConocoPhillips Alaska, https://alaska.conocophillips.com/sustainable-development /environment/air-quality/, para. 2.

30. Sabrina Shankman, "Surrounded by Oil Fields, an Alaska Village Fears for Its Health," *Inside Climate News*, August 2, 2018, para. 59, https:// insideclimatenews.org/news/02082018/alaska-north-slope-oil-drilling -health-fears-pollution-risk-native-village-nuiqsut/.

31. Rosemary Ahtuangaruak speech at Ken Salazar's public meeting on outer-continental-shelf energy development, April 14, 2009, ArcticOceanAlaska, at 1:28, 1:40, https://www.youtube.com/watch?v=zRsjTuNMHY8.

32. Rosemary Ahtuangaruak, personal communication, June 3, 2021.

33. V. Stepanyan, "The Danger of Industrialization: Air Pollution in Alaska's North Slope and Its Implications for the Community of Nuiqsut" (Anchorage: Alaska Community Action on Toxics, February 2019).

34. W. Yan, Y. Yun, T. Ku, G. Li, and N. Sang, "NO_2 Inhalation Promotes Alzheimer's Disease–Like Progression: Cyclooxygenase-2-Derived Prostaglandin E_2 Modulation and Monoacylglycerol Lipase Inhibition -Targeted Medication," *Scientific Reports* 6 (2016), article #22429.

35. Chen Xu et al., "The Novel Relationship between Urban Air Pollution and Epilepsy: A Time Series Study," *PLoS One* 11, no. 8 (29 August 2016): e0161992, https://doi.org/10.1371/journal.pone.0161992.

36. Lesley Fleischman et al., "Gasping for Breath: An Analysis of the Health Effects from Ozone Pollution from the Oil and Gas Industry," Clean Air Task Force, 2016, https://www.catf.us/resource/gasping-for-breath/.

37. Noah Scovronick (lead author), "Reducing Global Health Risks Through Mitigation of Short-Lived Climate Pollutants, Scoping Report for Policymakers," World Health Organization, Climate and Clean Air Coalition, hosted by the United Nations Environment Programme, 2015, http://apps .who.int/iris/bitstream/handle/10665/189524/9789241565080_eng.pdf;jsessi onid=D91C2FA393BE2FB55C5AD79161128AE7?sequence=1.

38. Rosemary Ahtuangaruak, personal communication, May 15, 2021.

39. State of Alaska Department of Health and Social Services, "Investigation into a Report of Increased Respiratory Illness in Nuiqsut Due to Possible

Exposure to Gas from the Repsol Gas Blowout and Smoke from the Alpine Fields Facility," June 2012, p. 7.

40. Ibid., p. 3.

41. Shankman, "Surrounded by Oil Fields," para. 32.

Scammon's Lagoon

1. Jonathan Amos, "Whaling's 'Uncomfortable' Scientific Legacy," BBC News website, June 25, 2017, para. 10, https://www.bbc.co.uk/news/science -environment-40385783.

2. Lyndall Baker Landauer, *Scammon: Beyond the Lagoon* (Pasadena, CA: Flying Cloud Press, 1986), p. 17, para. 6.

3. Charles Melville Scammon, *The Marine Mammals of the North-Western Coast of North America, Described and Illustrated; Together with an Account of the American Whale-Fishery* (San Francisco: J. H. Carmany, 1874), p. 32.

4. Smithsonian National Museum of American History exhibition, *On the Water*, "Fishing for a Living: Commercial Fishers—Whaling; Processing the Catch," para. 2, https://americanhistory.si.edu/onthewater/exhibition /3_7.html.

5. Wesley Marx, "The Scene of Slaughter Was Exceedingly Picturesque," *American Heritage* 20, no. 4 (June 1969): para. 29, https://www.american heritage.com/scene-slaughter-was-exceedingly-picturesque#3.

6. Roy Chapman Andrews, *Whale Hunting with Gun and Camera: A Naturalist's Account of the Modern Shore-Whaling Industry, of Whales and Their Habits, and of Hunting Experiences in Various Parts of the World* (New York: D. Appleton, 1916), chap. 15: "Rediscovering a Supposedly Extinct Whale."

7. S. Elizabeth Alter, Eric Rynes, and Stephen R. Palumbi, "DNA Evidence for Historic Population Size and Past Ecosystem Impacts of Gray Whales," *Proceedings of the National Academy of Sciences* 104, no. 38

(September 2007): 15162–67, https//:doi.org/10.1073/pnas.0706056104, abstract, para. 1.

8.   Andrew J. Pershing et al., "The Impact of Whaling on the Ocean Carbon Cycle: Why Bigger Was Better," August 26, 2010, abstract, para. 2, https://doi.org/10.1371/journal.pone.0012444.

9.   N. Pyenson, *Spying on Whales* (New York: Viking, 2018), p. 205, para. 2; p. 208, para. 1.

10. Ralph Chami et al., "Nature's Solution to Climate Change," *Finance & Development* 56, no. 4 (December 2019): para. 14, https://www.imf.org/external/pubs/ft/fandd/2019/12/natures-solution-to-climate-change-chami.htm.

Utqiaġvik: Whale Snow

1.   Kim Murphy, "U.S.-Japan Whale Feud Playing Out in Alaska," *Los Angeles Times*, June 17, 2002, para. 17, https://www.latimes.com/archives/la-xpm-2002-jun-17-na-whale17-story.html.

2.   Mark Sweney, "BBC Radio 4 Broke Accuracy Rules in Nigel Lawson Climate Change Interview," *Guardian*, April 9, 2018, para. 1, https://www.theguardian.com/environment/2018/apr/09/bbc-radio-4-broke-impartiality-rules-in-nigel-lawson-climate-change-interview; Fiona Harvey, "BBC Coverage of IPCC Climate Report Criticised for Sceptics' Airtime," *Guardian*, October 1, 2013, para. 1, https://www.theguardian.com/media/2013/oct/01/bbc-coverage-climate-report-ipcc-sceptics.

3.   Steve Jones, "A Review of the Impartiality and Accuracy of the BBC's Coverage of Science," in *BBC Trust Review of Impartiality and Accuracy of the BBC's Coverage of Science*, July 2011, p. 55, para. 1, and p. 66, para. 2, https://www.bbc.co.uk/bbctrust/our_work/editorial_standards/impartiality/science_impartiality.html.

4.   Dominic Ponsford, "BBC News Sticking Two Fingers Up to Management Says Prof Behind Trust's Science Impartiality Report," *Press Gazette*, March 26, 2014, para. 7, https://www.pressgazette.co.uk/bbc-news

-sticking-two-fingers-management-says-prof-behind-2011-report-science
-coverage-impartiality/.

5. O. C. Salles et al., "Strong Habitat and Weak Genetic Effects Shape the Lifetime Reproductive Success in a Wild Clownfish Population," *Ecology Letters*, November 26, 2019, https://doi.org/10.1111/ele.13428.

6. D. Laffoley et al., "Evolving the Narrative for Protecting a Rapidly Changing Ocean, Post-COVID-19," *Aquatic Conservation: Marine and Freshwater Ecosystems* 31, no. 6 (November 25, 2020), https://doi .org/10.1002/aqc.3512.

7. "Pteropods," in "Module 7: Ocean Acidification, Red Tides, and Monster Jellyfish," *Earth in the Future: Acidification: Effect on Plankton*, Penn State University, para. 1, https://www.e-education.psu.edu/earth103/node/648.

8. S. Uthicke, P. Momigliano, and K. Fabricius, "High Risk of Extinction of Benthic Foraminifera in This Century Due to Ocean Acidification," *Scientific Reports* 3, article 1769 (2013): abstract, para. 1, https://doi.org /10.1038/srep01769.

9. Cracks: singular *quppaq*; plural *quppaich*.

10. Brower and Brewster, *Whales, They Give Themselves*, 41 para. 3.

11. J. E. Zeh et al., "Current Population Size and Dynamics," 1993, in *The Bowhead Whale*, ed. J. J. Burns et al., Society for Marine Mammalogy Special Publication no. 2, vxxxi, 409–89, http://www.north-slope.org /assets/images/uploads/International_Whaling_Commission_History_ Page.pdf.

12. Thomas F. Albert, "Influence of Harry Brower, Sr., an Iñupiaq Eskimo Hunter, on the Bowhead Whale Research Program Conducted at the UIC-NARL Facility by the North Slope Borough," in *Fifty More Years Below Zero*, ed. David W. Norton (Calgary, Canada: Arctic Institute of North America, 2000), p. 268, para. 3, http://www.north-slope.org /assets/images/uploads/The%20Influence%20of%20Harry%20Brower, %20Sr.pdf.

13. B. Streever, "Science and Emotion on Ice: The Role of Science on Alaska's North Slope," *Bioscience* 52 (2002): 183.

14. Polar bear: singular *nanuq*; plural *nannut*.

NOTES

The Sea of Cortés

1. Joe Roman, "Of Whales and War," *San Francisco Chronicle*, February 14, 2008, para. 4, https://www.commondreams.org/views/2008/02/14/whales-and-war.

2. Shane Gero, Hal Whitehead, and Luke Rendell, "Individual, Unit and Vocal Clan Level Identity Cues in Sperm Whale Codas," *Royal Society Open Science* 3, no. 1 (January 1, 2016): abstract, para. 1, https://doi.org/10.1098/rsos.150372.

3. Hal Whitehead, personal communication, February 2021.

4. Debora Mackenzie, "Seismic Surveys May Kill Giant Squid," *New Scientist*, September 22, 2004, paras. 7, 8, https://www.newscientist.com/article/dn6437-seismic-surveys-may-kill-giant-squid/.

5. B. G. Würsig et al., *Gray Whales Summering off Sakhalin Island, Far East Russia: July–October 1997. A Joint U.S.-Russian Scientific Investigation*, final report by Texas A&M University, College Station, TX, and Kamchatka Institute of Ecology and Nature Management, Russian Academy of Sciences, Kamchatka, Russia, for Sakhalin Energy Investment Company Limited and Exxon Nefteygaz Limited, Yuzhno-Sakhalinsk, Russia, 1999.

6. J. Tollefson, "Air Guns Used in Offshore Oil Exploration Can Kill Tiny Marine Life," *Nature* 546 (2017): 586–87, https://doi.org/10.1038/nature.2017.22167.

7. J. Semmens et al., "Are Seismic Surveys Putting Bivalve and Spiny Lobster Fisheries at Risk?" (presentation at Oceanoise 2017 Conference, Vilanova i la Geltrú, Barcelona, Spain); R. Day et al., *Assessing the Impact of Marine Seismic Surveys on Southeast Australian Scallop and Lobster Fisheries*, FRDC Report (Hobart, Australia: University of Tasmania, 2016).

8. Linda S. Weilgart, "A Brief Review of Known Effects of Noise on Marine Mammals," *International Journal of Comparative Psychology* 20 (2007): 159–68, para. 12, https://escholarship.org/content/qt11m5g19h/qt11m5g19h_noSplash_927ab626a4957971501692989d0917d9.pdf.

9. M. E. Dahlheim, H. D. Fisher, and J. D. Schempp, "Sound Production by the Gray Whale and Ambient Noise Levels in Laguna San Ignacio, Baja

California Sur, Mexico," in *The Gray Whale:* Eschrichtius robustus, ed. M. L. Jones, S. L. Swartz, and S. Leatherwood (New York: Academic Press, 1984), pp. 511–41.

10. Anne E. Simonis et al., "Co-occurrence of Beaked Whale Strandings and Naval Sonar in the Mariana Islands, Western Pacific," *Proceedings of the Royal Society B* 287, no. 1921 (February 26, 2020), https://doi.org/10.1098/rspb.2020.0070; Weilgart, "Brief Review of Known Effects," pp. 159–68, para. 13.

11. NOAA (National Oceanic and Atmospheric Administration) and US Department of the Navy, *Joint Interim Report: Bahamas Marine Mammal Stranding Event of 15–16 March 2000* (Washington, DC: US Department of Commerce, 2001).

12. Discovery of *Sound in the Sea*, "Feature Sound: Acoustic Thermometry of Ocean Climate (ATOC)," University of Rhode Island and Inner Space Center, https://dosits.org/resources/resource-categories/feature-sounds/atoc/.

Utqiaġvik: Belonging

1. Inupiaq for "thank you very much."

2. J. C. George et al., "Age and Growth Estimates of Bowhead Whales (*Balaena mysticetus*) via Aspartic Acid Racemization," *Canadian Journal of Zoology* 77 (1999): 576.

3. J. C. George et al., chap. 21: "Age Estimation," in *The Bowhead Whale:* Balaena mysticetus: *Biology and Human Interactions*, ed. J. C. George and J. G. M. Thewissen (Cambridge, MA: Academic Press, 2020), p. 316.

4. J. C. George, S. E. Moore, and J. G. M. Thewissen, "NOAA Arctic Report Card 2020: Bowhead Whales: Recent Insights into Their Biology, Status, and Resilience," 2020, https://doi.org/10.25923/cppm-n265.

5. M.-V. Guarino, L. C. Sime, D. Schröeder, et al., "Sea-Ice-Free Arctic During the Last Interglacial Supports Fast Future Loss," *Nature Climate Change* 10 (2020): 928–32 (esp. p. 932), https://doi.org/10.1038/s41558-020-0865-2.

6. "Agviqsiugnikun: Whaling Standards for Barrow and Wainwright:

Honoring the Learning of Our Young Whalers," prepared by Jana
Pausauraq Harcharek, North Slope Borough School District, 2002.

7. "Bowhead Whale Overview," Species Directory, NOAA Fisheries, para. 2,
    3, https://www.fisheries.noaa.gov/species/bowhead-whale.

8. Kaj Birket-Smith, *The Eskimos* (London: Methuen, 1959), p. 100;
    A. L. Crowell and E. Oozevaseuk, "The St. Lawrence Island Famine and
    Epidemic, 1878–80: A Yupik Narrative in Cultural and Historical Context,"
    Arctic Anthropology 43, no. 1 (2006): 1–19, https://doi.org/10.1353/
    arc.2011.0105.

9. Craig George, personal communication, February 2021.

10. Barry Lopez, *Arctic Dreams* (New York: Scribner, 1986), p. 4, para. 4.

11. Ibid., 4 para. 2.

Palos Verdes to Monterey Bay

1. Dick Russell, *The Eye of the Whale* (New York: Island Press, 2001), p. 242,
    para. 6; p. 243, paras. 1–2.

2. P. S. Ross et al., "PCB Concentrations in Free-Ranging Pacific Killer
    Whales, *Orcinus orca*: Effects of Age, Sex and Dietary Preference," *Marine
    Pollution Bulletin* 40, no. 6 (2000): 504–15.

3. "Health Effects of PCBs. Learn about Polychlorinated Biphenyls (PCBs),"
    US Environmental Protection Agency, https://www.epa.gov/pcbs/learn
    -about-polychlorinated-biphenyls-pcbs#healtheffects.

4. J. N. Lauren et al., "Ecological Knowledge, Leadership, and the Evolution of
    Menopause in Killer Whales," *Current Biology* 25, no. 6 (March 16, 2015):
    746–50, https://www.sciencedirect.com/science/article/pii/S09609822
    1500069X.

5. Robert L. Pitman et al., "Humpback Whales Interfering When Mammal-
    Eating Killer Whales Attack Other Species: Mobbing Behavior and
    Interspecific Altruism?," *Marine Mammal Science*, July 20, 2016, https://
    doi.org/10.1111/mms.12343.

6. Nan Hauser, interviewed by Al Shapiro, "How a Whale Saved a Marine Biologist from a Shark," *All Things Considered*, NPR, January 12, 2018, transcript, para. 23, https://www.npr.org/2018/01/12/577713381/how-a -whale-saved-a-marine-biologist-from-a-shark.

7. For further reading on this, see Frans de Waal, *Mama's Last Hug: Animal Emotions and What They Tell Us about Ourselves* (London: Granta, 2018).

Utqiaġvik: Doreen Kaleak

1. E. W. Kenworthy, "Judge Orders Hickel to Delay Permit for Alaska Pipeline, Road," *New York Times*, April 2, 1970, https://www.nytimes.com /1970/04/02/archives/judge-orders-hickel-to-delay-permit-for-alaska -pipeline-road.html.

2. Brody, *Other Side of Eden*, pp. 12, 14.

3. Brower and Brewster, *Whales, They Give Themselves*, pp. 156–59.

4. Ibid.

5. https://www.snopes.com/fact-check/white-wilderness/.

6. Jenny Diski, *What I Don't Know about Animals* (London: Virago, 2010), p. 34, paras. 1–2.

7. Riley Woodford, "Lemming Suicide Myth: Disney Film Faked Bogus Behavior," Alaska Fish & Wildlife News, Alaska Department of Fish and Game, September 2003, https://www.adfg.alaska.gov/index.cfm?adfg= wildlifenews.view_article&articles_id=56.

Depoe Bay to the San Juan Islands

1. Russell, *Eye of the Whale*, p. 339, para. 3.

2. Alter, Rynes, and Palumbi, "DNA Evidence," abstract, para. 1; S. Elizabeth Alter, Seth D. Newsome, and Stephen R. Palumbi, "Pre-Whaling Genetic

Diversity and Population Ecology in Eastern Pacific Gray Whales: Insights from Ancient DNA and Stable Isotopes," *PLoS* (9 May 2012), https://doi .org/10.1371/journal.pone.0035039.

3. S. E. Alter et al., "Climate Impacts on Transocean Dispersal and Habitat in Gray Whales from the Pleistocene to 2100," *Molecular Ecology* 24 (2015): 1510–22, https://doi.org/10.1111/mec.13121.

4. T. T. Waterman, *The Whaling Equipment of the Makah Indians* (Seattle: University of Washington, 1920), 38.

Utqiaġvik: Sounding

1. Lowenstein, *Ancient Land*, p. 148, para. 1.

2. Aleqa Hammond, personal communication, September 2007.

3. K. Rasmussen and W. Worster, *Eskimo Folk-Tales: Collected by Knud Rasmussen* (London: Gyldendal, 1921), p. 113.

4. https://www.historymuseum.ca/history-hall/origins/_media/Nuliajuk -EN.pdf.

5. John Fisher, "An Analysis of the Central Eskimo Sedna Myth," *Temenos-Nordic Journal of Comparative Religion* 11 (1975), https://doi.org/10.333 56/temenos.6311.

6. Piita Irniq, "The Story of Nuliajuk," History Hall, Origins, Canadian Museum of History, https://www.historymuseum.ca/history-hall/origins /_media/Nuliajuk-EN.pdf.

7. Rasmussen and Worster, *Eskimo Folk-Tales*, p. 113.

8. Frank Boas, *The Central Eskimo*, Sixth Annual Report of the Bureau of Ethnology to the Secretary of the Smithsonian Institution, 1884–85 (Washington, DC: Government Printing Office, 1888), pp. 583–85, https:// www.gutenberg.org/files/42084/42084-h/42084-h.htm#page649.

9. Edward Moffat Weyer, *The Eskimos: Their Environment and Folkways* (n.p.: Archon Books, 1932), pp. 355–59.

NOTES

Glacier Bay

1. Ryan Tucker Jones, "Running into Whales: The History of the North Pacific from Below the Waves," *American Historical Review* 118, no. 2 (April 2013): 349, para. 1.

2. George, personal communication.

Return to Utqiaġvik

1. Glenn W. Sheehan and Anne M. Jensen, *Diplomacy on Ice: Emergent Cooperation, or, Checkmate by Overwhelming Collaboration Linear Feet of Reports, Endless Meetings* (New Haven, CT: Yale University Press, 2015).

Home

1. K. M. Stafford et al., "Gray Whale Calls Recorded Near Barrow, Alaska, throughout the Winter of 2003–04," *Arctic* 60, no. 2 (2007): 167–72, www.jstor.org/stable/40513132.

2. Leo Hickman, "BBC Issues Internal Guidance on How to Report Climate Change," Carbon Brief, September 7, 2018, https://www.carbonbrief.org/exclusive-bbc-issues-internal-guidance-on-how-to-report-climate-change.

3. Lukoye Atwoli et al., "Call for Emergency Action to Limit Global Temperature Increases, Restore Biodiversity, and Protect Health," *Lancet* 398, no. 10304 (September 4, 2021), P939–41, https://www.thelancet.com/journals/lancet/article/PIIS0140-6736(21)01915-2/fulltext.

4. "Amazon Guardian, Indigenous Land Defender, Shot Dead in Brazil," Survival, April 1, 2020, https://www.survivalinternational.org/news/12365.

5. Fredrik Christiansen et al., "Poor Body Condition Associated with an Unusual Mortality Event in Gray Whales," *MEPS* 658 (January 21, 2021): 237–52, https://www.int-res.com/prepress/m13585.html.

6. C. Rutz et al., "COVID-19 Lockdown Allows Researchers to Quantify the Effects of Human Activity on Wildlife, *Nature Ecology & Evolution* 4 (2020): 1156–59, https://doi.org/10.1038/s41559-020-1237-z.

7. Carlos M. Duarte et al., "The Soundscape of the Anthropocene Ocean," *Science* (February 5, 2021).

8. Fiona Harvey, "UK Facing Worst Wheat Harvest since 1980s, Says Farmers' Union. NFU Predicts Yields Could Be Down by a Third as Extreme Weather Hits Crops," *Guardian*, August 17, 2020, paras. 1, 2, 7, https://www.theguardian.com/environment/2020/aug/17/uk-facing-worst-wheat-harvest-since-1980s-national-farmers-union-nfu.

ABOUT THE AUTHOR

After studying engineering, **Doreen Cunningham** worked briefly in climate-related research at the Natural Environment Research Council and in storm modeling at Newcastle University, before turning to journalism. She has worked for the BBC World Service for twenty years, variously as a presenter, editor, producer, and reporter. This is her first book.